Anne Binney

About the Author

MARCUS BINNEY is an accomplished historian and writer who is the author of *Our Vanishing Heritage, Town Houses,* and *Airport Builders.* Binney attended Cambridge, and has lectured extensively to historical societies in New York, Boston, Rhode Island, and Virginia on architectural preservation and history. He also fronted a thirty-nine-part series—*Mansions: The Great Houses of Europe*—broadcast in the United States between 1993 and 1997.

Binney's interest in the lives of the agents of the Special Operations Executive is a personal one. His father, Lt. Col. Francis Simms, MC, walked seven hundred miles through the Apennines after twice escaping from POW camps. His mother, Sonia, had done secret work with the code breakers during the war and in 1955 remarried Sir George Binney, DSO, also a war hero who had carried out one of the most successful blockage running operations of WWII in 1941—bringing back five unarmed merchant ships from Sweden through the minefields.

The Women Who Lived
for Danger

Also by Marcus Binney

Our Vanishing Heritage

Chateaux of the Loire

Town Houses

Airport Builders

The Ritz Hotel, London

London Sketchbook
(*with Graham Byfield*)

The Women Who Lived for Danger

Behind Enemy Lines
During World War II

MARCUS BINNEY

Perennial
An Imprint of HarperCollinsPublishers

This book was first published in Great Britain in 2002 by Hodder and Stoughton, a division of Hodder Headline.

The first U.S. edition of this book was published in 2003 by William Morrow, an imprint of HarperCollins Publishers.

HarperCollins books may be purchased for educational, business, or sales promotional use. For information please write: Special Markets Department, HarperCollins Publishers Inc., 10 East 53rd Street, New York, NY 10022.

FIRST PERENNIAL EDITION PUBLISHED 2004.

Library of Congress Cataloging-in-Publication Data is available.

ISBN 0-06-054088-5

07 08 RRD 10 9 8 7 6 5 4 3 2

To my Parents

CONTENTS

ILLUSTRATIONS

ACKNOWLEDGEMENTS

My thanks are due first to the agents I have talked to for this book – Lise de Baissac, Paola Del Din, Alix d'Unienville, Pearl Witherington and Countess Clémentine Mankowska. Violette Szabo's daughter Tania and Count Jan Skarbek have also helped me greatly. I have also had valuable guidance from former SOE staff including Sir Douglas Dodds-Parker, Leslie Fernandez, Peter Lee, the late Leo Marks and Chris Woods. Thanks are due to the staff of the Public Record Office, the Imperial War Museum (both the Department of Documents and the Sound Archive), to the British Library of Political and Economic Science, to the Centre Historique des Archives Nationales in Paris and the National Archives and Records Administration in Maryland USA and to Clive Richards at the MOD Historical Branch (Air).

In Paris I have also had help from Louis Dalais, Patrick de Richemont, and his sister Edith, François Rude of *Icare*, and the Musée de l'Ordre de la Libération. In the US I owe special thanks to Dan C. Pinck and Arthur Layton Funk. Anyone working in this field, particularly on SOE in France, constantly draws on the formidable work of Professor M.R.D. Foot, and also the work of Professor David Stafford. Further valuable help and advice has come from Gervase Cowell, John Harding, Lt-Colonel John Pitt and Mark Seaman. John Sainsbury has given me much valuable and expert guidance. General Sir Michael Wilkes first inadvertently prompted my researches and Air Chief Marshal Sir John Cheshire directed me to RAF sources. Further thanks to Lord Montagu of Beaulieu, Michael Buckmaster, Ian Payne, Nicholas Gibbs and Steve Tomlinson. At *The Times* my thanks to Sandra Parsons, Ian Brunskill and Zazie Barnicoat. Crispin Hasler kindly read the typescript and offered many suggestions.

Above all my thanks to the SOE adviser at the Foreign and Commonwealth Office, Duncan Stuart, and his assistant, Valerie Collins, for their enormous help in providing material and guidance about all the agents in this book. My literary agent Belinda Harley first set this book in motion with her usual swiftness and acumen. At Hodders my warmest thanks to Roland Philipps, the publishing director, his efficient and tireless assistant Lizzie Dipple, to Juliet Brightmore, picture research, to Celia Levett, copy-editor, and to Sarah Such. And finally thanks to my wife and sons for encouragement and forbearance throughout this project.

A NOTE ON SOE

Churchill's Special Operations Executive was an entirely new departure in warfare. On 16 July 1940, Churchill gave Hugh Dalton, Minister of Economic Warfare, the task of shaping the new organisation, exhorting him to 'set Europe ablaze'. In *The Fateful Years* Dalton explains that SOE's purpose 'was to co-ordinate all action by way of subversion and sabotage against the enemy overseas'. SOE, initially known as SO2, was to absorb a Section D ('D' for destruction) set up within the Secret Intelligence Service in April 1938, but would be

on a much greater scale, with wider scope and largely manned by new personnel. It would be a secret or underground organisation. There would be no public announcement of my new responsibility, and knowledge of the activities of the organisation would be kept within a very restricted circle. As to its scope, 'sabotage' was a simple idea. It meant smashing things up. 'Subversion' was a more complex conception. It meant the weakening, by whatever 'covert' means, of the enemy's will and power to make war, and the strengthening of the will and power of his opponents, including in particular, guerrilla and resistance movements.

In a much-quoted letter that Dalton wrote to Lord Halifax on 18 July 1940, he said: 'We must organise movements in enemy occupied territory comparable to the Sinn Fein movement in Ireland, to the Chinese guerrillas now operating against Japan, to the Spanish Irregulars who played a notable part in Wellington's campaign or – one might as well admit it

– to the organisations which the Nazis themselves have developed so remarkably in almost every country in the world.'

SOE started in offices in Caxton Street near St James's Park but soon moved to Sherlock Holmes territory in Baker Street, taking over the offices of Marks and Spencer and steadily expanding to occupy six large buildings in the vicinity, under the cover name of the Inter-Services Research Bureau. Maurice Buckmaster was appointed to the newly formed F (French) Section in 1941; this was distinct from de Gaulle's parallel RF Section. In Italy SOE was known as No. 1 Special Force.

From the very start Dalton, known by his staff as Dr Dynamo, achieved a very judicious mix of open-minded, able and energetic insiders who had experience in government, with outsiders principally from the City, the law, industry and commerce who had drive and entrepreneurial flair and a willingness, indeed a positive relish, to mount daring, unconventional operations fettered by a minimum of red tape.

Churchill proposed that Dalton should employ as his chief adviser the wily Sir Robert Vansittart (who quickly saw the talents of Christina Granville) and Dalton himself obtained Gladwyn Jebb, private secretary to Sir Alexander Cadogan, the Permanent Under-Secretary of State at the Foreign Office, to smooth relations with government departments. Dalton's first chief executive was not a career civil servant but an outsider, the businessman and MP Sir Frank Nelson. When he retired prematurely from exhaustion, Dalton brought in Charles Hambro who, he said, 'kept more balls in the air than any man I knew'. Hambro was a merchant banker, who served on the Court of the Bank of England and was chairman of the Great Western Railway. The banking skills of Hambro and those he recruited were a great advantage to SOE, resulting in many financially beneficial transactions, including some £70 million made on currency deals, the equivalent of over £1,000 million today.

Nelson recruited the Australian, George Taylor, whom Dalton described as 'always belligerent, persistent and ingenious'. Julian Amery, in *Approach March*, says that Taylor was 'very quick to grasp new ideas [and] probed them until he had extracted the last ounce of relevant information. He would then marshal all the departmental and military arguments for and against the course of action involved. When these brought him up against a difficulty he never tried to evade it, but worried away until he had found a solution.'

Colin (later Sir Colin) Gubbins, who had impressed Dalton at a dinner by his account of the British Military Mission to Poland in 1939, was put in charge of training and operations, taking over as head of SOE from Hambro in 1943.

Recruitment from outside was essential not only to SOE but to the war effort in general. Max Nicholson, who was brought into the Ministry of Economic Warfare to run Allied shipping during the vital battle of the Atlantic, says: 'The home civil service simply could not supply from its own ranks people with the necessary drive and ability to undertake tasks essential to success in the war.' As the war spread across the globe, overseas headquarters were set up in Cairo and then in Algiers, as well as offices in India, Ceylon and Australia, with a large number of sub-missions in other countries, particularly neutral ones. At its peak some 10,000 men and 3,000 women were working in SOE offices and missions, helping an estimated two to three million active resisters in Europe alone.

In 1942, an American counterpart to SOE, the OSS or Office of Strategic Services, was set up under 'Wild Bill' Donovan, who had many friends in SOE's top echelons.

After the war, OSS was to develop into the CIA, while Baker Street was closed down, a number of its functions being absorbed within the Secret Intelligence Service.

Chapter 1

RECRUITMENT
AND TRAINING

A new form of warfare was developed and has come to stay and may prove in a future War even more important than in the last one . . .

A Brief History of SOE

The girls who served as secret agents in Churchill's Special Operations Executive were young, beautiful and brave. At a time when women in the armed forces were restricted to a strictly non-combatant role in warfare, the women of SOE trained and served alongside the men. They fought not in the front line but well behind it. If caught, as were fifteen of the fifty women sent from Britain to France, they faced harsh and sometimes brutal interrogation by the Gestapo and thereafter the horrors of a concentration camp – which only three of them survived.

SOE operated all over Europe, Africa, the Middle East and the Far East, but the majority of its women agents went to France. They were trained as couriers and wireless operators, and in a few cases took on an effective leadership role, charged with running Resistance circuits – known in French as *réseaux*. As able-bodied men became increasingly subject to the STO, the Service du Travail Obligatoire (forced labour in Germany), young women had the advantage of being able to move about more freely and were less subject to suspicion.

Couriers did essential work, carrying money and messages to and from Resistance groups concerning recruitment and arms drops. From the time of the D-Day landings, they were involved in ambushes and hit-and-run attacks on German troops, as well as sabotage on a vastly increased scale. Couriers had to be used because the post was subject to censorship; telephone calls had to be placed through local operators who often listened in to calls; and anyone wishing to send a telegram or make a telephone call from a post office had to produce an identity card.

Agents in the field communicated with SOE by radio, tapping messages out in Morse code and using increasingly sophisticated ciphers. As the Germans had remarkably effective tracking equipment, agents were supposed to limit their time on air, but they often had to send lengthy messages, which exposed them to great danger, particularly in city areas. As more agents were caught, SOE began to supplement their numbers with women operators. Women, of course, constituted the overwhelming majority of radio operators in Britain and at overseas bases, but from June 1943, when Noor Inayat Khan was flown in by Lysander to serve as radio operator to the Cinema circuit, increasing numbers of women radio operators were infiltrated into France.

Why did women volunteer for such hazardous work? The most common reason for people serving their country in the war was that they wanted 'to do their bit', a modest way of expressing a national commitment to defeating Nazi tyranny. To serve behind enemy lines required courage and commitment of an altogether greater order, and the quality that unites the women who became agents was a steely determination to play an active role in inflicting real damage on the enemy.

With Violette Szabo, it was burning anger at the death of her legionnaire husband in the fighting at El Alamein. With the 21-year-old Paola Del Din, it was the wish to carry on the work of her brother Renato, killed leading the first attack on the fascists in a garrison town north of Udine.

2

In the eyes of her instructors, Noor's willingness to risk her life appeared at first to be a reaction to a broken engagement. However, it soon became clear to them that she was in fact motivated by idealism and a longing to be more active in the war effort.

In almost every case women agents had to conceal the nature of their work from their family and friends. Paola Del Din was an exception, having the help of her mother in preparing for a dangerous solo journey to break through the German front line in Florence and contact SOE. In addition, there were cases where brothers and sisters – or even, in one or two instances, husbands and wives – both served SOE. The most notable examples are the impressive group of Mauritian agents: the three gallant Mayer brothers, Percy, Edmund and James, and Percy's wife Berthe who continued her husband's radio transmissions from Madagascar after his arrest; Claude de Baissac and his sister Lise; the sisters 'Didi' and Jacqueline Nearne and their brother Francis. In a few cases, notably Odette Sansom and Violette Szabo, it meant leaving young children behind. Not surprisingly some in SOE had severe doubts about this, even if the children were entrusted to loving grandparents, but the women who made this difficult choice approached it in the same way as men with young children, deciding that this was a time when service to country was paramount.

No less remarkable is the youth of many of the girls. Paolo Del Din set off for Florence four weeks before her twenty-first birthday. Violette Szabo was just twenty-three when SOE dropped her in France; Christina Granville and Peggy Knight were twenty-four when they embarked on their missions. Alix d'Unienville was twenty-five, Paddy O'Sullivan twenty-six, Pearl Witherington twenty-seven and Noor Inayat Khan twenty-nine when they were sent behind enemy lines.

The background of the men who initially ran SOE was predominantly public school, Oxbridge and the City. Yet within SOE there were no distinctions between officers and other ranks. Recruitment and promotion were on grounds of ability. Violette Szabo had been working at the perfume counter in the Bon Marché store in Brixton when war broke out. Peggy Knight was a secretary for the Electricity Company in Walthamstow when she was recruited.

The obvious special ability that all these women possessed was their command of languages. They were not being sent to serve as guerrillas based in the mountains of Greece or Yugoslavia where they would be unlikely to meet the enemy except in battle. Their mission was to pass themselves off as ordinary citizens and to move safely through the numerous checkpoints and controls operated by both the Germans and the Vichy authorities, whether the Gendarmerie or the hated French military police known as the Milice.

Just as escaping prisoners of war in Italy were under threat from the Italians' sharp eye for every detail of dress, so the French have an extraordinarily acute ear for subtle intonations of speech. Because of this, SOE agents would sometimes carry papers suggesting they were of Belgian or Swiss parentage or came from overseas colonies.

Mary Herbert, who worked with Claude de Baissac, was told when she was arrested that she had a queer accent and was asked to explain it. She replied that she had lived in Alexandria and spoke French, English, Spanish and Italian and a smattering of Arab, which was sufficient to upset anyone's pronunciation. (She did not tell them she spoke German and after a while the Frenchman who was questioning her said to the Gestapo chief in German, 'I do not think we shall get anything out of this woman.' All this she reported to SOE on her return in 1945.)

SOE's policy of recruiting increasing numbers of women must also have been influenced by the resourcefulness and success of two of its very early female agents. The first was the Polish countess, Krystyna Skarbek, better known as Christine

Granville, or Christina, who was one of SOE's bravest and longest-serving agents. She volunteered and was enrolled in December 1939, before SOE itself had been formed, entering German-occupied Poland over the snow-covered Tatra Mountains and later being parachuted into southern France. The second was Virginia Hall, who thanks to her American citizenship was able to operate under cover of being Vichy correspondent for the *New York Post* and was only forced to flee as the Germans poured into the Unoccupied Zone in November 1942.

Not surprisingly, the arrival of beautiful young women was to cause some serious heartache, in some cases among their fellow agents. While in Hungary Christina proved a latter-day Zuleika Dobson, prompting at least one rejected fellow agent to attempt suicide by throwing himself into the Danube – unsuccessfully, as it was frozen. Margaret Pawley, a FANY (First Aid Nursing Yeomanry) who was with Christina in Cairo, observed: 'She was not beautiful in the formal sense, but she had qualities of fascination which men found irresistible. When she entered a room every officer looked up.' Her mesmerising powers of attraction meant that throughout the war men around her were falling under her spell. Despite her feelings for her husband Jerzy Gizycki (also a British agent), whom she called her Svengali, followed by her long and fond attachment to her fellow agent the Pole Kowerski (later Andrew Kennedy), she had a succession of romances with other agents serving with her.

Pearl Witherington, by contrast, was to meet her fiancé within hours of parachuting into France, to serve with him and, indeed, take command over him. The young Mary Herbert, sent to Bordeaux to work as courier for the Scientist network, had a love affair with her circuit leader, Claude de Baissac, and became pregnant by him, giving birth to a baby girl at the end of 1943. Brave and dashing Sonia Butt was so taken with a French-Canadian fellow agent that she left to marry him without signing off, not a popular move with her superiors.

SOE did not recruit Rosa Klebbs or Mata Haris. Of course there were times when women agents used feminine charms to extract themselves from dangerous situations. Red-headed Paddy O'Sullivan chatted up a German officer for half an hour and ended up making a date with him to distract him from looking in her suitcase. Young Paola Del Din produced from her bag a wartime luxury – fresh fruit – when two SS soldiers adopted an alarming line of questioning outside Arezzo.

Nor were these women Bond girls in the modern sense, experts in ju-jitsu, karate or other martial arts. Of them all, Violette Szabo, a tomboy always seeking to outdo her elder brother at any physical challenge, was probably the strongest and most athletic. Christina Granville, although slender, was very conscious of keeping physically fit and she had exceptional stamina and powers of endurance. Paola Del Din had built up strength walking in the Alps with her soldier father. But this was also an age when young women were often discouraged from bicycling too much for fear of ending up with bulging thighs and muscular calves.

This was noted early on by Squadron Leader Simpson in the *Sunday Express* on 11 March 1945:

The interesting thing about these girls is they are not hearty and horsey young women with masculine chins. They are pretty young girls who would look demure and sweet in crinolines. Most of them are English girls who speak perfect French. Some were educated in French convents; others attended Swiss finishing schools. A few are French girls who escaped from France and agitated for a chance to go back and work underground. Cool courage, intelligence, and adaptability are their most important attributes. They have to be able to pass themselves off as tough country wenches, and smart Parisiennes.

Leslie Fernandez, who instructed some of them, says:

During training we attempted to prepare them physically, building up their stamina by hikes through rough countryside. All were taught close combat, which gave them confidence even if most were not very good at it. These girls weren't commando material. They didn't have the physique though some had tremendous mental stamina. You would not expect well brought up girls to go up behind someone and slit their throats, though if they were grappled, there were several particularly nasty little tricks that we handed on, given us by the Shanghai police.

The girls were good at role playing. During interrogation you have to be consistent. Very little stands up to hard interrogation and the Germans were expert at interrogation, even without resorting to brutality. The best defence is a partly true cover story, which is easier to stick to. There was a tendency in SOE at the beginning to dismiss the potential of young women but it increasingly became evident that survival did not just require physical toughness but the ability to live a cover story – which women could excel at.

For sheer sustained brilliance, Christina Granville was surely in a class of her own, imaginative, resourceful and full of initiative. If one could be a fly on the wall to any conversation in the war, a perfect choice would be her confrontation, unarmed, with a Gestapo officer, during which she talked and talked, and finally terrified him into releasing three of her comrades from prison, hours before they were due to be shot. The American Virginia Hall was also possessed of astonishing resilience and sang-froid, only leaving her post in Lyons two hours before the Germans swept in, as determined to arrest her as they were later determined to seize Jean Moulin, de Gaulle's personal representative with the French Resistance. In his citation of 19 June 1945, recommending Virginia Hall for a George Medal, Colonel Maurice Buckmaster paid tribute to her courage and persistence, especially given her handicaps: a transatlantic accent, a striking appearance and – amazingly – a wooden leg.

The SAS officer, Captain Blackman, praised Lise de Baissac for her stamina and her 'great skill' with firearms, and commended her willingness to risk her life, often in terrible conditions. Pearl Witherington demonstrated an ability to take command over men who were hostile to women playing any role at all, as well as being a crack shot. Peggy Knight, travelling enormous distances by bicycle as a courier in August 1944, seemed incapable of fear as she carried out Resistance work constantly encountering German soldiers.

Alix d'Unienville was not physically strong – her parachute instructors were worried that she lacked sufficient strength in her arms for a parachute jump, although in the event she managed well. Yet she had the inner resolve to endure horrific privations and, when all seemed lost, to seize the moment to escape. There are repeated comments that Noor Inayat Khan was clumsy, and not just with her hands, but she worked hard at her physical training and was fleet enough to outrun her pursuers on two occasions. If she was naive, or too trusting in others, she also had formidable reserves of spiritual strength to enable her to endure months alone in a prison cell with both her hands and feet in chains. Yet Noor was no ascetic, but a touchingly loving daughter and sister who felt desperate pain at her separation from her family and was frequently heard sobbing during the night by those in nearby cells.

All women agents were given commissions in either the WAAF (Women's Auxiliary Air Force) or the FANYs in the hope that they would be treated as prisoners of war under the Geneva Convention. The First Aid Nursing Yeomanry, self-defined as the 'First Anywheres' and soon popularly known as the 'Fannys', was founded in 1907, the first of the women's services. During the First World War about 400 FANYs drove ambulances and other vehicles in England, France and Belgium. In the Fannys there were no military restrictions on the use of arms as in other women's services. By the height of

SOE's activities in mid-1944, over half of the FANYs' strength was devoted to SOE. FANYs made up most of the 3,000 women working for the organisation, which then employed a total of nearly 13,000. Fourteen of the fifty women agents sent into France held honorary WAAF commissions; some had started their service there.

However, the reality was that, as women agents were not in uniform, if captured they would sooner or later be executed as spies. Their best hope was to deflect suspicion that they were British agents at all: Didi Nearne persuaded her captors that she was French and had been sending messages for a businessman without knowing that he was working for the British. If this failed, Hitler's notorious Commando Order, kept secret for fear of countermeasures by the Allies, ensured that almost all captured agents were shot, too many of them in the last few months of the war. The daily Wehrmacht communiqué of 7 October 1942, issued three days after the Allied Commando raid on Dieppe, read: 'In future, all terror and sabotage troops of the British and their accomplices, who do not act like soldiers but rather like bandits, will be treated as such by the German troops and will be ruthlessly eliminated in battle, wherever they appear.' On 18 October the top-secret Commando Order was issued from Hitler's headquarters. It ran:

I therefore order that from now on, all opponents engaged in so-called commando operations in Europe or Africa, even when it is outwardly a matter of soldiers in uniform or demolition parties with or without weapons, are to be exterminated to the last man in battle or in flight. In these cases, it is immaterial whether they are landed for their operations by ship, or aeroplane, or descent by parachute. Even should these individuals, on being discovered, make as if to surrender, all quarter is to be denied on principle.

A supplementary directive followed:

I have been compelled to issue strict orders for the destruction of enemy sabotage troops and to declare non-compliance severely punishable ... It must be made clear to the enemy that all sabotage troops will be exterminated, without exception, to the last man. That means that their chances of escaping with their lives is nil. Under no circumstances can they be expected to be treated according to the rules of the Geneva Convention. If it should become necessary for reasons of interrogation to initially spare one man or two, then they are to be shot immediately after interrogation. This order is intended for commanders only and must not under any circumstances fall into enemy hands.

In most cases, however, death was to be much longer in coming – in waves of summary executions in concentration camps, first after the Allied landings in Normandy and then early in 1945 as the Nazis sought to kill Allied witnesses to the horrors of Dachau, Mauthausen, Ravensbrück and other camps.

Three of the women agents were to receive the highest possible award for gallantry, the George Cross: first Odette Sansom, then Violette Szabo and Noor Inayat Khan, the last two posthumously. Christina Granville was also strongly recommended for a George Cross, although the recommendation was changed to an OBE by General Alexander (a man of formidable physical courage himself) and then raised to a George Medal by the Ministry of Defence to make it clearer that the award was 'for gallantry'. Many other women agents received MBEs, a few the more coveted military version. Most of them got the civil one, although Pearl Witherington successfully turned down it down and justly received an MBE Military instead.

The very existence of SOE was kept a secret during the war, particularly as far as any press reporting was concerned. The chase was on when, early in March 1945, Sir Archibald Sinclair spoke in the House of Commons in praise of WAAF parachutists. The *Sunday Express* article, quoted above, gave two names. 'One, Sonia d'Artois (née Butt), is the young daughter of a group captain. She married the French-Canadian officer who jumped with her. The other, Maureen O'Sullivan, is also young and pretty. She comes from Dublin.'

The head of SOE's French Section, Colonel Maurice Buckmaster, also had a crucial, although initially anonymous, role in telling the public about the exploits of his women agents. A *News of the World* report of 21 April 1946 runs: '"Colonel X", an intelligence officer whose name must still be kept a secret, has returned to England with more evidence of the heroism of Violette Szabo, the daring British parachutist, who died before a Nazi firing-squad at Ravensbrück concentration camp.' Colonel X, the article says, 'directed British aid to the Resistance in France', which indicates without doubt that Colonel Buckmaster was meant.

Puzzlingly the colonel tells a story in which Violette's capture is transposed from open country to a town, with Violette retreating from house to house in a street honeycombed with secret passages. Buckmaster was to make a similar transposition in his book, *They Fought Alone*, with the story of Christina Granville's daring rescue of her circuit leader Francis Cammaerts, saying he was picked up briefing saboteurs in Sisteron, not arrested at a check-point at Digne. The story that can now be told, using Christina and Cammaerts's own accounts, is even more amazing.

Many explanations present themselves – that stories change in the telling, that Buckmaster may have suffered from lack of access to documents as SOE closed down and he valiantly struggled to keep the memory of its great deeds and adventures from disappearing altogether. Some said there was a Walter Mitty side to Buckmaster. He could also have deliberately changed details to conceal the source of the information – SOE agents and their bosses were subject to the Official Secrets Act. In his first book, *Specially Employed: the Story of British Aid to French Patriots of the Resistance* (1952), he writes: 'I do not claim that the incidents described in these pages are completely factually accurate . . . but the incidents *did* take place; what is perhaps more important, the spirit that made these incidents possible at all is described . . . with all the exactitude of which I am capable.'

The main point in every case is that the truth is still more exciting than the fiction and the stature of the agents grows as more records come to light. Violette Szabo may have gunned down fewer Germans than the film *Carve her Name with Pride* suggests, but she emerges as an equally fearless and still more electric personality.

The great change came in 1966 with the publication of M.R.D. Foot's *SOE in France.* Professor Foot had been given access to a large part of the surviving SOE archive, including the personal files (PFs) of agents. Previous books had been based on the recollections of agents and SOE insiders – good examples being Ben Cowburn's *No Cloak, No Dagger* and Bickham Sweet-Escott's *Baker Street Irregular.*

Foot's was based on archives and he was discouraged from talking to SOE stalwarts, a point that caused immense chagrin to some. Foot nonetheless laid a foundation of scholarship that has been the touchstone of SOE studies ever since. His book was wide ranging, authoritative and comprehensive, providing a degree of thrilling detail about individual agents and their activities that has never been available for any other secret service.

Foot was scathing about certain popular accounts by 'sensation mongers', especially gruesome stories of torture that were the product of authors' imaginations. Particularly bad examples, he said, were the account in the book *Carve her Name with Pride* of Violette Szabo's supposed torture by the Gestapo, complete with dialogue, for which no source existed, and articles that appeared in the *Sunday Pictorial* in June and July 1958.

Another author to come under attack was E.H. Cookridge, whose account of Christina Granville was scathingly dismissed by Cammaerts. 'He took a story of 5,000 words and blew it up to 50,000,' he says in an interview in the Imperial War Museum Sound Archive. One tantalising aspect of accounts such as Cookridge's in *They Came from the Sky* is that they often include interesting items that cannot be verified or traced – for example, Cookridge's quotations from a BBC radio interview in which Christina provided details of her youth.

Further strides in historical research have been taken by Professor David Stafford in setting the work of SOE in the wider context of government policy. His *Churchill and Secret Service*, as well as telling an absorbing story, explores a rich seam of archives – cabinet and Air Ministry papers as well as those from Lord Selborne, who took over from Dalton as head of SOE in 1942, when Dalton had moved to the Board of Trade.

The study of SOE is all the more absorbing because it is the only part of the secret services at this time for which a substantial archive is available, not only illuminating operational successes and failures but the careers of individual agents. Thanks to SOE's system of training schools, we have numerous reports of agents' characters, capabilities and shortcomings.

Whilst quite a number of the male agents were army officers before they were recruited, the women often came to the work almost straight from normal civilian life. Very few SOE agents were professional spooks – and for this reason it is possible today for those with no service background to understand and identify with them in a remarkable way.

As a secret service, SOE could not recruit publicly and would not have wanted to. Initially, names were put forward through personal contacts. Later, as the demand for recruits grew, a more general call went out within the armed services for people with language skills. SOE's chief recruiter was the thriller writer Selwyn Jepson – several of whose books were adapted for the screen by Alfred Hitchcock. Jepson carried out his interviews in a bare room at the Victoria Hotel in Northumberland Avenue, then mostly occupied by the Quartermaster-General's directorate, or in Sanctuary Buildings in Westminster, a Ministry of Pensions office. In SOE Jepson was regarded as 'far ahead of anyone as a talent spotter' – although the ebullient Nancy Wake clashed with him. 'We did not like each other. He was so sarcastic I decided he either had an ulcer or was constipated,' she wrote in her autobiography, *The White Mouse*.

SOE had commandeered an impressive range of country houses – one wag suggested SOE stood for the Stately 'Omes of England. A list compiled in 1992 includes nearly eighty establishments, scattered across England and Scotland.

SOE's four-stage training was devised by Major F.T. 'Tommy' Davies and consisted of preliminary schools, paramilitary schools and finishing schools. With these came a flat in London where agents would be given a final briefing.

Many potential agents were sent first to Wanborough Manor, a large country house dating from Elizabethan times, on the Hog's Back near Guildford in Surrey. Mrs C. Wrench, who helped prepare agents for dispatch to France, wrote: 'As everywhere else the only language in use was French. The physical training was quite strenuous. The lessons in sabotage were not too specific and practical jokes . . . with bangs all over the place were the order of the day. Discipline was not too strict as the object was to allow the Agents to relax and so observe whether they were "made of the right stuff". This training, as did that in most of the other Schools, took three weeks.' During the Wanborough course no mention was made of SOE or the actual work it did, in case candidates were deemed not to be suitable.

Many candidates then went on to the paramilitary schools, based at ten shooting lodges on the west coast of Scotland near Mallaig. Loch Nevis and Loch Morar were nearby, and the rugged country was ideal for commando-style training. Here they were given instruction in handling weapons and explosives, silent killing, fieldcraft and raid tactics, as well as retrieving containers that had fallen in water.

In addition there were specialist schools such as Brickendonbury Manor in Hertfordshire, where Pearl Witherington hoped to be sent on a specialist demolition course, and Thame Park in Oxfordshire, where Noor Inayat Khan went for signals training.

Women agents, like the men, were sent for parachute training at Ringway airport near Manchester, staying at Dunham House nearby. This was the greatest physical challenge they faced, although at the end of it there was the prospect of earning the coveted paratrooper's wings. The training centre had every type of equipment for toughening and hardening people to make a coordinated exit from an aircraft and to withstand the impact on landing. In 'Top Secret Interlude,' Wing Commander B. Bonsey explains the importance of teaching the agent how to fall correctly on landing. 'There were ropes and swings to help with this technique,' and an old fuselage with a hole in it to help people to learn the correct way to drop out. 'Each country sent a conducting officer with their particular Joes, some of whom were highly strung and temperamental. It was found that most Joes reacted favorably to personal attention.' Five jumps were deemed sufficient, four from an aircraft and one from a balloon. Nancy Wake was offered the opportunity of waiting for better weather or jumping from a balloon. Her group, determined to have a weekend off in London, bribed her to go for it by each promising her a double whisky in a club there. I should have specified trebles, she thought as she descended in pitch darkness, waiting for the parachute to open.

Some agents also received training in identifying suitable night-landing grounds following their arrival in France, for use during the seven days on either side of the full moon when in good weather there was sufficient light to navigate by. Sir Robin Hooper, a Lysander pilot, wrote: 'My work between moons – for we lived by the moon – was to train some of the French who were to find fields . . . carrying out the delicate task of controlling the landing of an aircraft at night with no help but pocket torches.'

Often the most important part of an agent's training was the security course at Beaulieu Abbey, better known today as the home of the National Motor Museum. A plaque in a recess in the ancient cloister wall commemorates more than 3,000 men and women of at least fifteen European nationalities, as well as Canadians and Americans, who trained there as agents. SOE used a complex of a dozen comfortable country houses on the Beaulieu estate, built at the prompting of the 2nd Lord Montagu, who had offered friends parcels of land on which they could build in spacious grounds, out of sight of both their neighbours and his own family seat at Palace House. The principal course taught agents technique, clandestine life, personal security, methods of communication and recruitment in the field, as well as how they should maintain their cover and act under police surveillance. There was instruction on German, Italian, French and even Japanese secret police forces.

Mrs Wrench, always colourful, explains that here 'the Agents were required to carry out a bogus Mission in England. Perhaps they were required to collect information in a forbidden dock zone or to plant some bogus explosive in a war factory. If the Agent was caught, he or she had been given the name of someone who would extricate them from their dilemma.'

Precise details of a ninety-six-hour exercise are provided in the personal file of Noor Inayat Khan, which took place in Bristol on 19–23 May 1943. She was to visit Bristol under cover of gathering children's impressions of air raids for a book, and was also to provide articles for the BBC on this subject. This was considered quite a good cover story as she had written children's stories in the past.

Noor's initial contact was with a Mrs Laurie, head of the Irish Travellers' Censor Office, who had been primed by SOE. A meeting had been set up by post on the pretext that Noor was looking for a job. During this, the password was introduced naturally. A second meeting between them was then agreed, the 'cover' being that Noor was returning with her completed application form. This time Noor put forward her proposition that Mrs Laurie cooperate in a line of communication in the event of an invasion. Noor 'was very favourably impressed and considers Mrs Laurie a very suitable contact'. Mrs Laurie reported that Noor had 'put up a very good show', but added that Noor had something very suspicious about her manner. After talking further to Mrs Laurie, SOE put this down to nerves.

Next Noor had to set up live letter drops, which she did successfully with a porter at Bristol University and a secretary at the Empire Rendezvous in Whiteladies, explaining that she was moving to Bristol but as yet had no address. For her two dead letter boxes, Noor chose the ruins of the Bethesda Chapel in Great George Street and a call box at the end of Queen's Road, Clifton. SOE deemed Noor's positions – an oblique angle behind stone steps in the ruins and behind a fuse-case in the call box – very suitable.

Another task was to provide details of six rendezvous. Three of these were to be for a person of the same social standing as the student. Noor chose the University Library between 1300 and 1800 hours; the Clifton Lawn Tennis Club before midday on a Sunday; and the entrance to the Victoria Rooms after 2300 hours, which was when dances and parties finished.

Three further rendezvous had to be provided that were suitable for meeting an elderly working-class woman. This time Noor's choices were the waiting room at the Knowles

Centre bus station between 1300 and 1800 hours; St George's Church on a Sunday before midday; and the waiting room on Platform 9 at Temple Meads station after 2300 hours. Again, SOE deemed the rendezvous very well chosen.

Noor also had to find three operational sites where a wireless could be set up and used. This involved an extensive search for flats available for rent. Her first was at 34 Cornwallis Crescent ('voltage 210 – rent £80', she reported). SOE commented: 'There would seem to be little fear of being overheard as the only other person in the house is an old lady who is very deaf. Aerial already in position and good alternative exits.' Noor's second was at 99 Pembroke Road with a rather higher rent of £120 a year. Noor herself added that it had a 'spacious loft in which to conceal the set and easy fixing of aerial'. A third address, 10 Whiteladies Road (rent £75), seemed to SOE a very good place.

Noor had problems with her landlady, 'a very inquisitive person'; she would have moved if lodgings had not been so hard to obtain. She also made several 'stupid' mistakes during the standard police interrogation, 'which could easily have been avoided by a little forethought. She always volunteers far too much information when being questioned.'

Noor's own conclusion was: 'Bristol area as a whole suitable for operations', although, she added, 'Security precautions and well-founded cover most essential as police service extremely efficient, being coastal area.'

At Beaulieu, students were also put to the test with intense interrogations. Leslie Fernandez says: 'These were carried out under spotlights. We made these as realistic as possible. On occasion the interrogators would wear German Abwehr uniform, or that of the French Milice who were the most dangerous. On occasion a second or third student would listen in to try and learn.'

Once training was complete, preparation began for infiltration. Sometimes this was agonisingly slow, occasionally a desperate rush. Peggy Knight, recruited in April 1944, was dropped in France on the night of 6 May when, due to bad weather, she had made only one practice jump.

More, vivid details of agents' preparations are provided by Mrs Wrench. She had started work as a 'volontaire' at the French canteen, a club for de Gaulle's forces in London. The reward was a good meal with wine. This led her to Orchard Court, near Baker Street, which she learnt quickly was an SOE flat from which agents were dispatched to France.

Clothing was provided appropriate to each agent's cover story. 'Meticulous care had been taken that every article of clothing and all accessories should be an exact replica of items manufactured in France. The whole procedure was a model of thoroughness and every article that an Agent brought with him from France was studied and copied to the last detail. I remember one of the two tailors who were summoned to our flat from time to time demonstrating to me how even the buttons on the men's suits needed to be sewn on in a special French style.' After a while the section was moved to a house in Wimpole Street, where 'there were now a great many rooms where the Agents were able to shut themselves up with their files and study their missions and, not least, become word-perfect in their cover-stories. This entailed a good deal of verbal briefing and thus . . . much to-ing and fro-ing on the part of the Officers from Baker Street.'

The Wimpole Street address was a few doors down from the house from which Elizabeth Barrett had eloped with Robert Browning. The large ground-floor front room was lined with cubbyholes, each capable of containing 'all the assembled items which, when the signal for departure came, each Agent was to take to France. Each cubby hole had an Agent's number scribbled in white chalk, a wisely anonymous identification. Then, after the Agent had left for the Field, it was quite simple to erase the number and replace it with that of another Agent.'

Agents, she said, often appeared at Wimpole Street in the early days of their enrolment, before they were sent to training schools. Among them she noted Muriel Byack, 'an English Jewess who looked much younger than her twenty-three years. In fact she looked as if she was just out of school.' Byack was sent to join the agent Philippe de Vomécourt, but tragically caught meningitis and died. Nancy Wake she describes as 'large and handsome with enormous personality and drive, great courage and ingenuity and, a vital "plus", an enormous sense of humour'.

There are details of the SOE shooting range, 'a gallery over Baker Street Station where our Bods [SOE slang for agents] learnt to shoot from the hip. I had always been above average at shooting in fairgrounds and I longed to try.' Eventually Mrs Wrench gained admittance by pretending to be an agent herself. The scene that greeted her inside was pure James Bond, 'a series of quite long alleys with the life-sized metal silhouette of a man at one end. At my first attempt I cocked the pistol in the manner I had seen in the films. At this moment my instructor told me that if I indulged in this elaborate ploy I would be dead before I had time to pull the trigger.'

After the training camps, the agonising wait began while agents were on standby to depart. Violette Szabo spent the day before her departure trying to relax at Hasell's Hall in Bedfordshire, a handsome red-brick Georgian country house in a beautiful landscape park, laid out by Humphry Repton.

Alix d'Unienville recalls the strain, during each fourteen-day 'moon period', of having to remain by a telephone, day after day, waiting to find out whether she would be sent to France. Only if no call came before twelve o'clock, at which time an operation would be automatically postponed, would she know that she would not be going on that particular day. Until the following morning, at least, she was free. 'We frequented the bars, we sowed seeds of scandal in the dining rooms of solemn London hotels. Clients were indignant. Who had the right to frolic in war? Irresponsible youth.'

Chapter 2

AN AGENT'S LIFE

The Present struggle overrides all the inhibitions which purely humanitarian considerations imposed in the past, because at the end of it there will in any case be no victors and vanquished, but only survivors and annihilated.

Hitler's New Year's Proclamation on 1 January 1944

Agents were flown into France during moon periods – one week on either side of the full moon when there was sufficient light for night flying. Navigation was done by direct reckoning – following a line or series of lines worked out with a compass on a map. The big landmarks were the great rivers, notably the Loire, their still surfaces glinting in the moonlight. So many planes carrying SOE agents passed over Blois, where an island in the middle of the river was easy to spot, that one would have expected the Germans to be lying in wait for them, but by 1943 the scale of Allied air raids was such that their defences, whether anti-aircraft guns or night fighters, were fully stretched in protecting military and industrial targets. Hugh Verity records one rare but uncomfortably close incident when flying over Alençon with Lise de Baissac on the night of 16 August 1943: 'Just a mile or two ahead of me I saw an aircraft shot down in flames. It must have been done by a night fighter which I did not see. In the glare of the flames I hoped to see some parachutes but I saw none.'

Sir Lewis Hodges, who was first flight commander and then squadron commander at RAF Tempsford, flew both Lysanders and Halifaxes for SOE. He recalls, 'We flew across the Channel at about 600 feet [180 metres] to avoid radar detection, but climbed as we passed over the coast to get a broader view and pinpoint our position from the lie of the land. Then we would descend again to 600 feet to avoid radar.' Airfields in France were also given a wide berth, although, with heavy fighting on the eastern front, many of them were used by the Germans principally for training purposes.

While working out his route before take-off, the pilot would try to find a readily identifiable landmark about five minutes from the dropping zone. Distances from one pinpoint to another would be calculated in minutes according to the speed of the plane – about 240 kilometres per hour with a Lysander.

To land and take off, a Lysander needed an open grass field just 150–200 metres long. The plane would stop for no more than two or three minutes with its engines running, just enough time for the two passengers to disembark and be replaced by another two (three at a pinch), waiting to go back to London. Agents flown in by Lysander could take only a small suitcase – heavy items such as radio sets were usually dropped by parachute at a later date. As the Lysanders had a maximum range of 1,000 kilometres, even when provided with an enlarged fuel tank, they would usually be flown down from their base airfield to RAF Tangmere near Selsey Bill (or returned there) at the beginning of each moon period, shortening the journey to France. After the initial success of the Lysanders in 1941–2, larger twin-engined Lockheed Hudsons were also used. These could carry up to ten passengers but needed a landing field about 1,000 metres long, which was obviously harder to find.

When agents, or supplies, were to be parachuted in – as opposed to landing – the RAF used first Whitleys and then the new four-engine Halifaxes. By 1944, the Americans were also providing B-24 bombers for parachute drops. When parachuting, agents were usually dropped low at about 150 or 200 metres. This reduced the chance of their being spotted in the moonlight as they descended. It also meant that if more than one agent was dropped, there was less chance of their drifting apart or being blown off course. For this reason it was vital to avoid the slightest hesitation in jumping.

All too frequently agents suffered injuries on landing. Christina Granville badly bruised her hip. Paddy O'Sullivan temporarily lost consciousness but was saved from injury by the large number of banknotes stuffed into her clothing. Violette Szabo had badly injured her ankle during parachute training at Ringway, although she jumped well in June 1944.

Agents were sometimes dropped blind, but more usually they went to a dropping ground where a reception committee would be waiting to meet them and would receive and carry off the containers and packages. The reception committee was alerted by phrases broadcast on the BBC's daily *messages personnels*. A first message put them on standby, a second in the evening confirmed that the drop would or would not take place, a decision depending principally on weather forecasts. On Noor Inayat Khan's personal file is a message from one of her colleagues, requesting a BBC broadcast of a 'Message pour Don Quixote' on the day of the new moon (for example, 29 September, 29 October, 27 November and 29 December 1943) in preparation for the next period of moon drops. If a single Lysander was coming, it was to state: 'Les 15 pommes se vendront 8 francs'; a double Lysander operation would be announced by 'Deux panniers de 15 pommes vaudront 8 francs'; a Hudson by '15 grosses pommes vaudront 8 francs'. The first figure represented the landing ground and the second the date.

The pilot was guided in by lights set out by the reception committee, in the form of a T for a parachute drop and an L for a pick-up or landing. The lights were torches or bicycle lamps, or more occasionally bonfires, although these carried a greater risk as they were more visible, so they tended to be used only in remote areas. The pilot had to ensure that he had found the right landing ground, and as he made his first run the reception committee would flash an agreed Morse code letter to him to confirm he was in contact with the right circuit on the ground. When Pearl Witherington was dropped on the night of 22/23 September 1943, the pilot first flew to a 'target' flashing the letter F roughly thirty kilometres south-east of Tours, where he dropped fifteen containers and five packages, and then proceeded to a second 'target' flashing the letter D seventeen kilometres south-south-west of Châteauroux, where Pearl jumped. Inevitably there were occasions when the plane turned back, because of deteriorating weather, because the dropping ground could not be found, or because no lights were set out. The agent might then be flown out again during the next night or two, like Pearl Witherington, or be forced to wait till the next moon period. Paola Del Din's ten abortive sorties to north-east Italy from the SOE base in Apulia during the winter of 1944–5 were probably a record. But she was luckier than a fellow agent who parachuted right into the German barracks at Tolmezzo.

The agent or agents would be followed by the packages, then the containers would be released on a third run over the drop. The rear gunner usually had a view of these parachutes descending to the ground. Containers were stocked with supplies, principally arms and ammunition. They were of three types – a C and H type and an American type. The C containers were made entirely of metal and consisted of three cells or 'bins' enclosed in an outer shell. With a length of 1.6 metres, they could carry a load of 68–72 kilos. The H type, of identical length, consisted of five cells held together by steel strips with locking devices at either end. These had no outer shell. The American type was shorter at just over 1 metre and weighed just under 15 kilos yet carried a payload of 45–68 kilos. The cell was made of layers of thin, highly compressed cardboard, covered in fine fabric.

Items too bulky to fit in a container were made into parcels or packages, wrapped in Hair-loch, a mix of horsehair and rubber. At first some packages were very large, weighing up to 90 kilos but these were very difficult to manhandle in the plane and were also 'liable to rupture the dispatchers'. As a result, the size of parcels was limited to 54 kilos and then 49 kilos.

Edmund Mayer, brother of Percy (who was Paddy O'Sullivan's circuit leader), had one unfortunate incident when a plane, evidently lost, flew under another as it was making its drop, severing parachutes from containers. Two containers then collided in midair. One, filled with grenades and ammunition, caused an almighty explosion, although fortunately not injuring the reception committee below. On average, said Mayer, 'At least one container on every reception dropped without the parachute opening and the contents were destroyed completely.'

The accumulated skill of RAF pilots in finding dropping grounds in remote, often hilly areas, guided only by dim lights, was remarkable. On occasion, they had two extra navigation aids – Eureka and S-phone. The Eureka consisted of a transponder on the ground, which sent out a beam guiding the plane to the dropping ground, that was received by an instrument in the plane known as a rebecca. However, the Eureka was very heavy and for this reason was not liked by agents, who needed to be able to make a quick getaway. The S-phone allowed the pilot to talk directly to the agent on the ground.

Through their security training at Beaulieu, agents were very conscious of the need to leave the dropping ground as soon as possible, particularly when they were close to towns or German guard posts. On occasion, agents were surprised at the lack of any sense of urgency among those who came to meet them. Peggy Knight had to remind the head of her reception committee of the danger of waiting around for more than an hour, while she was questioned and relieved of cigarettes, chewing gum and other commodities that were luxuries in France.

Collecting containers could be problematic, particularly when they had drifted. Being heavy, they took time to unpack, so vans or carts were usually waiting to carry them off to nearby farms. The worst scenario was when a container burst on impact, damaging its contents or exploding. Pearl Witherington received some twenty-three drops, losing only one when a container of hand grenades burst on the ground and continued to explode for some time, helping the Germans to pinpoint the location of the drop.

Sometimes the containers were too heavy to move immediately. At Rochebrune, in the Charente, the Vicomte Jean de Richemont instructed his men to conceal them with piles of logs. When the Germans arrived, alerted by the sound of planes during the night, he coolly invited them out on a tour of the estate.

Edmund Mayer said containers could be located fairly easily but packages 'were invariably spread over quite a large area, sometimes as far as two miles away from the R/C [reception] ground'. This was a problem as the packages 'invariably contained important contents'. Initially, he said, members of reception committees would be people from nearby villages. Later, after D-Day, when security was not so tight, members of Maquis (Resistance) groups were used. Mayer's efficient reception committees consisted of twelve to fifteen men, with four people on the lights, four (or sometimes eight) sentries, and the remainder posted as observers on the extreme perimeter of the landing ground. To increase security, the truck was kept in a safe place about a kilometre away until the containers had actually been dropped, avoiding any undue movement in the field beforehand. After collection, care was taken to remove any undesirable tracks or tell-tale signs left by vehicles or people. As a result Mayer was able to use his two grounds during his whole period in the field.

By contrast, Commandant Paul Schmidt operated on a different principle for operations near Tours in July and September 1943. These involved fifty to sixty men, all recruited from villages about fifteen to twenty kilometres away for security reasons. 'Passengers waited in the cars until five o'clock when the curfew was lifted,' he said. On the night of the operation, the telephone exchange girl of the neighbouring village, who had been recruited, was warned. Her duty was to delay all telephone calls to the Gendarmerie or the Germans.

On one alarming occasion, Mayer was due to receive two drops, one on a new ground, when the waiting Maquis were attacked by the Germans and the ground overrun. Fortunately the cool-headed Mayer, using the S-phone, was able to contact the pilot and redirect him to the other ground, which was possible as the code letter was the same for all Mayer's grounds. After the containers had been taken into hiding, Mayer would go to them as soon as possible and carry out an inventory of the contents, or at least watch while they were opened.

Parachutes, usually made of silk, were eagerly retrieved – they could be used for tents and clothing for the Maquis. Edmund Mayer had to take stern measures to prevent locals from obtaining or stealing parachutes.

Agents were frequently offered a meal on arrival, which was often quite an occasion with wine flowing. Alix d'Unienville, under the impression that the French were half starved, was stunned, when taken to one farm, at the quantity of food on display. 'In the kitchen of the farmhouse our host began to make a colossal omelette on the stove,' wrote Benjamin Cowburn of Octraine, the rich farmer who also received Pearl Witherington.

Some agents were then allowed to sleep; others were immediately taken to another destination or sent onwards – either going to local stations to wait for trains or making for a safe house. Lise de Baissac, an SOE agent operating on her own, provided such a house in Poitiers. When debriefed back in England in August 1943, she explained that 'her job was to receive agents from England when they first arrived in the Field, arrange liaison for them, give them information about the life, and encourage them if they were nervous.'

In the early days, from 1941 to 1943, a large proportion of agents headed for Paris. While a large capital city offered a degree of anonymity, it also carried dangers of constant checkpoints, particularly at metro stations. As a result, agents often chose to walk long distances rather than take trains.

Each agent was given a typed set of mission instructions to memorise well before they set out, starting with an operational name (to be used by SOE), a first name in the field for use by Resistance colleagues and a cover name. The instructions given to Noor Inayat Khan survive on her file. They state her mission – to work as a wireless operator for a locally recruited organiser. They give details of her landing ground and its nearest villages, as well as a contact in Paris – actually the circuit organiser, with the address and location of an apartment ('8th floor opposite lift door') together with telephone numbers, a password and the reply. Noor was told to 'sever your contact with the people who receive you as soon as you possibly can and after that refrain from contacting members of any circuit apart from your own'.

Wireless communications were to be kept short and she was to 'send us as soon as possible the address of a postbox through which we can contact you personally, should the wireless communication break down'. She was also to send the address of a *cachette* or hiding place where she should go in case of difficulties. 'We will then contact you at the *cachette* with a view to getting you out.' In finding a *cachette*, she was to bear in mind that she might have to remain hidden there for up to six weeks.

A further form, headed 'Methods of Communication with H.Q. (apart from W/T [wireless telegraphy])', gave a postbox in a neutral country for postcards – in her case, Oporto. A series of 'convention phrases' were to provide information about the *cachette*. 'Un' + 'Madeleine' meant 'here is my *cachette* with the address'. A 'deux' + 'Madeleine' indicated 'the old *cachette* is no good, here is my new one'. A 'deux' and a 'trois' indicated that the old *cachette* was no good and that she had gone to the new one. 'Always refer to Madeleine as if she were in Portugal and not in France,' she was told. As a last resort Noor was to go to Spain, alerting Baker Street with a postcard with the word 'quatre' in the text as well as 'Madeleine'. On reaching Spain, she was to make for the British consulate at Barcelona and give her name as Inayat Khan.

Nancy Wake, who was involved in Resistance work in Marseilles even before she came to Britain and joined SOE, wrote: 'One always had to have a feasible explanation ready for every single action in case the police were, or became, interested in any person with whom we were seen.'

The natural talkativeness of French city people was a constant problem. Eugenie Roccaserra, who served on the escape line Passeuse, said: 'The situation in Cannes was very difficult for anyone wishing to do clandestine work. People talked too much, because of a natural vanity which made them boast of any operation they undertook.' In Ariège, on the contrary, she found the mountain people very security-minded, and the mass of the population ready to do all they could to help *résistants*: 'They never said anything outright, but one felt in a definitely sympathetic and secure atmosphere.' Often by indirect references she was warned of the dangers ahead on a journey, such as the absence or presence of controls, although the people of Ariège never indicated that they knew what she was doing.

Lieutenant Colonel George Starr (code name Hilaire) of the Wheelwright circuit had the following security rules: 'Never to try to find out more than he was told, never to try and find out who a contact really was, what he was doing or where he was living, only to use organisation names (usually Christian names) and never write anything down or talk unnecessarily'.

For the Diplomatic circuit near Troyes, Commandant Maurice Dupont laid down the following rules:

1. Cafés were out of bounds for ordinary rendezvous.
2. Two members of the organisation were not allowed to go out together without necessity.
3. After meetings or clandestine rendezvous no one was allowed to visit another member of the organisation straight away or go to a letter box.
4. Owners of safe houses were provided with innocent cover stories to explain the presence of a member of the organisation in their house.
5. Alibis were to be prepared for meetings, whether indoors or in the open.

Dupont never slept two nights running in the same house. Five or ten minutes before curfew he would arrive at a friend's house, stay the night and leave the next morning. The friends never knew in advance whether or not he was coming. Meetings with colleagues mostly took place on roads in open country. Circuit members would meet as if they were friends and cycle to a deserted road where the message would be passed on. A guard would watch to see they were not followed. Dupont would visit his radio operator in his house. An open window meant everything was in order; if closed it meant danger. Just in case someone had opened or shut the window by mistake, a broken branch was laid on the path in case of danger. On one occasion, finding he had been followed to the dining car on a train, the determined Dupont went back to another compartment, opened the door onto the track, waited for the man to come along the corridor and pushed him out of the train.

Francis Cammaerts was also specially security conscious, not least because of his hair-raising drive to Paris on the night of his arrival near Compiègne by Lysander on 17 March 1943. 'Although it was well after curfew they drove right through the capital, passing Le Bourget and other guarded areas.' Learning that his main contact had been arrested just as he was due to meet him, he set off to build his own new, secure circuit. After this was established he 'arranged that about eight men (two of whom were ex-Sûreté), should follow prospective recruits, and also men who had already been accepted in the organisation.' This included Cammaerts himself, who was frequently followed by his own people so that he could be sure his movements would not arouse suspicion. He insisted that his men 'should automatically work out for themselves a perfectly good reason for all their actions, in case of snap controls or surprise arrests'. All training was done in the open country, and arms and ammunition hidden in small scattered depots. Cammaerts briefed each leader and they in turn briefed their groups. Initially he gave sabotage lessons in the men's own homes but as material arrived he instructed them in the hills, 'where it was possible to use real explosive without attracting undue attention'. Material was hidden under fodder, occasionally in suitable grottoes or deep wells. Farmers were told exactly what they were being asked to hide, but although some served on reception committees, as a general rule they were not active members of the Resistance. Cammaerts informed recruits that they could not be sacked – in a case of bad discipline they would be shot.

Cammaerts never stayed longer than two or three days in the same house. Mostly he stayed with friends or their relatives and he never went to an unknown address without checking it or being personally recommended by a colleague. In the whole of his two missions he never stayed more than six times in a hotel.

There was nonetheless a danger that security precautions could become obsessive, inhibiting an agent's work. An example is provided in the debriefing of Michael Dequaire, a former schoolmaster. His file states: 'This man, with his seemingly wide knowledge of security theory, seems to be the type of person who would make a very fine agent,' but it soon became evident that security occupied him to such an extent that no positive results were ever obtained from him. 'Soon after his arrival he was being guided by Marianne (Secretary to Député) from Lyons to Clermont-Ferrand. He had on him the sum of 500,000 francs. This worried him to such an extent that he handed 250,000 to Marianne who was already carrying one million francs, a set of crystals and two new codes in a suitcase.'

Lise de Baissac's brother Claude had a lucky escape with his papers. He had been brought before a *commissaire de police*, who examined his papers with great thoroughness and then asked him: 'And how long have you been here? You should tell London to be more careful.' The man was pro-Ally and took no further action on the matter, but de Baissac naturally set about obtaining better papers. There were, he said, three types. First the *faux faux papiers* – those supplied by London. Second were the *vrais faux papiers* – those supplied illegally through the organisations in the field and forged by them. Third were the *faux vrais papiers*, supplied by a contact in the prefecture and generally made out in the name of a real person. Each, he said, had both advantages and disadvantages – the *vrais faux papiers*, for example, had no photograph or record on the police files, should the Gestapo try to check back.

Usually, the false papers supplied by SOE stood up well.

Pearl Witherington had a bad moment when a German controller spent a long time examining her pass with a colleague, only for him to pronounce: 'This is what a genuine pass looks like.'

Travel in wartime was mostly by bicycle, or by train for longer distances. Percy Mayer was understandably irate that his new radio operator, Paddy O'Sullivan, could not ride a bicycle – and was forced to spend a lot of time teaching her all too visibly on local roads.

Trains were subject to numerous checks, both during the journey and on arrival. Queuing for tickets could be a hazard too, as queues were easily watched. A number of agents were able to obtain passes, or season tickets, helped by staff of SNCF (French state-owned railways), who composed one of the largest band of *résistants* in the country. Maurice Southgate obtained such passes, which were used by several members of his circuit, notably Pearl Witherington, who not only had to make numerous long journeys, but for virtually three months had nowhere else to sleep but on a train – with no prospect of even the modest comfort of a couchette.

Virginia Hall sent the following account to her newspaper, the *New York Post*: 'Trains leave at discouragingly inconvenient hours in the morning such as 4 or 5 a.m., or awkward hours in the evening, so that connections with side lines are usually quite hopeless.' As cars and buses were restricted by a lack of fuel, everyone needing to travel tended to fill the few remaining trains to overflowing. In country districts where secondary lines no longer ran, villages were served by 'gazogene' buses, adapted to use charcoal instead of petrol.

As couriers, women agents were obviously exposed to constant risk as they went on their rounds. In Paris, once the Germans had identified a suspect house or apartment they would place a watch in it. When the agent or agents had been arrested, they would leave men there to seize any others who might arrive. Pearl Witherington's boss, Maurice Southgate, was arrested in this way in Montluçon. Noor Inayat Khan escaped such a trap when warned by a concierge.

Cammaerts in his debriefing says: 'Couriers were generally women, and each area had a live boîte aux lettres where the courier for that region could pick up or deliver messages . . . Messages were nearly always verbal, except on rare occasions, when informant [i.e. Cammaerts] instructed couriers to carry their messages on a small piece of paper in their hands, so that they could quickly be disposed of in the case of emergency.'

Another method of communication was the dead drop – which in a country area could simply be an inconspicuous tree. In provincial towns, blocks of apartments had letter boxes for each tenant. If a tenant agreed to supply a key, other agents could come from outside the town, and leave and collect mail from the box. In Paris, by contrast, mail was usually left with the concierge. In general, however, SOE advised the use of live drops, people rather than places.

Couriers played a key role in delivering messages to and from radio operators. If a message was found on a courier, whether in clear or in code, it meant instant arrest. So agents hid them in many ingenious places such as inside the handlebars of a bicycle. It was usually the job of the radio operator to encode and decode the messages. For security reasons radio operators tended to live separately from the others in the network. They were most at risk from direction-finding equipment which the Germans used to pinpoint the location of an outgoing signal.

Didi Nearne heard the Germans banging on the doors of the next-door house as she finished her transmission. Although she was able to burn her messages and hide her set, they were soon on to her, carrying out a thorough search of the house in which they located her radio, her codes and her gun. 'They also found the one-time-pad. They asked me questions about my code. I told them lies.' She was arrested on 25 July 1944 at Bourg-la-Reine at eleven o'clock in the morning, and was taken away to be interrogated.

Lieutenant Martin, who arrived in the field in April 1944, told how his watcher 'came to me and told me two big cars had crossed the village slowly and stopped a hundred yards from our house, hidden at the turn of the road'. He was at his radio in the cellar and coolly carried on until he was warned that the cars were reversing up the road. 'I stopped working and told him to pack. The Jerry's cars were about 30 yards [30 metres] away in front of the house. The Germans, three officers, two sergeants and one civilian, stood up in the cars and looked in the direction of my house, and pointed at it . . . they kept looking at the garden where my aerial was. I went to the staircase, whistled to my assistant and told him not to move the aerial. It had a good background, the slope of a hill, and they could not see it unless it moved. I got back to see the cars driving away at full speed.' He presumed they would return with reinforcements. Finding that the hideout was ready for the set, he handed it over, then took his code, his gun and half his crystals, giving the other half to his assistant to hide.

Still more dramatic was the experience of Captain Rousset – a radio operator who was transmitting from an isolated farmhouse in Brittany when he 'became aware that a plane, which had an aerial around it, was diving on the building. Informant stopped his transmission, hid his set in a barrel in the cellar and then left on his bicycle. On the way he saw several D/F [direction-finding] cars. He was not stopped or questioned.'

At one time Noor was the only radio operator left in Paris, repeatedly moving her set to avoid detection. Later on, some radio operators had several sets and would alternate from one to another. When sets had to be relocated it was usual for a courier to take the set, not the operator – in the agents' necessarily cold calculation it was better to lose the set or the operator, rather than both. For security reasons the crystals that were vital to operate early radio sets were often carried separately too.

Christina Granville's leader, Cammaerts, 'preferred his W/T operator to work in the country, as he considered the chances of being D/F'd [tracked by direction-finding equipment] were considerably less. He said that if a strange car drove up in a country district, that his operator had time to get rid of his set.' On one or two occasions Cammaerts had arrived by car at a farmhouse where Albert, the radio operator, was working and could find no trace of him at all. He later discovered Albert was hiding as he had not recognised the car.

Messages, whether incoming or outgoing, were potentially as incriminating as the sets themselves. But they were usually too long and complex to be committed to memory and had to be both collected from and delivered to the operator. Nor could the operator simply destroy them as soon as they were sent. SOE sometimes requested that a message be retransmitted. The average time for a reception and transmission was forty-five minutes, although in one case Captain Rousset transmitted information for a hazardous two hours. In the intensely busy period around D-Day, the responses were slow – and messages needed to be retained. Albert, who was very security conscious, had a small book where the numbers of all telegrams were inscribed with a résumé of their contents. This was kept buried in a biscuit tin.

Pearl Witherington's organiser, Maurice Southgate, told SOE on his return that while he was held in the Sicherheitsdienst HQ in the Avenue Foch in Paris, he had been shown some documents concerning wireless transmission.

I think the whole story started from the arrest of Prosper when approximately 400 of his men were arrested ... Having one contact with England it was easy for the Germans to organise reception committees on all grounds. Several times I have had proof of agents from SOE being dropped on grounds held by the Germans themselves. The Germans then used the wireless sets, codes and crystals of the new arrivals, but for a long time did not realise that there were two checks on outgoing telegrams (from the field to England), one the true check and the other the bluff check. These [the German] telegrams were sent out with one check only and most obviously should have been phoney to London H.Q. Time after time, for different men, London sent back messages saying: 'My dear fellow, you only left us a week ago. On your first messages you go and forget to put your true check ...'

Later Baker Street became more wary. When Cammaerts's second-in-command, Pierre Agapov, was arrested, the Germans sent messages back to London using his codes. They referred to this tactic as the *Englandspiel*, 'the English game'. However, according to Cammaerts, 'H.Q. were suspicious after the first few messages as the bluff and security checks were not in order.'

Wherever possible, mains electricity was used to run radios as batteries were cumbersome to transport. After D-Day, power for the sets became an increasing problem. Pearl Witherington commented afterwards:

My W/T [wireless telegraphy] operator had considerable trouble in keeping his batteries charged. The pedal *'rechargeur'* was quite out of the question, as also was the power plant, which needed thirty hours of heating and half a ton of wood ... There was no electric current in most of the farms and when we took to the woods still less. Consequently we had to spend most of our time going backwards and forwards to towns to have the batteries charged, and that was not always possible owing to the lack of electric current, due to bombing or sabotage.

The extraordinary achievements of the codebreakers at Bletchley are now widely celebrated but it is a bleak fact that the Germans had their own spectacular and prolonged successes in listening to Allied wireless traffic, not only by breaking codes and obtaining ciphers, but by playing back the sets of captured agents. Most notoriously, in Holland, the Germans arrested a steady stream of SOE agents as soon as they landed – and then played back their radios for a long period, convincing SOE that a large Resistance network was developing. Similar tragedies took place in France, on a lesser scale, although devastating damage was inflicted following the capture of Noor Inayat Khan and her set in October 1943. The Germans successfully played this back for several months before Baker Street became suspicious. The story is enthrallingly told in *Between Silk and Cyanide* by the SOE codemaster Leo Marks, who revolutionised the security of SOE's wireless traffic. Agents were using poems, or famous quotations, for their codes, on the basis that if agents were caught and searched it was better that their codes were in their heads. Marks explains, 'To encode a message an agent had to choose five words at random from his poem and give each letter of these words a number. He then used these numbers to jumble and juxtapose his clear text. To let his Home Station know which five words he had chosen, he inserted an indicator-group at the beginning of his message. But if one message was broken – just one – the enemy cryptographers could mathematically reconstruct those five words and would try at once to identify their source.' (Cammaerts had his own poem and codes but never used them as he considered it would show complete lack of confidence in his radio operator.)

Marks pointed out that the well-known poems and verse used by agents (one had been allowed to use the National Anthem) were vulnerable to any German expert with an anthology of English verse. Instead he largely produced his own poems, including the one famously given to Violette Szabo, 'The life that I have is all that I have'. Second, he introduced the one-time pad – rows of random numbers printed on silk. SOE held the duplicate, so they could be used at both ends for coding and decoding. Each line of numbers was used for one message only and then cut off and destroyed.

Agents in France were under threat from both German and French police. They could be pursued by both the German army's own secret police, the Geheime Feldpolizei under Admiral Canaris, or Himmler's security service, the Sicherheitsdienst (SD), which from the agent's point of view was as one with the Gestapo. According to Cammaerts: 'The Gestapo were particularly active against the clandestine work of the resistance rather than the maquis camps. Their rank and file were extremely incapable, and very much out for their own financial ends. They were stupid, and amongst themselves jealousy prevailed, especially against the Wehrmacht, as each man was trying to get "prize money" for arrests for himself.'

In 1943 the equally dreaded French Milice – military police – were formed. The agent Nancy Wake describes them as 'a small army of vicious Frenchmen dedicated to ferreting out the members of the Resistance and slaughtering them . . . They were arrogant, savagely cruel, treacherous and sadistic. They had absolutely no compassion for any of their compatriots who did not support their beliefs. They were hated intensely – far more than the Germans were.' According to another agent, Madame Gruner, the Milice 'were very rarely satisfied with a superficial exami- nation of papers. In the main they were scoundrels of the lowest type . . . composed of mainly young men who had joined the milice to avoid conscription for work in Germany . . . formerly pimps in Bordeaux.' She observed, 'The Germans had no means of knowing who was a stranger in the area, the milice did. Any stranger was automatically suspect.'

Controls on trains were usually carried out by Germans and as long as the photo on the identity card agreed with the passenger they were not normally suspicious. On the roads, Cammaerts said, 'It was impossible to tell who would be controlling [them], as the French, the Italians, the SS troops, the Wehrmacht, and the Gestapo in civilian clothes with milice to assist them were all carrying out this work.' He told, scathingly, of one occasion, when 'his car was searched for fifteen minutes by specially trained SS troops, who examined the car thoroughly but failed to notice that the boot was so full of arms and explosives that it was weighing down the whole back of the vehicle! Before reaching his destination on this particular journey, informant was controlled no less than three times and yet the material was never discovered.'

Cammaerts also noted that on the Côte d'Azur there were 'a considerable number of voluntary informers, who were of a very bad type indeed. One instance shows the attitude in Nice, where forty women were required as informers and the Kommandant of that town received 300 applications. Anonymous letters denouncing people were sent in daily in this region.' By contrast, there are many examples of the French Gendarmerie cooperating with agents, both early in the war in the Unoccupied Zone and in the run-up to D-Day.

Border police were important to agents too. André Flattot, an American who got to Switzerland, was told he had the choice of being interned or going back to France. Choosing at least temporary freedom, he was conducted to the border by the Swiss police who helped him under the barbed wire and told him to make for a hospital where the Mother Superior would offer shelter. By contrast, police on the Spanish border were not friendly and invariably arrested any agents they found as they descended from the Pyrenees.

Most SOE circuits complained that they were sent too many light weapons. When Christina Granville was in the Vercors with Francis Cammaerts, the failure to drop heavy arms was the prelude to disaster. Some circuits had arms instructors; others would have benefited from having one. Pearl Witherington, reporting on her Wrestler circuit, wrote: 'The heaviest arms we received were the Bren gun and Bazooka, the latter in far too small a quantity. Stens were sent in considerable numbers, but the Sten is hardly a weapon for country fighting. Several accidents happened with the Sten going off on its own. It is difficult to train at short notice peasants who have never held a rifle or seen a machine-gun.' The big advantage of the Sten was that it was cheap to manufacture and would fire captured 9mm ammunition.

One recurrent theme when agents returned to England was the lack of training in guerrilla warfare. 'Our greatest activity consisted in [this]. We have all been sent into the field without the slightest information on the matter . . . even so in the northern Creuse . . . we attacked the enemy each time we had a chance, killing 250 Germans without a single casualty on our side,' wrote Lieutenant D. Cameron of the Fireman circuit. Edmund Mayer felt the same, emphasising the need for training in the defence of camps, ambushes and withdrawals or disengaging actions – all of which were very common to his Maquis groups and of which he himself had little knowledge at the start. This, he said, 'was a great handicap at first' and he was 'obliged to use bluff and learn from experience'.

He also provides details of Maquis camps. 'Men going into the maquis were told they could not abandon it again, and leave was strictly forbidden. If they were found to be completely unsuitable, then they were given some other work to do.' Edmund Mayer emphasised the danger of allowing lorries and cars to drive up to isolated spots, leaving tyre marks and so giving away the location of a camp.

The men were therefore instructed to walk for two kilometres or so, and then meet the lorries, and take the supplies back in farm carts which did not arouse suspicion. The camps were in small woods but not in forests, as the Germans immediately suspected any activity near forests and would send planes to reconnoitre. The highest ground would then be chosen with thick shrubbery and trees, so that tents were well hidden and surprise attacks were impossible.

Training in sabotage and demolition was an important aspect of the work. Mayer would travel from camp to camp on his bicycle. At first he tried to train an instructor in each camp but he was not satisfied with the results and preferred to spend two or three days with the men himself, staying in the camp. In this way he trained about 800 men.

Between 1941 and 1943 SOE sabotage in France was usually aimed at targets such as factories and power stations. With the D-Day landings, there was a concentrated attack on railways, bridges, electric power lines and telephone and telegraph wires, with the aim of doing as much damage as possible to the enemy's communications of every kind. Edmund Mayer's Warder circuit is a good example. Railway tracks were attacked when there was no traffic on them, as 'Maquis groups did not want to derail the train for fear of injury to French people who might be driving, or be on, the engine': the Germans regularly trussed hostages on the front of trains to discourage sabotage attacks.

Another of Mayer's tasks was to harass the enemy by destroying road bridges over rivers and streams, in particular those carrying the main Limoges–Paris road. The intention was to divert German traffic to narrower roads where ambushes could be carried out more successfully. A substantial concrete bridge on this road was blown up by sinking six deep holes into the concrete arches and packing 13.5 kilos [30 pounds] of plastic explosive in each hole.

The charge blew a three-metre gash all the way across the fifteen-metre-wide bridge. Such work was carried out towards midnight when there was least traffic on the road, with sentries posted on either side of the bridge.

With pylons, the method adopted was to cut all four legs, placing the charges on two of the legs about one metre above ground and those on the others rather higher. This ensured that the pylons fell over; if all four legs were cut at the same level the pylons came down vertically and intact. Corner pylons were attacked wherever possible. Road blocks were effected by felling trees. For this there were abundant possibilities, thanks to Napoleon's policy of planting avenues along roads to provide shade for soldiers as they marched. Bren guns were placed on either side of the road to stop the first vehicle in a convoy. The rest of the party, usually about eight men, were stationed so that they could attack the vehicles behind with grenades and small-arms fire. There were strict instructions to withdraw as soon as there was any indication of a counter-attack from the Germans. This kept Resistance casualties to a minimum. On one occasion when Mayer's men had captured a train carrying petrol and torpedoes, the Germans successfully counter-attacked while the Maquis were arguing over what to do with the petrol.

Similar techniques were used effectively by Francis Hillier's Footman circuit in the Toulouse area.

Ambushes proved themselves a very economical form of warfare in areas where the ground was favourable. They involved heavy German losses at almost no cost at all, and they subjected the enemy to a very severe mental strain. Ambushes with automatic weapons did not give very good results, as there was a tendency to shoot from too far. The best results were always obtained when Mills and Gammon grenades were used. The Germans have a great fear of the latter. Two-inch [50mm] mortars and Bazookas gave very good results against lorries . . .

As regards guerrilla tactics, we found it essential to have large numbers of men available. It is impossible to place an ambush in a hurry, and a great many roads have to be guarded for a long time before a column is at last ambushed on one of them. We also found a good intelligence organisation essential, and preferably one set up by specialists working independently. We found we had cut too many telephone lines, and towards the end we were busy trying to reorganise our own circuits.

Most of our losses in men were due to vehicles moving without due care on roads, and falling into German ambushes. During attacks on [our] camps we lost few men, but transport and reserve equipment sometimes had to be abandoned owing to bad siting of the camp. In the end we kept a number of lorries loaded, and also kept our reserve food store separate from the camps.

Commandant Maurice Dupont of the Diplomat circuit described the use of weapons, during his interrogation:

Instruction was given in the use of Stens, revolvers, and light machine guns. While the team leaders were instructing their men, they were supervised by one of the two Lieutenants. At first the recruits were rather hesitant, but once a sabotage operation had succeeded, they became very enthusiastic. The training took place at night and a sentry was posted. If any stranger came into the village, the dogs would immediately give the warning but ... they never barked when villagers were moving at night, hence the 'practical' necessity of using locals as much as possible.

Following D-Day, Jedburgh teams or 'Jeds' began to arrive by parachute. These were teams of army officers in uniform – usually one British, one French and one American – with the aim of organising and arming the Resistance, very much as SOE agents had been doing for many months. In all, eighty-three Jedburgh teams arrived in France, thirteen in June 1944 (including six to Brittany) and the remaining seventy over the next ten weeks. The criticism was frequently made that they were too late, not least by the Jeds themselves who had endured frustrating waits at Massingham, SOE's Algiers camp. However, the arrival of uniformed Allied officers behind the lines was usually a big boost to Resistance morale, and their military training in many cases helped increase the effectiveness of attacks on the Germans. Jeds were to play a particularly important role in Christina Granville's daring mission to the French-Italian Alpine frontier.

Their arrival in many cases was also a surprise. Edmund Mayer recalled that one morning towards the end of July 1944 he was told that there were British officers only three miles away, 'who were promising anybody supplies and arms within twenty-four hours, and who were also training men in the use of any weapon within a few hours'. When Mayer met the Jed team, he explained that 'his men were fully trained and well armed, and that it was frankly quite useless to teach them the use of other weapons, as they were so enthusiastic that they would accept any amount of material which they did not need'. The Jed team immediately understood and went instead to help a neighbouring group with a large number of new recruits.

Major Hillier, code name Maxime, of the Footman circuit, a rare combination of administrator, diplomat, engineer and soldier, also highlighted a problem common to many SOE circuits:

Most of my time was spent in trying to deal with personal quarrels or political disputes; and I met very few leaders who were able to set aside all political loyalties and think only of fighting the Germans. In judging such a state of affairs it must be remembered that France is passing through a political crisis as well as a National crisis . . . [and] the resurgence of French national spirit . . . resulted in an unwillingness to take the advice of Allied officers, and in the failure of several operations.

Always there was the threat of vicious German reprisals. The worst were taking place in the very area and at the very time when Violette Szabo set out to begin her second mission. Pearl Witherington, to the north, wrote:

The Germans were active at the slightest provocation and set fire to many farms and villages, notably Valençay, where they destroyed thirty-five houses. There was a great amount of destruction on their retreat. They did not shoot many civilians but certainly did their best to scare the life out of them. Their treatment of maquisards when they caught one was appalling. After killing them they would proceed to atrocious mutilation beyond recognition.

The valour of SOE's women agents takes on an added dimension with their bravery during captivity and in the face of death. Odette Sansom tells a touching story of how, when she and a dozen other agents were herded together at 84 Avenue Foch in Paris, prior to transport to Germany, another agent, Diana Rowden, moved in front of her so that Odette could exchange a few whispered words out of sight of the guards with Peter Churchill, later to be her husband. Odette, who was one of the few to survive a concentration camp, was not only to be tortured but had to endure the most extreme form of prolonged solitary confinement. Noor Inayat Khan, the first SOE agent to be sent to prison in Germany, spent months of internment at Pforzheim with her hands and feet shackled; the chains on her hands were taken off only briefly at mealtimes. No sooner had her elderly gaoler ordered that they should be removed than the Gestapo telephoned to say they must be put back on. A determined and lucky few escaped: Didi Nearne towards the very end of the war in April 1945 when she was being moved from Markelberg in Silesia, and Alix d'Unienville as she was on her way to Ravensbrück on the infamous 'train of death' in August 1944.

Miss B. Bertram, who ran a base for French Resistance workers at her home, Bignor Manor in West Sussex, said:

I was told afterwards that on the whole it was the highly intelligent, sensitive ones that withstood torture best, not the 'tough guys'. Someone who had been tortured more than once said it was the smaller things that were hardest to bear, such as pulling out teeth or nails or sticking pins into a woman's breast, not the beatings, hangings by the wrists, electric shocks or near-drownings. These made them semi-unconscious after a time. Most agreed that if you could withstand the first quarter of an hour without 'talking' you probably wouldn't talk at all.

Chapter 3

CHRISTINA GRANVILLE

Miss Granville carried sabotage material, secret mail and large sums of money to Poland ... The routes she took over the High Tatra Mountains were of the most arduous description. On one occasion during the severe winter of 1940/1941 she walked for six days through a blizzard in temperatures as low as 30 degrees below zero. In this blizzard more than a dozen Poles lost their lives in this region while attempting to cross into Hungary ... The results of Miss Granville's operations were of the highest importance. She obtained and transmitted most invaluable intelligence including in the Spring of 1941, Germany's decision to attack Russia, in the summer of that year.

Lieutenant Colonel Philip Rea's award citation (recommending an OBE) for Christina Granville

Following her brutal murder in 1952 in a Kensington hotel, aged just thirty-seven, the world's press went wild over Christina Granville's exploits. 'The ace girl spy on either side in either world war', 'The modern pimpernel no man could resist' ... 'She ordered the Gestapo "Set agents free"' ran the headlines. One fellow agent said of her, 'The almost mesmeric attraction she had for men was a blend of vivacity, flirtatiousness, charm and sheer personality. She could switch that personality on and off like a searchlight and blind anyone in its beam.'

Christina was the longest-serving and most capable of all SOE's women agents, outstandingly brave, resourceful and alluring. Her lightning reactions repeatedly enabled her to extract herself from acute danger. Her extraordinary stamina and agility allowed her to survive extreme physical challenges, whether crossing the Tatra Mountains into Poland alone in deep winter snow or making vertiginous ascents in the Alps to meet the Italian partisans, as well as surviving brutal interrogation by the Gestapo. She was capable of magical warmth, but was without the pangs of conscience that hold others back from giving themselves to more than one person. Sweet-natured and intensely loyal to her friends, she also on occasion caused great hurt to those she most loved.

Puzzles about Christina have long abounded. Why did SOE sideline her for two crucial years in Cairo in 1941–3? Was this simply because of friction with her fellow Poles, failings on the part of SOE's often shaky Cairo operation, or jealousies and doubts of a more personal kind? Christina's extensive personal file sheds light on many of these questions.

Christina attracted a constant circle of admirers whom she actively encouraged, even if she described some of them as her lame dogs. Some were passionately in love with her, although their love went unrequited. To others, she gave herself almost impulsively. 'You always knew those who had been blessed, they had a special look,' I was told by one member of the 'firm'.

Dominating her life was her long, affectionate and occasionally tempestuous love affair with her fellow agent Andrew (Andrzej) Kowerski. She refused to marry him on repeated occasions, and she was about to rejoin him when she was murdered. 'When you saw them together they were like a couple,' says her cousin Jan Skarbek who is now head of the Skarbek family. Kowerski was powerfully built, brave, handsome and charming, and for much of the time Christina put out of her mind the accident that had left him with a wooden leg and a great deal of discomfort. Yet she was young, elfin and surrounded by handsome, adoring young men.

Numerous attractive photographs of Christina survive and the remarkable part is that in many of them she appears a completely different person, sometimes with film-star assurance and glamour, sometimes simply full of charm and fun. She could look alternately carefree and vivacious, wistful and retiring, gentle or playfully arch. Some of this was the result of the constantly changing way she wore her mass of beautiful black hair, flowing onto her shoulders or pinned back behind her small pretty ears. No less striking were her exquisitely delicate features and startlingly white skin.

In 1953 it was announced that Sarah Churchill, Sir Winston's actress daughter, was to play the part of Christina in a film, but the project lapsed and Christina's story was first told by a South African writer, Madeleine Masson. By one of life's strange coincidences, Christina served as Masson's stewardess on the voyage from Cape Town to London on the *Winchester Castle* in May 1952. 'I marvelled at the grace and fluidity of her movements. I thought perhaps she was an ex-ballerina assoluta who had fallen on evil times,' recalled Masson. The ship docked on 13 June 1952 and just a few days later Masson read of Christina's death in the newspapers. Masson explains how Christina's friends and family united, successfully, to prevent the publication of the sensational memoirs that numerous authors were evidently hoping to write. She herself was finally able to proceed when she won the confidence and cooperation of Kowerski.

Christine, as she was later known throughout British Special Forces, had been born Krystyna Skarbek on 1 May 1915 in Piotrkow, eighty kilometres from Warsaw. The Skarbeks were an ancient family who had helped drive the Teutonic knights from Poland in 1410. The crested gold ring that Christina wore on her third finger was embedded with a thread of iron, recalling a famous incident in Polish history when the Emperor Henry II was on the verge of invading Poland. Seeking to convince Jan Skarbek, the Polish plenipotentiary, that resistance was useless, the emperor pointed to his coffers, brimming with gold and precious stones that would fund his army. Skarbek calmly slipped off his ring, threw it into the nearest chest and said, 'Let gold go to gold, we Poles prefer iron.'

Count Frederic Skarbek was Chopin's godfather. Christina's father, the impoverished Count Jerzy, married Stephanie Gold-feder, the daughter of a leading Jewish financier in Warsaw. He bred racehorses on their country estate at Piotrkow, living extravagantly with a houseful of liveried servants. Christina's mother was 'a very charming lady', according to Jan Skarbek, but as a Jewess she would inevitably not have been wholly accepted in aristocratic circles at the time. For Christina, it was a tragedy that financial problems led to the sale of the family estate, doubly so when her father died soon after in 1930.

Although a lovable and loving child, she was also independent, strong-willed and at times ungovernable. When sent away to board at a convent school, her escapades became too much when she set fire to the cassock of a priest during Mass. 'Those poor nuns,' sighs Jan Skarbek. After a first brief failed marriage, Christine married a remarkable adventurer from the Ukraine, the handsome but irascible Jerzy (George) Gizycki. He had run away from home aged fourteen, working as cowboy and gold prospector in America before going on to become an author and foreign correspondent, a Polish Hemingway with a passion for Africa who even before the war was working for British Intelligence.

In the summer of 1939 they were living in East Africa. As soon as war was declared, Christina sailed on the first ship available for England where she arrived early that October. Determined to take up the fight, she made contact with the brilliant Australian, George Taylor, a key figure in setting up SOE, via introductions from Sir Robert Vansittart at the Foreign Office and the fearless Frederick Voigt of the *Manchester Guardian*, one of the first foreign correspondents to draw attention to the true nature of Hitler's National Socialism.

SOE's first report on Christina, written by 'Fryday' and dated 7 December 1939, begins: 'Madame G. visited me at four o'clock. She is a very smart-looking girl, simply dressed and aristocratic. She is a flaming Polish patriot. She made an excellent impression and I really believe we have a PRIZE.' Her husband Jerzy, it continues, has or had a post at the Polish consulate in London.

The young man R is a distant connection. I understand he will do anything for her and with her. [R was Radziminski, of whom more shortly.] Her idea is to bring out a propaganda leaflet in Buda and to smuggle it over the frontier herself. She is an expert skier and a great adventuress . . . It appears that she has visited the Polish winter resort of Zakopane for many years and knows every man in the place. It was her chief delight at one time to help the boys smuggle tobacco over the frontier just for the fun of the thing. She is confident that these men will help her now. She is absolutely fearless.

Christina told Fryday that the Germans were behaving with far greater brutality than the Russians. 'She thinks it most necessary to let the Poles know what is going on and that they are not forgotten . . . She says that sabotage is absolutely essential . . . to intimidate the Germans who are great bullies but not brave men when attacked singly.' Christina also promised regular reports from Austria to be sent by Slovenes who had lived for years in Vienna. 'She needs money for her work and I think she is going to earn it,' concluded Fryday.

By 15 December he was writing to Taylor: 'All her visas are in order and she is anxious to leave – *le plutôt possible*. She has had bad news about some of her friends, this enrages her and she is anxious to be up and away.' Christina was put on six months' trial. Her commission was to run for that period with £250 in financial support, and she was given the code name Madame Marchand. By her own wish, her salary was to be paid into Voigt's bank account.

Christina left England for Hungary on 21 December 1939, flying to Paris and travelling on via Italy. Soon after her arrival in Budapest she met Andrew Kowerski, who was already a legend, having won the Polish VC, the Virtuti Militari, fighting in the Polish army's only motorised brigade during the desperate three-week invasion campaign.

After Poland had been overrun, Kowerski had succeeded in crossing into Hungary where he was interned. Absconding, he established himself in Budapest and built up a series of escape lines. His object was to enable Polish and Czech internees in Hungary to escape from confinement and also to 'exfiltrate' volunteers from Poland and Czechoslovakia for service abroad. Among these were Polish pilots, who were to play a key role in the Battle of Britain in the summer of 1940. According to his citation in SOE files, he 'organized a number of posts on the borders of Slovakia and Jugo-Slavia and in the course of numerous operations transferred some 5,000 Poles and Czechs to appropriate destinations'.

The attraction between Andrew and Christina was immediate. Within days they had become lovers and were sharing a flat. Yet as always, other admirers were in constant pursuit. One of these was the Pole, Radziminski, who was also working for the British. A SOE note of 11 March 1940 says cryptically: 'Her attractiveness appeared to be causing some difficulty in Budapest and . . . one of our agents had attempted to commit suicide, first by attempting to throw himself in the Danube which was frozen and secondly by attempting to shoot himself.'

According to SOE, Christina recruited Andrew to work for the British to make use of his exceptional knowledge of frontier conditions. Although under constant Gestapo surveillance in Hungary, he distributed arms and explosives to Poles there and in Poland. He also arranged couriers operating in Poland and elsewhere in Central Europe, and helped Christina organise further escape routes for British POWs in Poland. In addition he carried out intelligence work on behalf of Britain in connection with enemy traffic on the Danube and on the Hungarian railways.

The loss of his leg following a hunting accident before the war made it impossible for Andrew himself to undertake long journeys on foot to Poland, but he drove huge distances from the Polish border to the Jugoslav frontier, constantly ferrying escapers and evaders. He was arrested four times by the Hungarian police. On one occasion he was captured on the Slovakian frontier while waiting for the arrival of some British escapees from Poland. Although roughly handled by the police, he managed to escape.

In a statement dated 23 February 1941 (a year later), Christina described her mission as follows: 'The Poles were of course receiving no news except German news and the main thing was to make them understand that Britain and the Allies had not forgotten them. I intended, therefore, to try and send them news each day by some regular radio service.'

In Budapest, Christina had met H.D. Harrison who, besides being the correspondent of the *News Chronicle*, was working for Taylor. He had been told to provide technical help for Christina's proposed radio bulletins and in turn asked her to act as an intermediary between him and the Poles.

As a result my flat in Budapest became a dump for everything being sent to Poland including high explosive . . .

I first went into Poland in February 1940 and took with me everything Harrison had given me. Since Radjiminsky had been dismissed I was asked whom I could recommend as an intermediary in my absence to which I replied that the only person I could trust was André Kowersky . . . [he] was an officer of the mobile Polish division which had escaped into Hungary during the war practically intact and which had later gone to Palestine. K was known to Generals Matsek and Sikorsky and had been ordered to stay in Budapest to help the remainder of this division to escape, a job he did with considerable success and at great personal risk.

Masson relates that Christina made her first crossing into Poland with a skiing instructor who was a member of the Polish Olympic team. A file note of 11 March 1940 tells a different story. It begins:

Mrs Marchand has left for the north-east frontier. She has told everyone she is going into Transylvania to get information for her newspapers. She will slip over the frontier on skis. Johan had promised help in getting over and given detailed instructions and a guide. At the last moment he refused to give any contacts in Poland itself and finally the guide's courage failed and he decided not to go as he was not too good on skis. Mrs M. seemed rather pleased than otherwise at the idea of going alone. She knows the mountains perfectly and has no doubt as to her own capacity to get over safely, make her contacts and get back.

With this come the first hints that Christina was having trouble with her fellow Poles, who were muttering that, 'because she was "in the pay of the English", she was no longer a trustworthy Pole'. However, a cable of 22 February announced that 'all friction with the Poles had been eradicated. Perhaps I should say that their fear was that Madame Marchand would be arrested and betray their line of communications.'

Christina entered a country where almost the entire population, from the youngest to the oldest, was hostile to the Germans and involved in active or passive resistance. Christina's statement continued: 'I stayed 5 weeks in Poland during which time I covered practically the whole country on foot, by rail, carts etc, collecting all possible information. I stayed 2½ weeks in Warsaw and there I found an organization called the P.P. whose activities included the secret publication of some twenty-seven newspapers. This organization has since been wiped out all over Poland by the Germans.'

The Poles had a long-standing tradition of underground struggle and revolt, developed during foreign domination in past centuries. The Home Army in Warsaw ran a whole series of small factories, supplying sabotage materials and building up stocks of arms for a general uprising. Some of Christina's Polish contacts belonged to an organisation called 'The Musketeers' set up under an engineer and inventor called Witkowski who Christina had met before the war in Paris. He became an important contact, though this was to lead to serious setbacks which could not have been foreseen. While in Poland, Christina wrote a discreet letter to Jan Skarbek's family who had now retired to live on a small farm in central Poland. In it, she said she had seen her mother in Warsaw and tried in vain to persuade her to leave.

An internal SOE memo of 14 April 1940 relates:

Mrs Marchand has returned from her trip to Poland. She has made many contacts there and has prepared a scheme of propaganda work. First and foremost this depends on her having at her disposal here a radio sending station of any ordinary commercial type (it need not be a special secret type of apparatus) which could be mounted on a motor-car or van and with which she can send messages which can be heard by ordinary commercial type radio receiving sets in Poland. She has made contact with the PPS – the Polish Socialist Party, which is the only well organised party in the country and which has united with itself the Peasant Party, the Democrat party, the socialist party and the former Trade Union party. This group has united some 18 militant organisations and has over 100,000 armed men scattered throughout both Russian and German Poland ready at any minute to revolt when the order is given.

Christina's plan was to broadcast at fixed hours on a fixed wavelength, providing 'a news bulletin giving a real picture of the situation and of what the Allies are doing. Poland is starved for real news – they are sick of German propaganda and they cannot get the news in Poland from England and other allied stations owing to German interference.' The bulletins would be taken down by stenographers and 'reproduced in multigraphed sheets which will be rushed all over the country and will serve as a news agency to supply the many small illegal sheets which already exist. Special secret newspapers will also be issued based on these bulletins and on special articles which will be smuggled in from here.'

Christina had also reported that she had had serious difficulties from 'Volksdeutsch' (ethnic Germans living in Poland) in the new administrative service – there were five or six in Warsaw – who alleged that they were British agents and said that if anyone came to Poland to do propaganda work they would have known about it. Christina was therefore suspected by the Polish organisations and was in danger of being killed as an agent provocateur. Fortunately friends vouched for her just in time.

She also proposed to work with General Balachowicz, who was famous as a fighter for Polish liberty before 1919.

His prestige is very great. He has some 500 officers organized for guerrilla work in Russia when the moment arrives. These will lead the Polish soldiers now demobilised and start a revolt against

Russia in [Russian-occupied Poland] and the Ukraine. They have small arms but need technical arms – anti-tank guns and rifles and ammunition and also money ... No work is possible on the German side of the frontier owing to the terrorist methods of the Germans who kill 100 men chosen at random for every act of sabotage. In Russia much more is possible and more is already being done.

The memo continues:

Mrs M. was astonished at the terrible disorder of the German administration. New orders are posted daily, withdrawn, cancelled, contradicted, re-enacted so that complete disorder exists. This is partly due to the intense hatred between the Gestapo and the Army. Now the Gestapo are being withdrawn to Germany as it seems there is need for more of them there. Only older men – Gestapo and troops – are being left. Many transports of troops have left German occupied Poland, crossed the Russian frontier and disappeared in a South Easterly direction. From Ljubljin troop transports were leaving day and night but it cannot be ascertained whether they were going to the Rumanian frontier or towards the Turkish frontier. The troops leave as a rule very drunk on vodka which is issued purposely to keep them in good spirits.

Christina relayed news of a terrible massacre, almost a second Katyn, by the Germans of their *own* men. 'Some three weeks ago 10,000 Bavarian troops were brought to Vutch where they were kept in trains guarded by troops with machine guns. For two weeks they were kept without food and Poles who tried to feed them by throwing food through the train windows were shot. Finally they were taken out, lined up and shot down with machine guns. It is believed they had tried to revolt.'

The news that Christina brought from Warsaw was equally grim. 'Over 100 Poles are shot every night. The terror is indescribable. Yet the spirit of the Poles is magnificent. Mrs M. went all over the country by horse and cart or in third class railway carriages and examined especially the military organisations. She would like to take a Polish speaking British officer over to show him.'

On 22 April 1940, shortly after her return, a memo states:

I find myself becoming something of a fan of Madam Marchand and would like to see her get her way . . . I suggest she be recalled to England for discussions, and that if you are impressed by what she says . . . sent to Paris to see whether the Polish mission would approve of her plan. Without such approval I feel the plan might lead us into trouble, but with such approval it may be a good egg, which could be carried on by Madame Marchand and her van driver wireless man as a unit entirely divorced from our own activities . . . in the event of things going wrong in Hungary for us, such a freedom station might manage to exist for some considerable time.

Meanwhile, Christina's husband Jerzy was in regular contact with London, writing on friendly terms to his controller, X.3 (whose name is blanked out but who was evidently a woman as he refers to her as mademoiselle). On 5 April 1940 he wrote from Col de Voza in Haute-Savoie, saying: 'I am still in the mountains, where am trying to regain my "form", seriously affected by a long "grippe" and its complications.' The reply of 12 April explained discreetly: 'Your wife is in your own country, visiting her relatives, consequently it is not very easy for her to write to you.' Jerzy was occupying his time writing a series of articles and reports designed to boost morale in Poland.

By 15 May, Jerzy is writing from the Hotel Danube in the rue Jacob in Paris: 'I am very much worried about [Christina] from whom I have not heard lately.' On 21 May he wrote again, saying that Christina had told him she 'will have to postpone her trip to London through Paris. Hard luck for me. I just hope she will not get into any serious trouble.'

On 6 June he wrote again, ruefully saying that Christina had failed to get the necessary transit visas. 'It does not look as if my desire to be with my wife or at least nearer to her, – should be fulfilled soon.'

Nearly four weeks later, on 1 July, he writes from London, with Christina still uppermost in his thoughts, complaining that his 'chances of finding here some interesting work are practically null, – I have decided to go to Canada and to prepare there some sort of home to which [my wife] could come when she gets out of her actual predicament.'

Christina had been prevented from returning to London from Hungary because the Italians had refused her a visa. It was necessary, obviously, for her to travel back south of the Alps, avoiding Austria and Germany. 'Harrison, however, who was going to England in any case, took an amplified version of my report.' Almost immediately after he left, Italy declared war and from that time on, Christina said, 'I was completely cut off from England.' She was also cut off from her source of funds but continued to send material into Poland via courier, helped by occasional sums from Andrew.

At the beginning of June 1940, failing to find anyone to act as a courier to Poland, she decided to go again herself. Unfortunately she was arrested while crossing Slovakia and quickly learnt that a reward of 10,000 marks had been offered for her capture.

They cross-questioned me, keeping me against a wall for several hours covered with revolvers but I swore I did not know 'the English' and so on. The Slovaks did not believe me and wanted to hand me over to the Gestapo, but having found 145,000 Zloty on me and 75 dollars, and 15,000 Kronen on a boy accompanying me, they apparently preferred that to the 10,000 Marks reward and we were able to escape.

On arriving in Warsaw on her first journey in the spring of 1940 she had sought out her mother and had begged her to go into hiding. As both a countess and a Jew, Stephanie Skarbek was certainly being watched, but nothing would persuade her to abandon her work teaching French in a clandestine school. Shortly after Christina's second visit to Poland, two men with swastika armbands dragged the countess from her flat. She was never heard of again.

Back in Budapest, Christina was now without money or a means of communication with London but was able to send a letter via the British Legation. This was the beginning of a relationship that was eventually to prove her and Andrew's salvation. With Andrew she now 'did everything possible to organize the evacuation of prisoners from camps, but finally in October we could carry on no longer as we were penniless. AA [the name has been blanked out in the document] however, at last began to help us and BB [also blanked out] said he could employ us on news work at 500 Pengoes a month.' The likelihood is that AA was no one less than Sir Owen O'Malley, the minister in charge of the British Legation in Hungary, or one of his senior officers. (At this time ministers and legations were more usual than embassies and ambassadors.)

Christina continues: 'We began by working on observation on the Danube . . . and on traffic between Germany and Rumania via Hungary.' During the first half of October 1940 a man came from Poland with the news that a new organisation existed. 'Its activities were sabotage and information only. The head of it was a friend of ours whom I had known for 12 years and he had sent me by special courier a long letter with a great deal of material.' This included a detailed description of all the work that the organisation had done: 'details of the work of German and Polish armament factories, plans of the factories, details of troop movements, of the numbers and colours of German regiments, plans of aviation fields, important information on new torpedoes and mines and very detailed information on new U-boats which were being constructed at Danzig'.

There was also information about sixteen prisoners of war, British pilots and aviators, who had escaped. They had been hidden in a Warsaw asylum for the deaf and dumb but as 'an order had just come out that the Germans were to shoot all lunatics, criminals, idiots, etc', Christina immediately set about organising their escape. After waiting for help for five weeks she decided she would mount the rescue herself.

Leaving Kacha Koshitza on 13 November 1940 she arrived in Warsaw five days later, only to find that the Englishmen had already departed for Russia. News had also come through that Hungary had joined the Axis. Christina heard that the English group had reached Białystok and had taken the train to Kiev, only to be handed over by the Russians to the Germans. But two had escaped and Christina was to find them safe in Belgrade.

On one of her journeys back from Poland, Christina fell in with a young Polish nobleman, Count Wladyslaw Ledochowski, who was also returning from a secret mission. As they crossed the Slovak border they were spotted and had to run deep into the woods, eventually spending a night there. Nestling together for warmth, they were soon in each other's arms and by the next morning Ledochowski was giddy with love. Although Christina had told him about Andrew, Ledochowski was convinced she was now his. When they arrived to relate their adventures at the flat in Budapest which Christina shared with Andrew, his feelings were all too obvious and Christina was forced to explain to Andrew what had happened. Andrew was naturally distressed but resolved to put the matter behind him. Ledochowski continued to see them at every opportunity and made no secret of his intense admiration for Christina. It was a situation that was to repeat itself again and again over the next three years, leading inevitably to a situation where Andrew himself was to fall for the advances of an admiring young girl.

Christina had brought back alarming news of new gasses

that the Germans were producing, complete with the formulas, as well as up-to-date information on ammunition factories in Germany and Poland. There were 'detailed plans of aerodromes, aircraft factories, the number of planes which existed in Poland, details of torpedoes, U-boats and a new torpedo invention'. During the summer of 1940 the Germans had seized a large number of workers from Poland, forcing them to work in munitions factories. Among them, the Resistance organisation had been able to place sixteen technical engineers, who were now at both factories and railway stations in Germany and were able to report almost exactly how many railway wagons left Germany, providing details of their contents and destinations. Christina explained: 'Like all the documents which I brought out, this letter and these reports had been photographed on 35-mm. film, the rolls of which I carried in my gloves.'

In all, Christina crossed the Polish border six times and the Slovakian border eight times. As Germany exerted pressure on Hungary, both she and Andrew came under increasing police suspicion. On 24 January 1941 both were arrested by the Hungarian police and handed over for separate interrogation by the Gestapo. Despite rough treatment they maintained the cover story they had agreed. Christina succeeded in biting her tongue hard enough to draw blood and feint a coughing fit. She was so convincing that a Hungarian doctor who was hastily called in diagnosed tuberculosis. He was encouraged in this by a shadow on her lung, which was the result of inhaling fumes while working in an office over a car repair shop. Andrew, still under suspicion, was temporarily released on account of her illness, partly in the hope that he might lead the Gestapo to other members of the group. In her report Christina briefly describes the incident: 'Questioned for 24 hours by the Germans. I again denied any dealings with the British other than a flirtation with [name blanked out] and we were released.'

Their new friend, the British minister, Sir Owen O'Malley, decided they had to leave Hungary immediately over the weekend. He recalls in his memoirs, *The Phantom Caravan*: 'The Gestapo had many curious habits, and among them was a great attachment to weekends without engagements.' Knowing that neither Christina nor Andrew would be allowed out of the country by the Hungarian border guards, he gave them both British passports. The names they chose were Christine Granville (appropriate in both French and English) and Andrew Kennedy. O'Malley then ordered a junior member of the legation to drive to Yugoslavia. He was to take O'Malley's own Chrysler, which had a boot large enough to conceal Christina as they crossed the frontier. Andrew travelled separately in his little Opel, using the ruse of pushing it across the border to await collection by a customer on the other side. Once across, he produced his new passport for the Yugoslav customs and drove off in jubilation.

O'Malley said of Christina: 'She was the bravest person I ever knew, the only woman who had a positive *nostalgie* for danger. She could do anything with dynamite except eat it.'

In Belgrade, Christina had the unexpected thrill of meeting her two 'boys' as she called them – actually the first POWs taken at Dunkirk to escape and return to England. She and Andrew then set off on an arduous trip via Sofia, where they met Aidan Crawley from the legation, handing him vital microfilms showing German troops massing on the Russian border. Ironically, although Stalin was given the clearest possible warnings by the British of the impending attack, he chose to disregard them.

After alarming delays at the Bulgarian–Turkish border, they were at last allowed to drive on in the valiant little Opel. In Istanbul, Andrew suffered the further affront of having the car impounded by Turkish customs, but they secured a receipt and promptly took a taxi to the Park Hotel, then the most comfortable in the city. After a few days exploring Istanbul at leisure, Christina was soon assisting SOE's Polish Section in their courier and contact work. Soon after came the news that Jerzy was going to join them with a view to taking over Christina's work in Hungary. For Andrew, this brought the prospect of a potentially disastrous confrontation. Christina, however, appeared serenely confident that she could handle the situation.

As Christina and Andrew were now 'burnt' as far as Hungary was concerned, Jerzy was indeed essential if the organisation they had left behind was to remain active. He wrote a lengthy report under his cover name, G. Norton, recounting that, after meeting them in Istanbul, he had been directed first to Belgrade and then on to Budapest, where he arrived on 1 April 1941, remaining for ten days and leaving at the same time as the rest of the British Legation with the intention of rejoining Christina and Andrew in Istanbul. His task, he says, was 'to establish a communication with our men in Poland, – a contact that would work after the closing of the Legation and the full evacuation of its staff'. He continues: 'I have made an arrangement with a Pole/absolutely trustworthy, intelligent, highly educated, courageous and having many friends among influential Hungarians,' who was to act as intermediary between 'our men in Poland and me at Istanbul/or elsewhere'.

Jerzy describes the increasing dangers at border crossings: 'The control on the borders, made easier by the melting of the snow in the mountains, [has] become much more severe and several Polish messengers [have] been shot by the Slovak and German frontier guards.' Jerzy had therefore left his man in Budapest with a second set of codes and messages in case the first fell into Slovak or German hands. He added: 'haste did not permit me to work out a more complicated, safer code and I had to recur to a simple code, based on dictionaries.' As the radio work with Poland was all to be done by Aidan

Crawley's office, he had sent them 'all the technical details – signals, frequencies, waves, times of transmission'.

Two days before leaving Budapest, Jerzy had received instructions for 'Lajos', a Hungarian Jew who had been carrying out minor sabotage work. Lajos was to be told to concentrate on lines of communication, particularly railways. Not knowing when he would be back in Istanbul, Jerzy had told his man in Budapest to address his communications to Aidan Crawley, who was interested in cooperation between 'our men in Poland [and] the RAF'.

Jerzy had wanted Christina and Andrew to remain and help him in Istanbul. But when he returned they had already set out across Turkey. In a cold fury, Jerzy explained in his report that he had sent a message to Istanbul 'asking my wife to remain there till my return. She was the only person fully au courant of the matters we were working on and would have been indispensable in Istanbul for liaison work during my absence.' His telegram had read: 'Please notify Granvil wait Istanbul my return.' This had been changed, he said, to read: 'Please notify Granvil not to wait Istanbul,' in his view 'a change too considerable to be due to faulty transmission'. The result, said Jerzy, 'was that my wife and Kennedy were sent away from Istanbul when they were most needed there'.

When diplomatic relations between Britain and Hungary were severed, Jerzy accompanied the British Legation staff on their way through Russia, smoothing their passage with his expert knowledge of Russian. This help was much appreciated but the irascible Jerzy saw the episode in a different light. 'I could have been back in Istanbul easily some ten days sooner if the Embassy at Moscow and the Legation at Tehran [had] acted promptly. Even so my trip Tehran–Erzeroum over the mountains – the normal route through Irak being closed at that time – was organized entirely on my own initiative and in spite of certain discouraging advices from the official circles, where I was told at first that the Turks will never give me permission to cross the frontier military zone.'

After returning to Istanbul, he stayed on to work for Colonel de Chastelain, who was in charge of the Intelligence Section in the British Embassy. De Chastelain said of Gizycki that besides being the most difficult man he had ever known, he was also the most capable and efficient individual he had ever worked with. But although Jerzy volunteered for service with the underground organisations in Poland, he was unable to get there.

SOE files offer a poignant glimpse of the dangers faced by the network that Christina and Andrew left behind. Marcin Lubomirski,

though much harassed by the Hungarian police and Gestapo, acted as a link between the Intelligence organization in Poland and the co-operative and pro-Ally Turkish Legation in Buda-Pest. He took an active part in the exfiltration of British POW's from Poland, some of whom stayed at his flat . . . After being arrested by the Gestapo Lubomirski was sent to Mauthausen concentration camp where he narrowly escaped the gas chamber. He was released after serving 1½ years imprisonment.

Another who actively helped exfiltrate British POWs was Antoni Filipkiewicz, also arrested and thrown into Mauthausen for a year. Six others who acted as couriers to Poland were arrested and met their deaths in the Mauthausen gas chambers. The author concludes: 'They were the best of the bunch, but as I only know the true names of three of them and little else besides, and as none of them has, to my knowledge, any surviving relatives, posthumous awards in this case would seem to have no point.'

Meanwhile, after paying a large bribe for the release of the Opel from customs, Christina and Andrew had set out on an epic journey across Turkey and round the eastern shore of the Mediterranean to reach SOE headquarters in Cairo. While in

Ankara, they had stayed at the British Embassy where they met the young Julian Amery who was later parachuted into Albania by SOE. In his book *Approach March* (1973), Amery recalls: 'Kennedy had an artificial leg and many valuable rolls of microfilm were brought out in it. Christine was one of the gentlest looking girls I have ever met, and it was hard to credit her with some of the bravest clandestine achievements of the war.'

The drive round the eastern end of the Mediterranean took them through Syria, then under Vichy French control. Evidently using all her personal charm and diplomatic skill, Christina succeeded in obtaining transit visas from the Vichy representatives in Turkey. The Polish Deuxième Bureau, which covered intelligence and counter-espionage, put a different spin on it – only German spies could have been offered free passage in this way, they said.

As Christina and Andrew crossed the border into Syria, they saw thousands of storks gathering to migrate northwards. For a while they sat in silent admiration, poignantly aware that, unlike them, the great birds were free to fly to Poland. Arriving at the legendary St George's Hotel in Beirut with its private beach, they came face to face with a group of smartly dressed German officers sitting in the hall. But their spirits rose as the receptionist, seeing their British passports, promptly offered them the best room in the hotel at a standard price.

A still bigger fillip awaited them at the Palestine border where they found they were expected by the British. They were immediately issued with petrol coupons and ration books, and told to drive on to Haifa where they were booked into a hotel. The warm welcome continued in Jerusalem where rooms had been reserved in the cool and attractive Eden Hotel. Here Christina had the added pleasure of finding a great friend, Sophie Raczkowski, who lived with her husband in an old house in the hills overlooking the city.

Finally the little Opel reached Cairo, where they were to

stay at the Continental, a pleasant rambling hotel with a wide shady veranda. Here they encountered the Polish Carpathian Lancers, recently returned from the desert. In command was Colonel Wladyslaw Bobinski, whose horse Christina had ridden as a teenager. Andrew's cousin Ludwig Popiel was also with the regiment.

Jerzy's report, quoted above, continues with an irate account of the problems Christina and Andrew now encountered with SOE.

I have been informed by my wife that Maj. Wilkinson has notified her that she, Kennedy and I are suspect as the organisation in Poland, we were in touch with and which counts between its members well known Polish patriots and friends of Gen. Sikorski, – is a Gestapo organisation.

This is the reward from the British Government for all our efforts, our sincere desire to do some useful work, and the grave risks my wife and Kennedy were running, – she while crossing repeatedly into Poland and he while getting hundreds of the Polish military men out of the Hungarian detention camps.

In Jerusalem, he continued, the whole Polish colony was talking about Christina 'and us two with her, being suspected by the British of espionage and of our being called to London to justify our acts. This sort of information could only have come from the Cairo office.' Jerzy protested against this unfair, ungentlemanly attitude, adding that although finally they were cleared by 'a message from London stating that we, personally, have acted out of patriotic motives and are free from suspicion . . . collaboration with our countrymen has been rendered impossible'. This was the reason, he said, that he did not accept an offer of work in Persia, thereby bringing his own remarkable work for Britain to an abrupt end.

SOE's Peter Wilkinson describes his meeting with Andrew and Christina in his book *Foreign Fields* (1997). On his arrival in Cairo he had found a telegram instructing him to break off contacts with any Polish organisations with which he had previously been in touch in SOE's Balkan network, including Christina and Andrew's. 'It proved a painful interview which I handled badly; I was just back from Crete, more over-stressed than I cared to admit. Impatient with their special pleading I made life long enemies of both of them, which I later came greatly to regret. However, I neglected to have them struck off the SOE pay-roll so both of them were able to subsist in Cairo for the time being,' he wrote.

Wilkinson's own memo dated 10 October 1941, commenting on Jerzy's remarks, goes some way to providing a final word on this desperate interlude. He acknowledges 'the disgraceful treatment' of Christina but points out that the source of the problem was that

we had been asked by Sikorski to break all contact with the Witkowski organisation [also referred to as Witkowski's Musketeers] as soon as possible ... We had information that the Witkowski organisation had, in fact, been penetrated by the Gestapo largely because it was mainly composed of amateurs. In these circumstances I warned I.b. M.E. [deputy chief Middle East] to keep an eye on Kennedy and Gisycka while they were in Cairo. This came to the ears of Colonel Ross who, I understand, informed Kennedy of whom he was a personal friend. As you can imagine, the fat was then properly in the fire. Actually there was no doubt about their loyalty though it was alleged that, owing to the indiscretion of Madame G. [Christina], one member of the VIme Bureau organisation was killed when they were crossing Slovakia in the same party.

This allegation, although not rebutted in the memo, was certainly never substantiated.

Andrew's case was taken up in London by Colin Gubbins, who wrote to General Sikorski on 17 June 1941:

Last year before I came to this appointment a Polish citizen named

Kowerski was working with our officials in Budapest on Polish affairs. He is now in Palestine with the officials for whom he was previously working. I understand from Major Wilkinson, who is out there now, that General Kopanski is doubtful about Kowerski's loyalty to the Polish cause, owing to the fact that Kowerski has not reported to General Kopanski for duty with the Brigade. Major Wilkinson informs me that Kowerski had had instructions from our officials not to report to General Kopanski, as he was engaged at that time on work of a secret nature which necessitated his remaining apart. It seems therefore that Kowerski's loyalty has only been called into question because of these instructions.

Gubbins continued: 'I am anxious that this man should not suffer through any fault of ours and I should be very grateful if General Kopanski could be informed.' The reply of 24 June 1941 from Polish General Staff HQ at the Hotel Rubens confirms that 'a W/T message has been sent to General Kopanski explaining the situation'.

SOE telegrams show genuine concern in London at Christina's and Andrew's plight (they are referred to as X and Y). 'I would like to make clear that we are under strongest possible obligation to X . . . Whilst we have no obligation to Y we would in all the circumstances be prepared to repatriate him,' runs a cable of 3 August 1942. Another adds, three days later: 'She has been offered a passage to England but prefers to stay here. She is financially provided for and lacks nothing except employment. We are trying to remedy this.'

Despite these troubles Christina and Andrew were entrusted with occasional missions by SOE. Soon after her arrival in Cairo, Christina was able to continue her courier and contact work on an important mission in Syria, 'where she proved particularly useful during the Syrian campaign against the Vichy French'. The Syrian armistice terms were initialled at Acre on 12 July 1941. In October, Christina and Andrew were sent off on a reconnaissance of the bridges over the Tigris and the Euphrates. The aim was to draw up a contingency plan for blowing up all the river crossings in the event that the Germans suddenly reached an accord with Turkey and attempted to make a dash for the Middle East oilfields. This took them to Aleppo where they explored the miles of covered souks and stayed at the Baron Hotel. Its Oxford-educated proprietor, Koko Muzlumian, produced one of his last bottles of whisky in their honour.

In Aleppo, Christina attracted another admirer, Hissam, the son of the Emperor of Afghanistan. He was serving in Prince Albert Victor's Own Regiment, which was stationed outside the city.

Christina and Andrew's problems with SOE were a reflection of the difficulties that the 'firm' itself was having in Cairo. Some felt, perhaps with justification, that SOE was lax and ineffective. Lady Ranfurly, who considered that SOE's 'good-time Charlies' were behaving offensively, pulled rank and demanded to speak to Anthony Eden alone when he visited Cairo in March 1941, telling him 'that the whole of this hush-hush organization is not only in a state of chaos, but that any amount of public money is being wasted'. SOE's Bickham Sweet-Escott wrote in *Baker Street Irregular* (1965): 'Nobody who did not experience it can possibly imagine the atmosphere of jealousy, suspicion and intrigue which embittered the relations between the various secret and semi-secret departments in Cairo during that summer of 1941, or for that matter for the next two years.'

But for those who had endured the hardships of wartime Britain or occupied Europe, Cairo was also a welcome haven of luxury. 'We were staggered by the shops . . . where fabulous bales of silk were unfurled before us. Tea at Groppi's where the cakes outdid even Gunters further amazed us,' wrote Annette Street, a FANY working for SOE in Cairo.

Because of the heat, work started at eight o'clock in the

morning, breaking for a three-hour siesta at lunch and continuing from five until eight-thirty at night. 'There were a lot of parties . . . we were always tired when we went to bed,' Gwendoline Lees, the senior FANY officer in Cairo, recalled. Christina spent much of her time at the Gezira Country Club, set on an island in the Nile studded with villas in well-watered grounds. All her life she loved the sun and here she was in her element. Patrick Howarth, who was with SOE in Cairo, described her as 'stretching in cat-like delight with the Gezira sun, dull dark-brown jacket, dull light-brown shirt, brilliant brown mobile arresting eyes'. Lees, who named her eldest daughter after Christina, said: 'She was one of the most remarkable women I've ever known.'

The problems and possibilities for Christina and Andrew were set out in detail in a memo on 16 December 1942.

The difficulties involved in finding employment for these people are numerous, and follow partly from their somewhat complex personalities, partly from violent opposition to them by practically all Polish organisations, and partly because they are probably well enough known to the Gestapo . . . G [Granville] would very much dislike being separated from K [Kennedy] and vice versa. She considers that K is not really able to look after himself without her supervision. K thinks the same of G. He has made offers of marriage to her (confirmed independently by both), but she has turned down these offers. She has also turned down a further offer of marriage from a certain Captain Cookham, belonging to an Indian regiment and a very decent sort. In any case she is not formally divorced from Gizycki, although he has promised to place no obstacles in the way of a divorce. Therefore, it is difficult to find employment for one without the other, – they form a sort of team.

The note continues, suggesting that Christina, despite her relaxed appearance, was under severe stress:

G has very strong prejudices against any form of office work, no matter what its nature would be. This prejudice is due partly to a feeling of incompetence on her part, and partly due to a general inferiority complex. If her employer was to tick her off for making slight mistakes in what she did, she would probably burst into tears and drop the job forthwith. In general she is very diffident and timid in meeting new contacts, and so tends to give the worst possible impression of herself. She is, moreover, extremely obstinate and if she has once made a decision no amount of argument will shake her.

K is a far less complex type in that he definitely has no inferiority complex and is on the whole very simple and straightforward . . . He is, however, of a very independent nature and will not submit to off-hand treatment. According to G he has a weak character, and can readily be persuaded to spend his substance in riotous living. He, however, told me that this was an illusion . . . which G unfortunately had, and that he really was not as careless in money matters as she thinks. On the whole I am inclined to agree with him.

I am afraid it is practically hopeless to induce the Poles to change their mind about G and K. If they were to employ them they would certainly insist on their resumption of Polish nationality, and this they are definitely and absolutely unwilling to do, claiming, probably with truth, that they would thereupon be put in the 'cooler' by the IIème bureau at the first convenient opportunity.

Although they both think that the Gestapo know very little of them and that they could move in enemy occupied territory without the least risk, I personally rather doubt this . . . One reason is their somewhat striking personal appearance and mannerisms, which together with K's wooden leg, make them the sort of people who once seen are never forgotten. What makes things worse is that they have literally hundreds, if not thousands, of friends, enemies, relatives and acquaintances, fairly liberally distributed all over Europe, Africa, and Asia Minor, so that there is always the risk of the disclosure of their identity in a perfectly innocent way as a result of a chance meeting.

I do not think that either of them have any special talents for conspiratorial work. They would shine under conditions in which personal courage and determination are essential ... G would be quite happy as a nurse, especially if this were to be within a danger zone, and would be perfectly ready to function as such with our forces, with the Americans or with the Fighting French. She would also be willing to do low grade wireless work, or to work with prisoners of war, or do any of the hundred little jobs that might justify her existence to herself. She does certainly feel rather humiliated at receiving pay without giving equivalent services in return ... As to K, I think he really does know quite a lot about cars and if he could be found a small job, similar to that which he already performed fairly successfully in Cairo as O.C. transport, or garage, this would be quite suitable ... I may add that General Kopanski told me in August that he would be ready at any time to find K employment in his Division, but G was against this on the grounds that under desert conditions sand infiltrating into the stump of his leg would very soon cause abrasions of the skin, and put him out of action.

Whatever the difficulties, it remains a poor reflection on SOE's Cairo operation that the talents of two such intrepid and resourceful agents should have been left so long unused. But during 1943 their prospects at last began to improve as both Christina and Andrew were sent on a series of training courses – with a view to Christina being sent back as an agent in the field and Andrew becoming an instructor.

Just before Christmas 1943, Andrew was sent to England for briefing before going to Italy, first to Bari, and then on to Ostuni, where he was to work in a new Polish school for parachutists. After three years of intense closeness, Christina and Andrew were to be separated for nearly twelve months – with disastrous results for their relationship. In London, Andrew received the warmest of welcomes from the O'Malleys, but while in London attracted the attention of a young girl he had known previously. By the time he left London, Andrew was more than a little in love himself. Although he had had to endure more than the occasional infidelity from Christina, not to mention her constant circle of adoring admirers, Christina was hurt and upset by Andrew's lapse and never let him forget it.

As late as March 1944 serious consideration was given to sending Christina back to Hungary. A memo of 25 March notes that by the end of the month she would have been trained in 'W/T, the set with which she is most familiar being a "B" set; parachute jumping; use of elementary explosives; SIS course; preparation of reception committees; simple personal disguises; in addition, arrangements have been made for her to be trained in the use of S-phones at Bari'. All this made Christina one of SOE's most highly trained agents, able to act as both courier and W/T operator and, thanks to her experience, able to do the work if needed of a circuit organiser.

The aim of the proposed mission to Hungary was 'to establish W/T communication and make reception arrangements for SOE parties to be dropped into Hungary'. The country's strategic importance was considered great enough to warrant infiltration even if the operation involved 'the greatest risks' and promised 'only a slight chance of success'. Hungary was unusual as there was no SOE presence or, indeed, communication with any Resistance group. Shortly before the German occupation, the Americans had dropped the Sparrow group at a location suggested by the Hungarian government but SOE had no knowledge of whether it had survived or been blown.

The first option was therefore to send her to the Sparrow group, if the Americans agreed. The second was to drop Christina blind into Hungary. 'This has the advantage of simplicity, and it would not compromise any existing organisation.

However, as a course to be adopted it would probably amount to little short of homicide . . . while this would not deter the operator.' A firm 'no' is pencilled in the margin.

Christina's qualifications for the mission, as set out by SOE, are also interesting.

She has a number of close personal friends in Hungary, mostly among the landed aristocracy. A number of these people exercised considerable influence in Hungarian affairs up to the time of the German occupation of Hungary. She also has, or had certain contacts of a more Left-Wing nature. She speaks perfect Polish, almost perfect French, good English and some Russian and a little Italian. She knows only a few words of Hungarian and knows no German at all. She is a person of quite outstanding courage with exceptional charm and powers of persuasion.

Evidence that the Hungarian mission was being considered at the highest level comes in a report of a visit by General Jumbo Wilson to Monopoli in Italy early in May 1944. Hungary had recently been included in his operational theatre and he was emphatic that 'penetration was necessary and that it was imperative we should have some stake in the country before the arrival of the Russian armies in order that we might have a say in the future of Hungary'.

A telegram from Cairo of 7 April 1944 requests documents for a Polish woman named 'Marja Kaminska living in Lwowun born 1914', adding, 'This should be done without knowledge of Poles.' Soon after, another telegram of 14 April 1944, also from Cairo, casts serious doubts on the project, as information suggested that the Sparrow group was 'in the bag'. Flying first to Yugoslavia also promised little hope of getting to Hungary. The alternative was 'to drop Kris [Christina] blind somewhere in Hungary. At present moment this seems quite pointless since if operation succeeded there is little she could do to help us for some time to come. In view of fact that she is well known to Hungarian Police and speaks little Magyar do not feel justified in taking large risk involved . . . If therefore you have some other project in mind for her for example France please let us know soonest and we will release her at once.'

Three days later, on 17 April, Bickham Sweet-Escott wrote from Cairo to London, again suggesting that Christina should be used in France, saying: 'She is a Polish lady of considerable beauty and great courage . . . as brave as a lion and as SOE minded as the best of Poles.'

Yet at the end of April, as D-Day loomed ever closer, Christina's future was still undecided. Only in May was the decision taken to send her to the SOE base at Algiers to prepare to be dropped in southern France. Massingham, as it was known, was housed in the Club des Pins, west of the city, a resort of villas set amidst the sand dunes on the beach. Here she began the final agonising weeks of waiting, making friends with fellow agents due to be dropped and being included in the counsels of the senior officers who ran the establishment, notably Brooks Richards, in charge of the French Section, and Douglas Dodds-Parker, the station commander. Dodds-Parker recalls Christina's determination to get to France and his own concerns that she was simply too flamboyant and too valuable. Clearance, he says, finally came quickly – when over dinner at Massingham she was able to exert her powers of fascination on General Stawell.

Short though Christina's French mission was to prove, it was to bring her more glory and excitement than anything yet. She would act as a much-needed replacement courier for one of SOE's most successful circuit commanders, the young Francis Cammaerts, known through his circuit as Roger.

Cammaerts, born in 1916, was the son of the Belgian poet Émile Cammaerts. At Cambridge, where he won a hockey blue, he was a pacifist like many of his contemporaries, determined that the slaughter of the 1914–18 war should never be repeated. When war broke out again in 1939,

Cammaerts became a resolute conscientious objector, working on the land and only narrowly escaping a term in prison, but following the death of his brother in the RAF in action, he decided to enlist.

He was sent out to France to take over from Peter Churchill, who had been acting as liaison officer with the Carte organisation in which SOE had initially placed great hopes. Cammaerts told SOE that 'Carte was an ambitious and temperamental man who had set out to make himself the "General de Gaulle" in resistance work.

Recruiting, however, was not carefully controlled, and a great many young and irresponsible men joined the organisation, who were extremely careless about security precautions.' But, he acknowledged, there were some excellent aspects of Carte and the organisation had handled some important operations using feluccas, small sailing vessels used in the Mediterranean.

Cammaerts was landed by Lysander in March 1943 and, after returning to England for debriefing, he rejoined his organisation in February 1944. He had an alarming moment as he flew over France. The plane, headed for a reception ground in the Alpes Maritimes, ran into very bad weather and, unable to distinguish the pinpoint for the dropping ground, turned back. About sixty kilometres from Lyons it caught fire and Cammaerts had to jump from 3,000 metres – very different from the usual low drops. He landed in a potato field with no idea where he was. There was a farm nearby and he decided to take the risk of waking the farmer, who promptly gave him a meal and showed him exactly where he was on a map. By good fortune he was only about twenty-five kilometres from one of his own safe houses at Beaurepaire and the next morning he borrowed a bicycle, returning by car to collect his belongings.

Christina flew out from Algiers on the night of 7 July 1944, this time with the code name Pauline. She parachuted in with Paquebot mission whose leader, Captain Tournissa, was an engineer. He was being sent to the Vercors to supervise construction of an airstrip near Vassieux to enable supplies and reinforcements to be sent to the large Maquis contingent there, which had brazenly declared the Vercors plateau liberated even though it was well behind German lines.

Christina bruised her hip badly on landing but within a very short time was active again. Part of her mission was to attempt the subversion of satellite enemy troops, particularly those guarding the Alpine passes into Italy – a new tactic for SOE.

A 'résumé of Pauline's activities' in the National Archives in Maryland, USA, describes Christina's swift progress. 'On 13 July Pauline reported that she had done preparatory work with Polish troops . . . and the possibilities for subversion were considerable. On July 17 [Cammaerts] reported that Pauline's work . . . with the Polish troops was proving so widespread it was essential to send a lieutenant to help her.'

Very soon Christina and Cammaerts were swept up in the great battle of the Vercors, a natural mountain fortress to the south-west of Grenoble surrounded by steep cliffs, where a large Maquis contingent had congregated. Parts of the plateau were covered with dense forest where, according to popular belief, bears still roamed. The extensive areas of forest on the thirty-mile-long plateau made it suitable as a Maquis base; that of Lente was said to be one of the largest virgin forests in Europe. There was also extensive grazing on the plateau and a population of several thousand in villages and scattered farms.

Vivid accounts of the battle of Vercors are provided by officers of the inter-Allied Eucalyptus mission sent in by SOE to aid the Maquis, notably by its head, Major Longe, and the American OSS radio operator, Lieutenant André Paray. Their mission was to act as liaison between the commander of the Maquis, Colonel Hervieux, and Allied Command.

Entry to the Vercors, said the instructions to the Eucalyptus mission, 'can be prevented by blocking eight roads', five along gorges and three over the crest. The Maquis there consisted of 500 armed men, 500 *semi-sédentaires* and 2,000 *sédentaires* (non-mobile troops). London clearly foresaw the danger of massing in the Vercors. 'It is certain that large numbers of men are at the moment or will in the near future – be flocking to the Vercors . . . this movement . . . should be discouraged, as the gathering of a large number of men whom it will not be possible to equip will result in German attacks.'

The Eucalyptus mission had set out from Algiers on 24 June in a plane brimming with equipment but tragically one of the engines failed as they flew past the Balearic Islands and they were forced to turn back, ditching supplies as they went to reduce loss of height. First to go were the propaganda pamphlets, then packets of arms and clothing, and finally the containers in the bomb bays in which were packed the heavy machine-guns essential for effective defence against German attack. When the mission parachuted in four days later on the night of 28/29 June, they found the heavy machine-guns had been replaced with Stens, and that the Welbikes – folding motor bicycles, enabling rapid movement in hilly terrain – had been omitted.

The next morning one village after another turned out to greet them. The French flag was flying everywhere. They met Hervieux and immediately struck up a warm rapport. They also found Cammaerts, who had come to the Vercors to serve as senior British liaison officer to Colonel Zeller, the commander-in-chief of the FFI (French Forces of the Interior) in the region. Longe and his colleagues were surprised that Hervieux had received orders to hold the Vercors at all costs when the whole conception of the Maquis was to use hit-and-run tactics and avoid standing fights if at all possible.

Between 1 and 23 July, Paray transmitted about eighty

to eighty-five messages, urgently requesting arms, especially heavy machine-guns and mortars. 'During this period only five cables were received from London having little bearing on ours. We therefore asked London whether they were interested in our signals, to which they finally answered that they appreciated them and found them of great interest.'

Longe describes 'Pauline's' arrival at the end of the first week in July.

One day, we were advised that 4 French Commando instructors were to be dropped to us and also a Fanny named 'Pauline' who John and I had known in London. We went to the dropping Zone at about 11pm to receive supplies and the 'bodies', first a lone plane dropped supplies, then another two came over, one of them dropped the four instructors, they had a very nasty jump due to conditions of wind and they were very scattered. One, poor fellow broke an arm and fractured his skull on the rocky ground where he landed, we picked him up and rushed him to the hospital in St Martin . . . After endless circling, the plane carrying Pauline did an approach and Pauline jumped. The plane was higher than was usual for dropping and the wind had got up – Pauline drifted a very long way and we had to run for a very long distance in order to 'Mark her down' and gather her into the fold.

Meanwhile the Germans bombed and strafed the villages around the Vercors with the aim of inducing such terror that the villagers would not dare send supplies, especially food, to the Maquis. But the Maquis became bolder in their sorties against the Germans, and reprisal atrocities began. Following an attack on a convoy on Route Nationale 75, which left fifty or sixty Germans dead, one captured Frenchman was taken to the village of Lalley. His eyes and tongue were torn out and he was bayoneted in front of the whole population. Before tying the prisoner to the post, the German officer informed the villagers that they were going to see how terrorists were treated. The prisoner replied that he was not a terrorist but had been fighting as a regular soldier with an American commando unit. As a result, said Paray, the village was not burnt down, but the Germans threatened to return if help was given to 'terrorists and assassins'.

Then, on 14 July, Bastille Day, came the long-awaited arms drop by the Allies. Longe describes the moment:

At about 9.30 A.M. we heard the roar of planes, there they were, eighty five silver flying fortresses laden with supplies for us because we had asked for them, how our hearts warmed to the folk in the London office. It was a lovely morning and these huge four engined planes supported by fighters circled us three times, twelve in line and flying very low, on each circuit there was a glorious view of different coloured parachutes filling the sky at Vassieux ... To see a mass daylight drop coming to you when you are some three hundred miles behind the enemy's lines, completely encircled by the swine is a sight which does not fade, but only becomes more vivid each time you recall it.

The long-range Allied fighters bombed the German aerodrome at Chabeuil but within an hour of the drop the Germans were furiously on the counter-attack.

They bombed and strafed us all day, Vassieux was [razed] to the ground and La Chapel burned for 36 hours. Many civilians ... were killed and wounded and much of our transport, waiting to remove the newly arrived containers, was destroyed. As the fighter and fighter bombers came onto us at St Martin it was a very difficult job for us to get the civilians to disperse. Instead they stood scared stiff in their hundreds in doorways making lovely targets for the guns of fighters.

Only at night, says Paray, was it possible to gather in some 200 of the containers. 'They were packed with ammunition, Stens and heavy clothing. Mortars, heavy machine guns were lacking.'

The wireless operators tapped repeated messages to London

and Algiers, asking for supplies, particularly mortars and heavy machine-guns, only to receive a message back: 'We believe you are about to be attacked in great strength, cable what we can do to help.' This was irony indeed, commented Longe; 'All we could say was "Carry out our requests in previous cables".'

As their cables became more frantic, Longe vented his fury against the Algiers office which, he said, 'always end their cables with love to P[auline], etc for which I would gladly break their necks, we have no time for love here'. Not that Christina was sitting idle, having almost immediately set off on a dangerous mission to the Italian frontier. No less remarkably, she succeeded in returning to the Vercors, avoiding the gathering Germans. By 20 July, said Paray, the Vercors was completely bottled up. All passes and roads were guarded by troops equipped with artillery. The Iser bridges were guarded. Machine-gun nests had been set up along the river.

The Germans now began to tighten the noose. Additional planes arrived at the nearby German aerodrome at Chabeuil. The Engins tunnel was blown up, denying a possible escape route. A bridge east of Pont-en-Royans was blown. Battalions of mountain troops arrived at Grenoble.

A ferocious general attack began the next day. As villages in the north were occupied, Paray describes the scene: 'Hostages were shot, farms were burned down . . . Mountain passes and roads all around us were attacked . . . The Germans with the use of their mountain troops were infiltrating, scaling the mountain ridges. The enemy columns, fearing mines, compelled peasants to walk ahead of them. Others had to carry ammunition. They would be sent back and while walking away, be shot in the back.'

On the morning of 21 July at about 9 a.m., German gliders landed on the new airfield at Vassieux built by the Resistance. Two were shot down, two more were damaged.

But 250 or more SS troops leapt out and managed to entrench themselves in the ruins of nearby houses. While the Germans received extra supplies, the Maquis were now running out of ammunition. Longe says: 'Impossible odds face our exhausted maquis, the Germans are using overwhelming forces including an armoured division and an Alpine Regiment. Our forces are armed only with light weapons and apart from two anti tank guns captured from a German practice range we have nothing heavier than Bren guns. We are being mortared out of the ground.'

Paray continues: 'At Vassieux the SS killed on sight, even whole families ... At the Château hamlet ... Mr and Mrs Blanc, their 19 year old daughter, their daughter-in-law with four young babies were trapped under the ruins of their house. Only one eleven year old girl, Arlette Blanc, remained alive. Her leg was caught under the wreckage. To the passing Germans the girl asked for water. They laughed. For five days they went by without helping.' Arlette was finally rescued by a curé but gangrene had set in and she died. The massacres continued. Captured Maquis had their eyes and tongues torn out, and were then strung up to die slowly. 'The Germans would eat their lunch in front of the struggling men,' said Paray.

As the German assault became overwhelming, Hervieux called a conference at about 1 a.m. on the morning of 22 July. Here he said it was no longer possible to hold the Vercors against impossible odds. It was agreed that Cammaerts, Christina and Zeller should leave immediately as their presence would not alter the outcome of the battle and they had important work to do in maintaining resistance in other areas. 'They left the Vercors on Saturday 22 July, at about 8.30, in the South which was the last remaining exit route,' says Paray.

Christina quickly turned her mind to future tasks. A cable from Brooks Richards on 5 August, now in the US Archives, runs: 'Christine reports in contact four hundred Poles in Briançon area requires definite information regarding status of rival Polish governments and authoritative propaganda in Polish language without which she is unable to get hold of the serious elements.' The report on her activities in US National Archives states that after leaving the Vercors, 'She immediately took up her work with satellite troops and reported that the Polish garrison at Briançon would be prepared to come over to Maquis as soon as Poland was made free.'

Her thrill at being in France emerges in an earlier letter to Brooks Richards, the head of the French Section in Algiers, dated 27 July 1944. It is written in a familiar tone, conveying how strongly she figured in the counsels of her senior officers.

Dear Brooks,

I am very happy with my work. Roger [Cammaerts] is a magnificent person. The unity in the whole of the South of France depends on him. They treat him as the only 'neutral' person and take all his advice having known him and his work for the past 18 months, when there was nothing and nobody at all to be with them and to help them. You must support him and back up his prestige as much as you can. Tell all our missions that contacts got through him are guaranteed. Every Frenchman I have met during the three weeks, and I have met many hundreds, trusts Roger entirely. We need as many Jedburghs and Missions as possible, and for God's sake do not wait until the war is over. Send at least 1 Jedburgh and 1 mission to each department, and instruct them all to listen to Roger's orders or advice.

Cammaerts, for his part, was delighted with Christina's work. 'Pauline is magnificent, what couldn't I have done if she had been here three months ago,' he said in a report to Brooks Richards on 27 July 1944.

Christina also reported to Brooks Richards on the subversion of foreign troops.

The only important group are Poles. There are very few Serbians and Checks, some Ukranians, Russians and Armenians. They move constantly which does not make the work any easier. We had excellent contacts, but lost them temporarily in Vercors. I am going tomorrow to Gap where there are about 250 Poles. Again we must tell them NOW if we want immediate action, or do you want just information: and will you send a specialist later to deal with them . . . The Maquis want the Poles (whom they trust) to join them with arms and if possible German prisoners.

Christina demanded immediate instructions and information about the attitudes of the British government, the Polish government-in-exile and the Polish army fighting with the Allies in Italy.

Send me . . . as soon as possible as many declarations, official papers and papers in Polish. Do you realise that now the Poles are almost like the Ukranians. I cannot promise them a free Poland, and I do not want to tell them that the Polish army is a foreign legion fighting as a mercenary army . . . The morale in the German army is bad, they know that the war is lost. Propaganda is almost unnecessary, and with the help of the Maquis one can get from the coast to Lyons almost without hindrance, but you must warn Roger at least ten days before D.day [this is D-Day for the South of France landings].

Christina concluded with advice about Andrew – evidently there had been thoughts that he might work alongside her mission. 'The conditions now on the Swiss frontier are too difficult for him. There are no means of transport at all and everything has to be done on foot. Send him to Switzerland to deal with the Poles there and send them to us.'

She also talks of the imminent arrival of Major Havard Gunn, who had trained with Christina at Massingham and had chosen his unusual *nom de guerre*, Bambus, from a clump of bamboo he and Christina had encountered there. Gunn, an accomplished painter, lived near St Tropez before the war. He joined the Seaforth Highlanders, later transferring to SOE. 'If his work is to be of any use you must send them immediately to Roger's [landing] ground Turriers. We need him for the Var and Alpes Maritimes very badly. With Roger's contacts and advice he can produce miracles.'

The background to Christina's imminent Alpine venture was that early in 1944, SOE in Italy (No. 1 Special Force) had proposed Operation Toplink, which would attempt to link Italian partisans and French Maquis in a joint operation in the high Alps. A group of four British majors, ten captains and one sergeant began training in Algiers with a view to being dropped by parachute at the time of the Normandy landings to work under Cammaerts. The aim was to protect the planned landings in the South of France from possible flanking attacks over the Alps by German troops based in Italy. Equally the Germans wished to safeguard their forces from any Allied attacks across the passes, especially those of Tende, Larche and Montgenèvre.

The chief in this area was a Frenchman, Gilbert Galetti, a good friend of both Christina and Cammaerts, who had his base in a group of chalets above Bramousse. His men used the trails over the Col de la Mayt and the Col de la Croix to keep in contact with Italian partisans under Marcellini, who was attempting to harass the German convoys supplying the mountain strongholds from Turin. The first Toplink mission finally parachuted in on 1 August, consisting of three Italians, one Frenchman and two British officers, Major Hamilton and Captain Pat O'Regan.

Christina now went to join Galetti at Bramousse. From here a helpful ski instructor, Gilbert Tavernier, took her on the back seat of his motorcycle up the Guil valley to L'Échalp. Crossing the 2,000-metre Col de la Croix into Italy, she met Marcellini (sometimes Marcellin), busy re-establishing his base further north after they had been struck hard by the

Germans. Cammaerts had given Christina the task of making the first contacts with the Italians on behalf of the Toplink mission. He observed that Christina

realised at once the possibilities of Marcellini as a leader, and did all she could to help him when he was attacked by over 5,000 Germans, and finally put him and what was left of his band into contact with Major Hamilton whose mission was to contact Italians all along the frontier . . . Pauline accomplished this mission at very great personal risk, as she went in there at the time of a big attack, and had to pass the German lines under fire to get there and back, and made a 24-hour trip on foot in difficult and dangerous mountain country.

It speaks volumes for her energy and tenacity that she found Marcellini, while Hamilton, following the same route, only learnt of the German attack when he returned to France and met with Christina. Immediately he set about supplying the partisans by using mules.

On the night of 4 August Major Gunn parachuted in, followed on 7 August by a further group, including two close comrades of Christina, Major R.W.B. Purvis and Captain John Roper. The next morning Cammaerts and Christina drove over to Savournon where they had landed and conducted them to a meeting with Resistance leaders in a forest east of Gap. Among them was Paul Héraud, the great Resistance leader in the Hautes-Alpes. Tragically, the very next day Héraud was stopped by a German patrol and summarily shot.

Christina's most legendary exploit was to secure the release of Cammaerts and two companions just hours before they were due to be shot. Over the years this story has been retold and embroidered in various ways. Now we have Christina and Cammaerts's own reports, his dated 23 October 1944 and hers 1 November.

The events leading up to Cammaerts's arrest are best described by Xan Fielding in his *Hide and Seek: the Story of a War-Time Agent* (1954), which he dedicated to Christina. He was dropped into France early in August from Algiers with the code name of Cathédrale. The waiting Maquis took him the next morning to the safe house where Cammaerts and Christina were staying. Set in the village of Seyne 1.5 kilometres down the valley from the point where they had landed, it belonged to the local grocer, Monsieur Turrel, and his wife who had 'placed their home at our disposal since the beginning of the occupation, thereby endangering their lives far more than any member of an armed maquis band . . . Monsieur Turrel, fat and jovial, in a waistcoat three times too small for him, looked as carefree and contented as an actor in a documentary film. He offered me a glass of wine while his wife . . . went upstairs to wake Roger and Christine.' Cammaerts surprised him – 'a smiling young giant' with sloping shoulders and an easy poise. Christina had the appearance of an athletic art student with short, carelessly combed dark hair and no make-up of any kind on her delicately featured face.'

After breakfast they climbed together up to the dropping ground – Fielding still in uniform – and spent the day in leisurely fashion, gathering containers and packages. The Alpine scenery of meadows and high peaks left Fielding stunned with delight – he could hardly believe he was on a military mission. At this stage in the war, there were no fears here of Germans appearing in pursuit. That evening, while Christina set off for the Italian frontier, Cammaerts and Fielding drove to Cammaerts's wireless station a few kilometres outside the village and spent a comfortable night after an excellent dinner with the two French radio operators. One of these, Auguste Floiras (Albert), was SOE's longest-serving operator, eventually sending 416 messages and changing his lodgings fifteen times in sixteen months.

The next morning they set off on Cammaerts's rounds, in a Red Cross car equipped with a special licence. The driver was Claude Renoir, son of the famous Impressionist painter. With them was a French officer, Commandant Christian Sorensen, whose family produced wine in Algeria and who had trained at Massingham with SOE. His code name was Chasuble. As they checked their papers before they set out, Fielding counted out the money he had with him. 'Such a large sum might have looked suspicious if discovered in the pockets of one man, so Roger and Chasuble between them relieved me of over half of it,' he wrote. As an extra precaution they agreed that if stopped they would say they did not know each other and were simply hitching a lift.

It was the morning of 13 August 1944, two days before the Allied landings in the South of France. Fielding recalled: 'Our drive was so uneventful and enjoyable that I had to keep on reminding myself that I was not on holiday but on active service – a fact that escaped me in each of the delightful villages, where, while "Roger" conferred with each of the local leaders, I drank a glass of wine outside the café under the plane trees.'

This idyll was shatteringly interrupted. As they drove back to Seyne in the Red Cross car, they were on the outskirts of Digne when an Allied air raid began. They waited for the all-clear as they knew a special German road block was set up during air raids in place of the ordinary police control.

When the air raid ended, they approached the road block, realising too late that the Gestapo had not yet been relieved. Cammaerts, Fielding and Sorensen declared they were hitch-hiking and the Red Cross car was allowed to proceed without them. Fielding noted that Cammaerts and Sorensen appeared utterly unconcerned as they showed their documents and emptied their pockets, Cammaerts with an expression of surprised amusement on his face, Sorensen with a look of contempt.

Suddenly he saw a spark of triumph in the expression of the interrogator and sensed immediately that something had gone wrong.

'You say you don't know these two men,' barked the German.

'No, I don't,' replied Fielding.

The next question was addressed to all three of them.

'Then can you explain how these banknotes, which each of you was carrying individually, happen to be all in the same series – no, don't answer; I won't have any more lies. Into the car, the whole lot of you.'

For the next three days they were moved back and forth between the prison, the German barracks and the Gestapo headquarters on the edge of the town. Like many Gestapo establishments, this was installed in a gracious house, the Villa Marie Louise. Their story now was that they had all been involved in a black market deal, and even if this was not believed, there was no suspicion yet that Cammaerts was the major Resistance leader in the region. Cammaerts explains: 'By the 13th August their communications had been non-existent for a couple of months.' Even so, although they did not yet know it, they were sentenced to be shot.

Cammaerts continues:

Pauline spent three days and three nights trying to get together a *corps franc* who would attack the small German garrison at the barracks, and offered to lead them herself. The French Commandant of the FFI decided that the risk was too great, so she chose the last possible solution, knowing that we were due to be shot on the night of the 17th, and went and interviewed the Gestapo herself, bluffing them with stories of the proximity of American troops, the imminence of heavy bombardments, the great importance attached by the Allies to our safety, and her own exalted relations . . . The way in which she handled these thugs, whom I had occasion to meet myself, and who were entirely without normal human reactions, was unbelievably skilful. She took voluntarily one chance in a hundred, and undoubtedly if it had not come off she would have been shot with us.

Fortunately, the Gestapo did not realise what a catch they had. 'Having questioned us, not tortured us, they decided to get rid of us,' Cammaerts told SOE afterwards.

Christina's own account fills out the story. 'I had been working as Roger's second-in-command in South East France, and on the night of August 13th heard that he together with Chasuble and Cathédrale had been arrested.' Having failed to persuade the FFI leaders to mount an attack, she contacted a gendarme, an Alsatian named Albert Schenck, who acted as liaison officer with the Gestapo, and emphasised that he was in grave danger. 'I said that I was English, General Montgomery's niece, and that when the Allied landings took place in the South of France, he would be handed over to the mob. I was very fortunate in that purely as a shot in the dark I told him that an Allied landing in the South of France was imminent and that Digne would be bombed.' Schenck told her there was one person who perhaps could help, Max Waem, a Belgian who acted as an interpreter for the Gestapo.

Two days later she again saw Schenck, 'who in the meantime had done nothing'. Christina continues: 'I was able to terrify him because the Allied landings had by then taken place and I told him (untruly) that the Allies were 30 kilometres away, and that Digne was surrounded. He then arranged an interview for me with Waem at Mrs Schenck's flat.' By arrangement Christina went first and at about 4 p.m. Waem arrived. She talked to him for three hours.

When he came he at first covered me with his revolver. He was dressed in Gestapo uniform. After a time he put his revolver down. I began to work upon his fears by telling him of the extreme danger in which he and other collaborators were, that the Allies would be upon the scene the same night, that his only hope of escaping destruction at the hands of the French populace was to save his life by rendering some service to the Allies. From the beginning I openly told him that I was a British parachutist, that I had worked there for two years and I also said I was General Montgomery's niece, and a relation of Lord Vansittart. I made as much as I could of Roger and Chasuble's importance in the eyes of the British and French authorities, and furthermore stated that Roger was my husband. I said I knew that they were to be shot that evening, but I had no fears for them because I knew the Allies would be there in time to rescue them. I said that General Montgomery would attack Digne and that the civilian population would in consequence suffer casualties, unless the Allies knew that they had already been freed. I said I could make an immediate wireless contact with General Montgomery and let him know that they were free; to convince him I produced from my pocket some [wireless] crystals (which although he did not know it were broken). I told him that he was known among the French population as the chief of the Gestapo there and one of the principal torturers. After three hours of that kind of talk during which he became obviously terrified, he said, 'I will get them out for you'.

Christina explained that Waem made three conditions, which she promised to fulfil in the name of the British government. First, that he would be saved from the vengeance of the French population. Second, that he would be treated as a free man and would never be put in prison or a concentration camp. Third, that the British government would do its best to bring about his rehabilitation and for this purpose would bring it to the notice of the French or Belgian authorities, or whatever authorities were concerned, that he had rendered the Allies an important service.

Crazed by fear and guilt, Waem went on to say that he wanted to come back to France and even to Digne, to convince the French people that he had never worked against them. When Christina suggested he might find this most difficult, Waem said he wanted to undertake some really dangerous work for the British. He said he knew all about the workings of the V1 and V2 rockets and was willing to go alone on a mission to Germany, enemy-occupied Holland or Belgium.

Christina continues: 'Waem then left and I remained in Mrs Schenck's flat, after having made an appointment with him in one hour's time. I was fetched to the rendez-vous by a man sent by Waem and Schenck, and Waem arrived with Roger, Chasuble and Cathédrale. We then made our escape by car.'

Fielding takes up the story, describing Waem as a *milicien*. 'Slamming the door on us, he got in himself beside the driver, and at once we were skidding round the nearest corner and heading for a road block on the outskirts of the town. The sentries there, seeing . . . a uniformed man leaning out of the front window, automatically drew back; and we flashed past them into open country.' Not long after, on the edge of a steep embankment, the car stopped and Waem jumped out. Beckoning Fielding to follow him, he slithered down the slope to a stream. Here Waem took off his uniform and, helped by Fielding, buried it beneath pebbles and stones at the water's edge.

Christina omitted one vital element in the story. Schenck had demanded a huge ransom of 2 million French francs – ostensibly to pay Waem. 'Brooks Richards got two million francs in 48 hours – the quickest drop ever,' Cammaerts recalls.

Shortly afterwards, Schenck was found murdered, presumably for the money. Why is there no mention of the ransom in the official record? Was it a wish to conceal the payment of the money or the failure to recover it? 'Knowing the tricks SOE were up to, it was probably fake money anyway,' volunteered one SOE stalwart I talked to.

In fact, Vera Atkins, Buckmaster's brilliant assistant, had tracked down the details shortly after the end of the war and set them out in a memo of 13 August 1945 to Captain

Hazeldine. Cammaerts had told her that Schenck was a double agent. The money – either one or two million francs – had been paid not to Schenck, as is usually thought, but to Madame Schenck for her own use. Atkins continues: 'She is apparently not aware of the fact that her husband was a double agent and is an honest woman. Roger warned the husband not to return to his home as he definitely ran the risk of being bumped off. He ignored this advice and was promptly executed by members of the Resistance.'

Christina concluded her report: 'I most earnestly ask that my promise to Waem is honoured and wish to make it clear that I feel very strongly about this, as Waem undoubtedly saved the lives of Roger, Chasuble and Cathédrale.'

Christina's demand for an amnesty for Waem caused problems. Sir Douglas Dodds-Parker, who saw Christina in Naples, told me: 'Waem was one of the most wanted men in France. I said to Christine, "I can't just let him off. I'll put him on a plane back to France and give him forty-eight hours." Christine would not accept this and said, "I'll never forgive you."' Dodds-Parker put Waem as top priority for the daily shuttle to France. When he asked the duty officer if Waem had got off, he was told that General Stawell had ordered that Waem should be flown to Cairo, telling no one.

General Stawell recommended the immediate award of a George Cross to Christina: 'The nerve, coolness, and devotion to duty and high courage of this lady which inspired and brought to a successful conclusion this astonishing *coup de main* must certainly be considered as one of the most remarkable personal exploits of the war.' Very surprisingly, the great General Alexander, the Supreme Allied Commander of the Mediterranean Theatre, reduced the recommendation to an OBE. The War Office raised it to a George Medal, 'which would make it obvious that she had been decorated for gallantry'. The George Medal was duly approved in June 1945, Christina receiving it 'as a Pole'. The OBE was given to her later, as a British subject, in May 1947.

Throughout this dramatic episode, Christina was carrying out her normal duties. The report on [Cammaerts] in the US Archives states that after the arrests, 'Pauline acted with great calmness and carried on her work with no pause. She directed British Liaison Officers then arriving in the field to the appropriate contacts . . . and put the newly appointed successor to [Cammaerts] in touch with as many as possible of [Cammaerts]'s connections.'

There were two types of German military forces in France at this time, the regular army and the occupation forces. The occupation army, which was under separate command, had small detachments in various towns all over France made up of second-rate garrison troops including administrative personnel and a lot of Slavs, who were frequently hostile to their German commanders. In Franche-Comté, a group of Ukrainians killed all their German officers and joined the Resistance. Larche was especially vulnerable as 60 of the 150 members of the garrison were Poles.

After Cammaerts's release, Christina's movements become confused but efforts continued to woo the satellite troops on the passes to lay down their arms. On 19 August Captain Roper and others put an ultimatum to the German commander at the Col de Larche. Initially he refused to surrender but he gave them dinner. He was cut off and half his garrison was mutinous. After the meal, says Captain John Halsey, a British liaison officer, 'The commander assembled practically the whole garrison in the hotel and we argued . . . the Poles deserted with all their arms and at 0230 the German commander accepted my terms and I took him away with his dog which I have kept to this day.'

Cammaerts attributed the surrender largely to Christina's efforts:

While Christine Granville was operating in the Col de Larche area, she obtained, by her own personal efforts, the surrender of the Larche garrison. Working entirely on her own, she approached foreign elements in the German Army, particularly Polish troops, and persuaded them to steal all the arms of the garrison and surrender, carrying with them the breech-blocks of the heavier weapons. This work was of extreme danger. The Germans were fully aware that we were attempting this type of subversion and had taken every possible step to prevent it, including the moving of their troops constantly from one area to another.

French accounts suggest that a local gendarme, Macari, also played a key role in persuading the garrison to surrender. The Allies knew through Ultra that the Germans had no attention of attacking over the Alps. The Germans nonetheless were determined to hold on to the Larche pass and began an attack on the 23rd that drove the FFI out of Larche, allowing them to hold points on the French sides of the passes and so hamper any Allied attack across the mountains.

From her time in the Alps probably date two often-told stories about her which, even if not authenticated, are probably not apocryphal. One day she was held up at gunpoint by two young Italian conscripts but immediately raised her hands to reveal two hand grenades. 'If you shoot, I'll drop them and we shall all be blown up,' she called. Her captors stood aghast as she retreated out of sight. 'Hand grenades are much better than rifles, revolvers or Stens,' she later remarked.

On another occasion she dived into a thicket to avoid a passing German patrol, only to find an Alsatian dog bounding up to her. Putting her arms round its neck, she hushed it until the Germans, sensing an ambush, fled in terror. The dog remained with her for weeks. Another time, seeing a German checkpoint ahead and fearing that the SOE silk map in her bag might be discovered, she promptly tied it round her neck and went smiling past the soldiers on duty.

In September 1944, Christina and Cammaerts were overrun by the advancing Allied forces. On 5 October, she made an official report in Avignon of her mission, thereafter returning to England.

In September a heated discussion had begun about whether she should be given British citizenship. An SOE official insisted that normal bureaucratic procedures should apply, prompting a strong rebuke on 30 September from Lieutenant Colonel H.B. Perkins: 'This does not reflect the spirit with which we have built up S.O.E. and obtained the loyalty of those working for us. To tell a good and trusted servant who has often risked her life for our interests that if she requires nationalisation she should make a personal application to the Home Office through a solicitor is not my idea of service. I think we should help.' Scrawled at the bottom are a series of questions and answers: 'Why has she gone to France? – went back with Rouget. Who sent her? – obtained permission from CO. What is she doing? – Insuring R. does not get into trouble.'

In November 1944, Christina was being considered for a mission in Poland. The memo, dated 9 November, ran: 'Will you please allot a code name urgently to Miss Christine Granville, who has been chosen to act as courier in Poland between the various Missions and Sub-Missions such as Freston, Fernham, Flamstead, etc. She will be entirely separate and have her own ciphers and it is necessary that she should be treated as a separate operation and have her own code-name.'

At the same time her superiors decided that a routine security check should be carried out, perhaps because she had been enlisted so early that no check had ever been set in motion with MI5. The reason was that, unusually for an agent in the field, Christina had 'circulated fairly freely at H.Q. both here and in Cairo, and Algiers. So far as I can trace from our records she has never been put through the cards. It is rather late in the day but I feel that before finally leaving the U.K. the opportunity should be taken to vet her while particulars are available.' A week later the form came back from M15 with the standard 'No objection'.

Meanwhile Christina had been given the code name Folkestone – all the sub-missions of Flamstead began with an F. Simultaneously Christina was enrolled in the WAAF and granted a commission as a flight officer. The memo requesting it, dated 14 November 1944, read: 'Miss Granville is one of the most distinguished of our female agents . . . She has been working for S.O.E. since 1939 and is a woman of very considerable influence, not only with the Poles but also in the Middle East and with the Hungarians. It is necessary, therefore, in our opinion that when giving her an emergency commission of this sort for cover purposes she should not be treated as a junior officer.' Christina evidently approached her new mission with determination; a memo dated November 15, the next day, is annotated: 'I am going to make sure that I keep on Christine's side in future,' in one hand, and then, 'So am I. She frightens me to death,' in another.

Christina's commission was issued on 21 November 1944. Two days later details of the mission were provided in a letter to Major General Stanislaw Tabor, CB. Christina was to be one of a number of British officers attached to the Polish Home Army as observers. 'It is our desire that the maximum value shall be obtained from these observers, and under no circumstances will it be in our mutual interests if after arrival in the country they fail to give us the independent and reliable information, or rather, confirmation, of which we are in need.'

Christina was to fulfil a special role.

Miss Granville has now had five years' experience as an S.O.E.

officer. This experience, together with her intimate knowledge of Polish affairs will make her invaluable to Colonel Hudson as personal assistant. She will also act as liaison officer between him and the sub-missions. She has, as you know, been closely associated with the British for many years and understands our character and temperament as well as she understands that of her own people. I feel very strongly, therefore, that her knowledge and experience will be invaluable in smoothing over any difficulties which may arise through possible misunderstandings . . . She will be leaving for Italy within the next few days, and it is our intention that she shall go into the field as soon as possible.

Before leaving, Christina left instructions for funds to be remitted, if requested, to her aunt Countess Helene Skarbek at the Hotel Beau Séjour at Brides-les-Bains in Savoie and also to her husband in Montreal. A note states that Gizycki was believed to be doing the job of superintendent in the Polish Home on Drummond Street. 'After having been employed for some time as a manager of a resort hotel in the Canadian Rocky Mountains, he applied to the Association of Polish War Refugees in Montreal for aid in the autumn of 1942.'

The importance and delicacy of Christina's mission to Poland is evident in a note of 23 December 1944. The Poles had agreed to allow her to pass messages to and from Britain on any London–Poland wavelengths that existed. 'Folkestone will have her own cyphers and has the right to communicate independently with London.'

Her mission was to observe 'political conditions in the whole of German occupied Poland'. She was to report 'all possible political information' and advise the Freston mission and the other sub-missions 'on the political conditions and personalities in their areas'. She was also to 'do all in her power to explain H.M.G. policy with regard to Poland and the Poles. It is realized that this is a very difficult task. However, it is hoped that the Poles may be brought to an understanding of the expediency of the suggested solution.' She also signed a receipt on 23 December 1944 for two 1-carat diamonds, value £80 16s 8d each. In addition she was to take $1,000 in gold and $500 in notes.

The background to this mission was that from the middle of 1942 Soviet propaganda had increasingly put about the view that resistance in Poland was not significant; that the underground movement was a myth created by the government in exile for political ends; and that the only real resistance came from Polish communists and Soviet partisans. As Russia was a valued ally, these ideas gained more currency than they deserved. It was decided at the beginning of July to send a reliable officer, Colonel D.T. Hudson, who had carried out a similar mission in Yugoslavia, to the scene of the fighting to report back first hand. The mission was endlessly delayed but Hudson and his group finally took off from Brindisi in a Liberator on the night of 26 December 1944, landing at a secret dropping zone near Czestochowa.

A letter to the mission of 26 December 1944 gives further details. 'Dear Bill . . . Christine will be bringing this to you . . . I think you know her quite well already, so there is no need for me to eulogise on her many and various good qualities. There is no question about it whatever that she is better informed on Polish political conditions in this country than almost any other single personality.'

Christina left for Bari on 27 December, hoping to join Hudson within days. It was not to be. The last flight from the West to Poland took place just two nights after Hudson had been dropped. Meantime, in the heart of winter, on 12 January 1945, Stalin launched a broad attack, surprising both the Western powers and the Germans, whom he drove back in disarray. Hudson's mission quickly received radio instructions to make their way to the nearest Soviet Command. This they did on 18 January. All the members of the mission were arrested, it is thought on Stalin's orders, and thrown into prison at Czestochowa. They were released on 12 February, the day that the Yalta Conference ended. They returned to Britain via Moscow, Odessa and the Near East. Christina, although deprived of a long-awaited mission to her homeland, had had a lucky escape.

Her stay in Italy also marked a crucial turn in her long relationship with Andrew. He was in Bari, living in acute discomfort with other male agents in a house without heating, while Christina was rather better accommodated at the Imperial Hotel. In an attempt to snatch some time alone with Christina, Andrew had booked a room in a picturesque small hotel for a short holiday, hoping to rekindle the romance of their blissful months in the Middle East. Tragically, for reasons Andrew either never wholly understood or could not bring himself to speak about, things went agonisingly wrong. As soon as Christina arrived, she announced that she was leaving immediately for Cairo. It was a shattering moment for Andrew, who felt that at this moment they had ceased to be lovers. He now steeled himself no longer to be bound exclusively to her.

At about this time Peter Lee, who was head of SOE security in Rome, received an urgent message that he had to rush to Naples to look after an important agent. Arriving at the house that SOE used in Vomero on a hill above the city with a superb view of Vesuvius, he found Christina. Here they dined together on two successive nights. 'I saw this slim, oval-faced, rather olive-skinned, dark-haired girl with beautiful features come in,' he recalls. Christina, he says, was completely without nerves and described to him how, circling over a dropping ground, waiting for the green light to go on, she had fallen asleep while waiting to jump.

Arriving in Cairo, Christina took up a job with the Movement Section of GHQ and slipped back into the life she had enjoyed at the Gezira Country Club. But it rapidly became clear that there was little further prospect of work with the 'firm'. An officer who showed particular concern for her at this time was Colonel H.B. Perkins. Before the war he had lived in Poland where he owned a small textile factory in Bielsko. As a result he spoke Polish quite well and knew Polish likes and dislikes. He succeeded Bickham Sweet-Escott as head of SOE's Polish Section, which got under way in the late summer of 1940.

On 15 March 1945 Perkins wrote to Christina in Cairo, breaking bad news as gently as he could: there was no more work for her. Christina's handwritten reply of 25 March vividly captures her mood:

Perks Kochany [Darling Perks]

Thank you very much for your very nice letter. I was expecting something like that since our Polish scheme fell through – but you always put things in a kindest way. I am very grateful to you for the three month pay you are offering me. I should like to stay here in Cairo for at least these three month and, in the meantime . . . look around for another job. If I do not succeed – then I will again ask for your help. I have already put in an application for a work with R.A.F. but I am afraid that it's too late. If I need it – will you write and tell them that I am honest and clean polish girl? . . . for God's sake do not strike my name from the firm . . . remember I am always too pleased to go and do anything for it . . . I could be useful getting people out from camps and prisons in Germany – just before they get shot. I should love to do it and I like to jump out of a plane even every day. Please Perks, if it's not for your section – maybe somebody else.

Christina asks after her husband and adds, 'Please do look after Andrew and don't let him do anything too stupid.' There's also news of romance: 'By the way – do you know that I have become very fond of Henry? We're getting on very well together.' This was the handsome and dashing Henry Threllfall, who had worked with Perkins and who had been put in charge of the Italian end of the Polish Section, based in Bari, where Christina presumably first met him. Xan Fielding also saw her in Cairo, lending her £150, which is the subject of a note she wrote in February 1945.

Whether Christina's idea of a mission into Germany to rescue some of her fellow agents from execution in concentration camps ever received serious consideration is doubtful. Certainly it was timely. Noor had been executed at Dachau in September 1944; Violette Szabo had been shot at Ravensbrück early in 1945 with Denise Bloch and Lilian Rolfe. On the face of it, this would certainly have been the most impossible of missions. Even as the war drew to a close, the Germans remained ruthless and almost universally bestial in their treatment of concentration camp prisoners. Could Christina, armed with suitable quantities of cash, have been successfully dropped by parachute and, speaking little German, have talked her way into Ravensbrück or Belsen and carried out further incredible rescues? Only one thing is certain. She would not have hesitated for a moment to attempt it.

Interestingly, another SOE agent in France, Philippe de Vomécourt, had also been thinking on these lines. In his book, *Who Lived to See the Day*, he wrote:

My plan was to drop three-men teams, including radio operators, in the vicinity of the concentration and prison camps. We already had the papers showing us as civilian workers. We would make contact with the prisoners' leaders and ask them what arms they would like ... Then by arrangement with the air forces, fighter-bombers would pretend to strafe the camp, the guards would take cover, and the containers of arms would be dropped to the waiting prisoners, the weapons already assembled and loaded.

In a matter of a minute, Vomécourt reckoned – before the guards had recovered – the prisoners would be able to kill them and escape.

A note of 25 April 1945 reports that Christina 'has been approached by the Poles who would like her to work for them. Christine is inclined to exaggerate at times, but I feel there is something in what she told me, very confidentially.' The reply came back nearly a month later, raising no objection and saying this 'would seem an admirable solution for her future'. Meanwhile Christina's WAAF commission had come to an end on 11 May. There was a flurry of memos as London realised that Christina might still be using her WAAF identity documents in Cairo; instructions went out, saying that they should immediately be replaced by ordinary civilian ones. With SOE itself being wound up, her case was being handled by a man, who said: 'I know nothing about this woman save that she is Polish national [and] ex-agent . . . I consider that arrangements should be made for her immediate return.' A hastily scribbled note points out: 'She was considered an outstandingly good agent . . . at one time there was talk of recommending her for the George Cross.'

Christina's ongoing difficulties were recognised in a memo of 22 June. 'The ordinary Pole has the right to be looked after by his or her own Government. Christine appears to have forfeited that right by working for us and, therefore, I think we are under an obligation to pay her some sort of maintenance allowance until such time as she can arrange to maintain herself.' Andrew had told SOE that she needed about £30 a month to live in Cairo. SOE agreed to keep her on half-pay of £21 6s 4d a month until the end of the year.

Christina's plight continued to be the subject of genuine concern – a telegram of 17 November 1945 says: 'Christine intends remain Middle East until Europe situation becomes more normal. At present employed special Middle East move-ment job which fortunately does not require any secretarial or clerking qualifications which she does not possess . . . Her prospects not bright. I estimate present job will not last more than one year.'

A report of 18 December 1945 adds: 'when her present job finishes, it is unlikely that she will be able to obtain further work in Egypt and she will most probably have to emigrate. She has applied for British naturalisation and if and when this is granted, has expressed a desire to go to a British colony.'

There was, of course, no question that Christina would go back to a Russian-dominated Poland. Instead, returning to London, she had to take any work she could find, serving as a switchboard operator, shop assistant and housekeeper in a hotel. Stanley Moss, author of the classic *Ill Met by Moonlight*, described her plight in the *Picture Post* of 4 October 1952:

Following the murder of her mother by the Germans, her only surviving close relatives – a young niece in Poland and an aged aunt in the south of France – now looked to her for support. She took a job in a Paddington hotel, where her duty was to care for the linen-cupboard. Next, she took a job as a waitress in a tea-shop. A little later, she found employment in the dress department at Harrods' store. Throughout this time she was too proud to trade on her medals or even to mention her war record, but – incredible though it seems – she never lost her sense of humour. When being interviewed for a job in a chain of hotels, she was told that only married women could be employed. She asked if men also had to be married, and was told for them it didn't matter. 'All right then,' she said, 'give me a list of your unmarried managers and I'll marry one of them.' And that was the end of that job.

Seeking work in the British Section of the UN in Geneva, she was told, 'But you are not British at all – you're just a foreigner with a British passport.' In desperation she took a job as a second-class stewardess on the Shaw Savill liner *Rauhine*, making its maiden voyage to Australia. The captain ordered all crew to wear the ribbons of their decorations, and the dazzling array on Christina's blouse caused a hideous outbreak of jealousy that such awards should have gone to a foreigner and a woman to boot.

One steward, Dennis George Muldowney, took her part and in return Christina introduced him to her friends in London. But Muldowney became a pest and Christina decided to leave London to shake him off. Andrew had made contact and in the summer of 1952 invited her to join him in Brussels. Suddenly the end of her troubles was in sight. But on 15 June her plane was grounded by engine failure and she went out that night for a final dinner with friends in London. Returning to the Shelbourne, the small family hotel in Lexham Gardens where she had lodged for several years, she started up the stairs only to hear a voice behind her. The night porter heard a desperate cry of 'Get him off me,' and rushed to find Muldowney standing over her, clutching a knife. 'I killed her,' he said. Christina was just thirty-seven.

At the trial, Muldowney pleaded guilty to murder, and the judge pronounced the death sentence. It was not quite the end of the drama as Mr Roger Frisby, representing her relatives and friends, stood up to say that 'there was not one particle of truth' in allegations by Muldowney that he had had a romance with Christina. Afterwards Andrew told the *Daily Mail*: 'To Christine rank and birth meant nothing. She brought him to see her friends and said, "This is Dennis. He has been kind to me and I want you to be kind to him."' Yet it will for ever remain a puzzle as to why a woman who had lived with danger for so long, whose antennae were usually so finely tuned, allowed such a threatening situation to develop. She recognised the warning signs, of course, but for once only when it was too late. Had life lost its edge for her after so many setbacks?

Andrew settled in Munich but never married. In his will he expressed the wish that his ashes should be placed in the grave in Kensal Green cemetery where Christina was buried.

The earth placed on her coffin was brought from Poland so she lies beneath her native soil. Andrew's ashes lie under a tablet on her grave bearing his name and decorations.

Christina (or Christine) Granville, born Krystyna Skarbek, came to London soon after Poland was invaded. She volunteered her services and set out for Hungary in December 1939 with the mission of entering German-occupied Poland.

The American Virginia Hall went to Lyons in August 1941 for SOE, using the cover of working as a correspondent for the *New York Post*.

(*above*) Christina Granville and the Pole Andrew Kennedy, her lover and lifelong friend. They met in Budapest where he was running escape lines out of Poland.

(*below*) Christina Granville with the Maquis in the Haute-Savoie in August 1944. From left to right: Gilbert Galetti, Captain Patrick O'Regan, Captain John Roper, Christina Granville and Captain Leonard Hamilton.

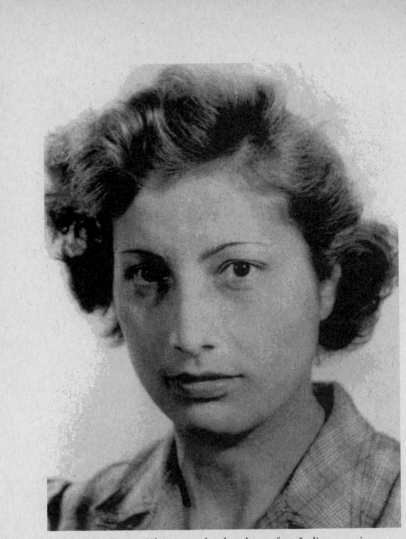

Noor Inayat Khan was the daughter of an Indian mystic and an American mother. Brought up in France, she joined the WAAFs with her sisters, trained as a wireless operator and was landed in France by Lysander on the night of 16 June 1943.

Mauritian by birth, Lise de Baissac went with her family to France when she was fourteen. When France was invaded, she crossed into Spain and made her way to London via Lisbon. Described by her SOE instructors as 'imperturbable', she parachuted into France on the night of 24/5 September 1942 with a mission to establish herself in Poitiers.

Violette Szabo was working at the Bon Marché store in Brixton when war broke out. After the death of her French Legionnaire husband Étienne Szabo at El Alamein, she joined SOE and was first landed in France by Lysander near Azay-le-Rideau on the night of 5/6 April 1944.

Pearl Witherington grew up in Paris and escaped via
Portugal when France was invaded. She parachuted into
France near Châteauroux on the night of
22/3 September 1943.

Carte d'Identité

NOM _Leroy_
Prénoms _Corinne Reine_
État civil _VII_
Profession _Secrétaire Commercial_
Né le _26 Juin 1921_
à _Bailleul_
Département _Nord_
Nationalité _Française_
Domicile _64 rue Thiers_
Le Havre

SIGNALEMENT

Taille _1m 64_   Dos _rect_
Cheveux _châtains_   Nez
Moustache   Dimensions _moy._
Yeux _marrons_   Forme du visage _ovale_
Signes particuliers _néant_   Teint _mat_

Empreinte digitale   Le Titulaire,   Les Témoins,

Vu pour la légalisation
Le _1 5 MAI 1943_   19

Violette Szabo's fake identity card, brought back from her first
mission to France in 1944.

Chapter 4

VIRGINIA HALL

A remarkable woman, of extraordinary courage and formidable tenacity. Despite her transatlantic accent, her memorable appearance, her wooden leg, she succeeded in remaining almost three years in occupied territory without being arrested. She did not submit easily to discipline, she had the habit of forming her ideas without regard to the views of others, but she rendered inestimable services to the Allied cause and is a very great friend of France.

Colonel Maurice Buckmaster's citation of 19 June 1945,
proposing Virginia Hall for a George Medal

Virginia Hall is a commanding figure in the early history of SOE – a resourceful and brilliant agent playing a key role in helping numerous other agents establish themselves and make vital contacts. Almost all the early agents who went to France had dealings with her – a procedure in itself completely at variance with SOE's tight security procedures. This was no lapse but was possible thanks to Virginia's unusual cover. She was an American citizen, using the cover of a journalist working for the *New York Post*, accredited to the Vichy authorities.

Another early SOE agent, the Frenchman Philippe de Vomécourt, described her as an 'extraordinary woman . . . hiding her artificial leg with big strides, so effectively that no one who did not know her was aware of it'. He added: 'She had carried messages for us, she had gone where we could not go. She wheedled the police into releasing many prisoners, including escaped P.O.W.s and agents.'

Ben Cowburn, a tough Lancashireman who was one of the first SOE agents to be dropped in France, wrote: 'If you sit in [her] kitchen long enough you will see most people pass through with one sort of trouble another which [she] promptly deals with.'

Virginia was blown – badly 'brûlé' – after the Germans swarmed into the Unoccupied Zone in November 1942. However, she made her way back to England and in 1944 embarked on a second career as a secret agent, this time working for the newly formed American OSS, the Office of Strategic Services, later to develop into the CIA. The story of her activities has to be pieced together from many sources: from letters, cables and memos in her personal file, her own activity report to OSS in US National Archives, and the reports and recollections of other agents.

In Vichy France, Virginia operated under the code names of first Marie, then Philomène, returning to Brittany in 1944 as Diane. In correspondence with SOE she is referred to, and signs herself, DFV.

She was born in Baltimore on 6 April 1906, the youngest child of Edwin Lee Hall, who had married his secretary, Barbara Virginia Hammel. Her grandfather had made a fortune in shipping. After a private day school in Baltimore, she attended Radcliffe and later Barnard College from 1924 to 1926. Then her father allowed her to continue her studies in Europe; she spent a year at the École des Sciences Politiques in Paris and two years at the Konsularakadémie (Diplomatic School) in Vienna. Indefatigable in her quest to improve her French, she also studied for a short time at the universities of Strasbourg, Grenoble and Toulouse.

Returning home in 1929, Virginia took further courses in French at George Washington University in Washington, DC. She then entered the diplomatic service, working in the US Embassy in Warsaw, at the consulates in Smyrna and Venice and at the US Legation in Tallinn. While stationed in Turkey, she had a hideous accident. When shooting snipe with friends near Izmir, she accidentally shot her own foot. Gangrene set in and her leg had to be amputated just below the knee. She was given a wooden leg, which with characteristic brio she christened Cuthbert. Ironically, this accident was to lead directly to her career as a secret agent, as the State Department at the time had a regulation that barred employment of anyone who had lost a limb.

When war was declared in September 1939, Virginia was in Paris, where she joined the French ambulance service. After France fell in June 1940, she set off for England by way of Spain. When she was recruited by SOE in late 1940 she was working in London as a code clerk for the US military attaché.

The first mention of her on SOE files is a memo of 15 January 1941 to Maurice Buckmaster from a colleague about

Miss Virginia Hall (34) who works at the US Embassy, [and] talked in my house last night of wanting to go for about a month to France via Lisbon/Barcelona. In the latter place she said her old chief would give her a visa for France ... It strikes me that this lady, a native of Baltimore, might well be used for a mission and that we might: a) facilitate her voyage to Lisbon and back; and b) stand her expenses while on her trip in exchange for what service she could render us. I am getting further details on her and will put her through the cards.

'Nothing recorded against' was MI5's routine comment a month later.

SOE's first thoughts were that she should obtain cover as a correspondent of the American magazine *P.M.* The publication's London representative, Ben Robertson, was agreeable but approval was also needed from the proprietor, Ralph Ingersoll. A memo written to Buckmaster on 1 April 1941: 'Please make it clear that we are paying all expenses and that Miss Hall need only be paid space rates by him for any material used. She has journalistic experience. Also please make it clear that we are not asking Miss Hall to do anything more than keep her eyes and ears open.'

Some time during the next few weeks the plan changed and Virginia was accredited to the *New York Post*. On 21 May, a memo to Buckmaster talks of putting her on the priority list for a plane at the beginning of June. Virginia was also to receive guidance on a suitable kind of code that she could include in the newspaper articles she sent to New York. It was suggested that she have two or three days in Bournemouth where officers from Beaulieu could come to see her, in addition to 'a certain amount of instruction from me'.

Another memo that same day confirms her newspaper accreditation. 'I saw Mr Backer yesterday at Claridges, when he handed me an attestation that Virginia Hall was a fully accredited correspondent of his newspapers, together with a Cable Company Identification Card, which she would need. Mr Backer, without saying anything, was obviously aware of an ulterior motive to the issue of passes for 27-land [SOE code for France], and was extremely cordial.'

She left for France on 23 August 1941 and took an apartment at 3 Place Oliviers in Lyons. In a story sent to the *Post*, dated Vichy, 4 September 1941, she provided her vivid first impressions:

The years have rolled back here in Vichy. There are no taxis at the station, only half a dozen buses and a few one-horse shays. I took a bus using gazogene, charcoal instead of gas, to my hotel. Vichy is a tiny town used once by summer visitors to take the cure. It is an infinitesimally small place to accommodate the government of France and the French Empire which has commandeered most of the hotels . . . I haven't seen any butter and there is very little milk. I also see little clothing in the shops and that is extremely dear . . . Women are no longer entitled to buy cigarettes and men are rationed to two packages a week.

A glimpse of the milieu that Virginia was entering is provided in a memo of 7 November 1941 to Buckmaster about Flight Lieutenant Simpson, then in the Queen Victoria Hospital at East Grinstead, who had passed on names of contacts to Virginia. These included 'Germaine Guérin, a woman of considerable attainments who incidentally works the Black Market, and is part owner of a brothel. This woman has in particular a friend who is a well-known French Engineer, in a high position and who is able to travel about freely between the two Zones. His is an official job, and he could work for us without hindrance.' Germaine Guérin is described as 100 per cent and working hard for what she calls 'the revolution against the German occupiers'.

The memo goes on to say:

Simpson declared that Lyon is full of extremely phoney people, who go around proclaiming that they are engaged in subversive work, and that the greatest care must be taken in making any contacts. Among the American people in Lyon, Simpson was in contact with Miss Harvey, now U.S. Consul at Lyon, who is reliable but talkative. He is somewhat suspicious of the Vice-Consul and his assistant, George Wittinghill and Houston respectively, the latter of whom is in charge of British interests. Houston also he suspects of being pro-German and quite capable of working against us.

Another contact introduced by the redoubtable Madame Guérin was 'Dr Rousset, a prominent gynaecologist, ardent de Gaullist, ready to help the allied cause in any way'.

Virginia avidly devoured German, Swiss and Italian newspapers as well as French. Her report of 14 November 1941 quotes the *Koelnische Zeitung* as stating that the first houses in the Polish city of Posen (Poznan) destined for Dutch families will be ready in March; that 10,000 Dutch farmers are to settle in the province of 'Posnanie'; and that in future only German name signs will be used on Polish stations.

A memo of 2 December 1941, giving instructions to an SOE

agent code-named Raoul, illustrates how SOE put agents in touch with Virginia. On arrival in Lyons, he was to go to the Hôtel de Verdun near the station and then

get in touch with Miss Virginia Hall, an American journalist, who is at the Grand Nouvel [*sic*] Hôtel in Lyon. I think you will probably be able to see her and if you do you will introduce yourself, when you are alone with her, with the Marcel formula [a phrase such as 'Has Marcel come back from the country?']. Naturally you will talk to her in French ... If Miss Hall is not there when you call, you should leave her a note. You can say somewhere in the text of your note: 'J'aimerais vous voir pour avoir des nouvelles de Marie'. Then sign 'Raoul', four letters underlined.

A report from 'Marie' [Virginia] of 23 December 1941 gives an insight into the extraordinary range of contacts and intelligence that she was now handling:

The inventor of Mazout burners used on the S/S 'Normandie' has escaped from the occupied zone. The Germans are seeking to capture his patents, which he places at the disposal of the British Admiralty. We can easily get in touch with him ... We have organized a political information service based on people in the Marshal's [Pétain's] entourage and several politicians of the first rank, both now serving and formerly in office. This service has already given us a certain number of tips which have proved 100% correct regarding the Pétain–Goering and Ciano–Darlan interviews. Moreover it has provided us with news of the probability of an attack on Portugal through Spain with the consent of Spain and the eventual passivity of Portugal.

Early in March 1942 there is a laconic report from Marie on two agents:

George thirty-five [initially all SOE radio operators were referred to as George with a number affixed] and Jean ... I contacted them in Marseilles on February 24th. It appears that the pilot made a mistake of about thirty kilometres and they landed in the fields near Vaas in the Sarthe. George landed in a vineyard, luckily between two rows of stakes and the idea of having been impaled for public view rather shook him – or rather, his faith in the infallibility of pilots. Jean came to a rather more comfortable rest on the other side of the fence. As there was no reception committee and the dog at the farm began to raise a row, they buried their gear for safe keeping and took a stroll. They went to Tours, from there to Paris, and finally to Perpignan where they contacted a man who sent them to Marseilles where I picked them up and brought them home with me!

... Both men are in good spirits and frightfully pleased at having contacted us, because a month of aimless and seemingly hopeless wandering, without reliable means of obtaining food tickets etc, has been discouraging, especially after having been landed in the wrong place and almost been split upon a stake. It really isn't good enough.

Her droll style typically makes light of the whole affair but according to Colonel E.G. Boxshall, one of SOE's early chroniclers, by this rescue 'she probably saved the whole set-up'. George was of crucial importance to F Section, as some months earlier, in October 1941, following a trap set by the Marseilles police, about a dozen British agents had been arrested in quick succession, making a virtual clean sweep of British organisers in the Unoccupied Zone. Agents arrested included Georges Bégué and Lieutenants Clement Jumeau, Jack Hayes and Bruce Cadogan. Subsequently Michael Trotobas had been arrested in Châteauroux during an identity card check-up, and Philippe Liewer (later Major Staunton, Violette Szabo's organiser) had been arrested in Antibes.

Virginia sent George to Châteauroux to pick up a wireless set that Bégué had left there, to bring it back to Lyons and re-establish communication with London. She also provided Philippe de Vomécourt with his means of communication with London until he received his own radio operator in September 1942.

Gerry Morel, an insurance broker trilingual in English, French and Portuguese, was another agent saved by Virginia. He had been dropped by Lysander with the task of contacting numerous friends and persuading them to form groups that would carry out sabotage when arms and explosives came from Britain. After six weeks, one of his contacts betrayed him but he became seriously ill. Immediately after an operation, he slipped past a policeman dozing by his bed and escaped on the arm of a nurse who helped him over a wall. A friend of de Vomécourt's was waiting outside with clothes. They passed him on to Virginia, who set him on to an escape line over the Pyrenees. By March 1942 he was back in England, working as Buckmaster's operations officer.

Another agent who made his way straight to Virginia was Marcel Clech, who landed by felucca from Gibraltar in April 1942. She sent him to Puys to look for suitable landing grounds – information on two were sent back to England. The agent Charles Hayes also first landed in France from a felucca on 14 May 1942 and was put in touch with Philippe de Vomécourt by Virginia. Hayes reconnoitred several possible sites for sabotage, including power stations at Toulon and St-Jean-de-Maurienne on the edge of the Alps, but found them too well guarded. When Virginia told him that the Gestapo had a full description of him, he decided it was time to leave and she found him an escape line across the Pyrenees, which enabled him to reach England by August.

Virginia also provided crucial help to Ben Cowburn on his second mission. On the night of 1/2 June 1942, he had para-chuted into the Limousin, forty miles (sixty kilometres) wide of the intended spot, with an RAF officer, E.M. Wilkinson. They desperately needed a wireless operator and Virginia introduced them to Denis Rake, a promiscuous homosexual who was one of SOE's more colourful agents.

At the end of June, Virginia warned Denis Rake that the police were looking for him and advised him to return to England. Rashly, Rake decided first to go to Paris, and Hall agreed to send on his wireless set and luggage by another route. By now the police had Rake's name and they were able to arrest him as he crossed into the Occupied Zone at Montceau-les-Mines. He was transferred with 100 other prisoners to Châlons-sur-Marne and then sent on to Dijon but, remarkably, he persuaded his guards to let him escape, jumping out of the train at Dijon. Arriving in Paris but finding no sign of his set or luggage, he decided to go back to Lyons to obtain another set, hiding in the fuse box of the electric train. Virginia sheltered him in her flat and, in an attempt to resolve his very dangerous predicament, went to Cannes to discuss his future with the agent, Peter Churchill. Churchill decided that Rake should return to England. Instead, the ever-rash Rake set off back to Paris but was arrested en route at Limoges, this time as a black marketeer, and sent south to Castres. However, he was released in November 1942 by a friendly prison commandant who thought his life would be in danger when the Germans swarmed into the Unoccupied Zone. Rake later followed Virginia over the Pyrenees but broke his ankle and was eventually imprisoned, finally reaching England in May 1943.

Virginia's reports provide a commentary on French opinion, particularly following the surrender of Singapore. One of late February 1942 reads:

People take a pretty sour view of the British these days, but they are still hoping for their victory and many, many of them are willing to help, but they would appreciate seeing something concrete besides retreating. They acknowledge the vastness of the task that the British have taken on, but are not able to take the really broad view ... The propaganda of the Germans showing that the German soldier is shedding his blood to defend France from the Russians is received here with good humour and a great willingness to let them shed as much blood as they like – the more the better, indeed – but it does get through to certain mentalities and the constant drumming of German propaganda has its effect. Everyone is, alas, agreed that British broadcasts in French are very poor. In fact the B.B.C. has lost many auditors [listeners] in the last weeks, but everyone is listening to Boston and to Switzerland.

Virginia also makes a plea for a good circuit organiser. 'Actually we could use about six clever chaps in various centers this side. It's a snowball, but you do need a certain number of perfectly and utterly reliable persons – persons from "home".' As an aside she adds: 'If you could ever send me a piece of soap I should be both very happy and much cleaner.'

Big cities always held dangers for SOE agents and Virginia was one of the first to point to the growing sympathy of people in country areas, which towards D-Day were to become F Section's great strength. Her report of 20 March 1942 notes: 'The country folk are turning more and more against the government and more and more toward the English whom they don't like, fundamentally.' Farmers, she said, were soured by the fact that they had to ask the authorities for seed and 'in order to get it must promise from 50 to 99 per cent of the harvest . . . Many are not planting wheat this year because they have to give it all back.'

Her report of 22 April 1942 brought further news of public feeling.

Laval's return [as head of the Vichy government] has caused the rise of a lovely tide of hate and the Maréchal's stock has slumped very sharply. The army is disgusted with its new head, but there is so much apathy and fear in the country that there has been no decided reaction – nothing spectacular, that is, although everyone who was on the fence before has gone over to whatever is against Laval. He has brought you a lot of partisans. Unfortunately everyone fears internment or prison . . . The French have got the habit of meekly accepting during the past year. They have accepted stricter and stricter rations, lessening of rations, restrictions on wine, less bread, less alcohol, no beer, until finally they have arrived at the state of eating rutabaga for supper, washed down with mineral water – no beer or wine is served in the evening with meals . . . It is incredible but true.

Virginia's cable of 22 June 1942 to the *New York Post* brought two items of interest: first, that air attacks on Germany were prompting the authorities to send children out of danger (as had happened earlier in Britain), in this case from the Ruhr to Hungary, to stay with German-speaking Hungarians. 'The age limit of the children . . . is not given but considering the fact that German children from the age of ten years are under the obligation to perform their "work service" it would seem the children in these convoys which are shuttling about Europe must be under ten years of age.' Meanwhile numerous French workers, laid off because of lack of raw materials, such as those from the shoe factories in Limoges, were going to Germany. 'One eats to live these days and to eat one must work and for work one must go to Germany. Malnutrition has a very bad effect however, on the quality and quantity of work produced and it is distressing that the workmen whose reactions have become slow and dull these days are constantly having minor accidents in the manipulation of machinery. The loss of fingers becomes phenomenal.'

A report from Virginia of 30 September 1942 (she is now using the code name Philomène) provides interesting details of her brushes with the police. An agent – Justin – who was left alone in a café,

looked so obviously nervous that an inspector of police felt he had better question him . . . Justin said he was *chemisier* in Lyon. Asked how much he earned a month he said eight thousand a month and added 'Mais c'est pas énorme, vous savez'. The good inspector positively jumped at that and decided he was an agent of some sort. He had a look at the contents of his pockets and the money he had was nice and new, not pinned and all in series, so of course he must have come from England or Germany. He waited for the other two and picked them up as well.

The other agent, described simply as F., was 'also well supplied with money, unpinned and in series. It appears that all thousand franc notes come out of the bank pinned together in the left hand corner in bundles of ten, so when the inspectors find a thousand franc note without pin marks on it, they are immediately on guard. Furthermore, F. and Alex had cards of identity from different towns but made out in the same hand writing.' The inspector, continued Virginia, did not know if they were English or German agents, but took them to the police station. There, a friendly officer allowed them to burn their papers and confiscated the automatic Alex was carrying, so there were no serious charges against them.

Virginia next mentions an interesting means of sending agents to Germany disguised as French workmen. 'They can go to any part of Germany you wish, or be placed in any factory you desire. The man who places them will not know that they are not good Frenchmen.' She adds: 'I think a good job could be done over Limoges way, if you would send me a good man for it, or else let me undertake the job myself. The only trouble is that I am doing too much as it is and find it hard to swing around the circuit fast enough.'

Back in London, on 19 October 1942, Virginia was recommended for the CBE (a manuscript amendment improves the typed OBE to a CBE). The citation reads: 'She has been indefatigable in her constant support and assistance for our agents, combining a high degree of organising ability with a clear-sighted appreciation of our needs. She has become a vital link between ourselves and the various operational groups in the field, and her services for us cannot be too highly praised.'

Cheeseparingly, in July 1943 Virginia was only awarded a more modest MBE.

A lighthearted letter of 25 November 1942 from Virginia reports that a 'nice red headed doctor' is taking her shooting and that she will 'keep Cuthbert well out of the way'. A postscript adds: 'I've made some *tart* friends. They tell me their Jerry bed companions are not so bright as once was. In fact many are downright pessimistic. Excuse my acquaintances – but they know a hell of a lot!'

A note of her accounts gives some idea of the scale of the Resistance network she had been supporting: a total of 225,000 francs paid out to nine agents in October, with a similar sum for November. Even so, as she left, almost all of them were broke and in need of money.

Virginia describes her hurried departure and escape across the Pyrenees in a letter from Barcelona of 4 December 1942. On 7 November she had been warned of the imminent invasion of North Africa, which was likely to prompt the Germans to swarm south and take over the Unoccupied Zone. The next day news of the invasion duly came and a man from the Deuxième Bureau told her the Germans were expected in Lyons some time between midnight and the next morning. 'I packed my bag and left for Perpignan on the 11 p.m. train,' she wrote. She was right to leave in a hurry – the incoming head of the Lyons Gestapo said that 'he would give anything to put his hands on that Canadian bitch'. Before she left, she made one last use of her contacts, arranging the escape of several prisoners from Castres.

In Perpignan she sought out a man she knew, Gilbert, who could always be met on the main square between two and three every day, and he found guides for her. She picked up three more men, two of whom she thought might be useful to SOE. The normal cost for guides to Barcelona was 20,000 francs a head – Virginia paid for all of them as the others had no money, negotiating a price of 55,000 francs. They went to Villefranche on foot and over the Col de Tivoli, then down from Camprodón to the small mountain terminus of San Juan de las Abasedas, aiming to catch the 5.45 a.m. train to Barcelona, which they believed was not subject to controls. Unfortunately, the police were up early that morning and when they arrived at the station at 4.30 a.m., they were promptly picked up and put in gaol. Whilst some agents spent a long time in the notorious camp at Miranda before securing their freedom, Virginia was released two and a half weeks later through the efforts of the American consulate in Barcelona. She was back in London with remarkable speed in January 1943, reporting all this to SOE.

Not surprisingly, Virginia had problems with her wooden leg on the journey. London received a now legendary message from her, saying: 'Cuthbert is giving me trouble, but I can cope.' The reply was terse: 'If Cuthbert is giving you trouble, have him eliminated.' 'God knows how she made the journey over the mountains,' exclaimed Philippe de Vomécourt.

Virginia's debriefing in London on 15 January 1943 provided SOE with a useful summary of the mainstays of her circuit in Lyons. There was Germaine (owner of a part-share in a brothel) whose 'main interest was helping prisoners' and who 'used to get food, clothes, etc, for them'. Then there was Pepin, 'useful as a postbox' and for arranging 'a clinic, ambulance service, doctors, nurses, anaesthetists, etc. for our men, as long as we provide food cards, etc. He will put them up at the clinic (originally an asylum) whenever they need a place urgently, or a hide-out.' Earlier she had reported: 'He is most devoted to the good cause. I hope you give him a large medal some day.'

Next came Eugène, whose girlfriend had a sister and brother-in-law 'ready to do anything for us. The brother-in-law can travel round and will take [wireless] sets, etc. for us.' They could be contacted through Eugène or his girlfriend, Andrée Michel 'de la part de Philomène'. If a further password was required the contact should ask about 'the flat out in the Armenian quarter of Marseilles'.

Another contact was Madame Landry of 2 rue Bailli de Sufresne in the old port. 'She is able to get all sorts of fake papers for people. She works principally for the Austrians – has an Austrian boy named Muller who travels around the country and helps refugees of all sorts with fake identity cards and fake ration cards.' Madame Landry also passed messages to Paris for Virginia, using her contacts in refugee organisations.

A further contact was the Marquis d'Aragon in the South, 'who is willing to do anything, has a few trained men ready. He only has one servant in his château, near Albi, and people can go in there and hide for a few days without being noticed.' There was also a woman at the St Joseph prison in Lyons who was willing to help in any way she could, 'particularly any prisoners of ours in the prison. She said that if ever a safe house was needed, anyone brought to her would be taken into the country into safety, though not comfort.'

In a further report of 17 January 1943, Virginia passed on details of conditions in France.

There appears to be no more control on the trains now than before the occupation. One has to be a little careful going into frontier towns as the control on buses etc. is strict and one has to have a good reason for moving about. There was talk of making a 'Zone Interdite' along the Pyrenees but this has not yet been carried out. Food cards: they are stricter over the issue of coupons, more questions asked as to where you live, what you do, and they can ask you to show your work ticket. This started in November . . . Workers for Germany are only wanted voluntarily and they cannot be sent without signing a contract. In one case, workers refusing to sign this contract were arrested and incarcerated in a fort outside Lyon, were kept there for ten days under pressure to sign, but had to be released finally without signing. V.H. [Virginia Hall] gave instructions to one man to tell the others to hold out.

To this was added a list of the vital radio sets known to Virginia. There were two safely stowed with friends in Lyons at 21 bis rue Xavier Privat, without crystals. One of these had been sent to her for the agent Georges 60. Grégoire had another set. Justin's set was in the hands of the Sûreté in Paris. Eugène had one set sent out to Nicholas during the September moon. Another set bound for Eugène had been seized when 'the *camionneurs* had been arrested, the depots found, and the house where the set was'.

Virginia describes the problems associated with sabotage and arms in the early days of SOE. Nicholas had given a large quantity of explosives to clandestine organisations but these had been used to carry out acts designed to irritate the Germans but of no real value, such as blowing up newspaper kiosks. Material given to the communist-run Francs-Tireurs, Combat and other resistant groups had been stored very badly in damp places and was ruined and rusty, even the plastic showing signs of mould. The Francs-Tireurs had suggested blowing up the rails in front of a train carrying Marshal Pétain to 'frighten him' but Virginia had managed to dissuade them from this 'ridiculous' act. Guns had not been properly looked after, she said: 'It is imperative that only our own men trained over here, or men trained by them over here, should handle material.' With regard to sabotage in factories, she reported there were 'many people willing to carry out anything possible, they only needed material', but SOE instructions were to avoid all small acts.

Virginia was now enlisted to work for D/F Section, which operated escape lines. A memo of 5 May 1943 sets out her brief on a new mission to Spain – referred to as 23-land. 'She will be acting as foreign correspondent for the *Chicago Times* . . . She will, however, undertake no work of any kind for us for a minimum period of two months, and during this time she is to confine herself entirely to journalistic duties.' This was to enable her to establish her cover firmly with the Spanish authorities. She was not to make contact with the controller at the embassy but was given the name of a contact in the press department 'whom, in the course of her journalistic duties, she is bound to meet'. Her work was to indicate safe houses and possible personnel for future recruitment. She was also to take verbal and written messages as instructed, with the aim of accelerating urgent correspondence from provincial towns, the port of Bilbao particularly.

The memo continues: 'I think you will find her both intelligent, useful and pleasant to work with. She is certainly capable of getting things done as is proved by the fact that she obtained her visa literally within a couple of hours although she had, of course, no support from us. If therefore, at a later date you feel that she could actually run a line, there is no reason why you should not set her to do such a task.'

She was to travel by the first plane available after 15 May 1943. Although she had expressed an interest in wireless work, she had been told that such work was sufficiently covered in the peninsula, but she was asked to keep her eyes open for likely recruits. She was also told to be careful to contact only those who had fought on Franco's side during the Civil War, as serious diplomatic complications would ensue if the Spanish government discovered that men of Republican sympathies were being recruited. Nonetheless, SOE made eager use of exiled Spanish Republicans at Massingham, its Algiers base. As to any Americans involved in secret work, she was told not to cold-shoulder them but also to give no hint she was working for SOE.

Next arose the question of her pay. A cable sent from Madrid to D/F Section on 8 July 1943 says that if Virginia 'stays on here we must provide her with adequate money since her American editors will pay almost nothing for articles on Spain. Since much of her usefulness will depend on her being able to give and accept entertainment her net income must be at least 3500 pesetas per month as compared with 2500 pesetas per month paid to embassy typists.' At least 2,500 pesetas had to be cashed at the official rate; the remainder, as well as travel expenses, could be paid from the SOE pesetas fund 'unless she finds official inquiries being made into [the] source of her income'.

Ten days later a cable from London brought news that Virginia had been 'awarded MBE repeat MBE', adding that 'in view of her nationality and cover essential celebrations remain strictly private'.

To protect her cover, Virginia's pay came in the form of monthly payments from the USA as if from her employers, via BOLSA (the Bank of London–South America) in New York. Conveniently two senior SOE figures held positions in the London branch of the bank. A further memo of 8 September 1943 says the bank must be in a position, if questioned, to be able to state the origin of the funds. It also states that neither the American authorities nor the *Chicago Times* should know Virginia was being paid by SOE.

After the danger and excitement of life in France, Virginia soon tired of neutral Spain, writing to Buckmaster:

Dear F.

I've given this a good four months' try and come to the conclusion that it really is a waste of time and money. Anyhow, I always did want to go back to France, and now I have the luck to find two of my very own boys here and sent them on to you. They want me to go back with them because we worked together before and our team work is good . . . I suggest I go back as their radio, or else as aider and abetter, as before. I can learn the radio quickly enough in spite of scepticism in some quarters.

She explains: 'When I came out here I thought I would be able to help . . . but I don't and can't. I am not doing a job. I am simply living pleasantly and wasting time . . . I think I can do a job for you along with my two boys. They think I can too and I trust you will let us try, because we are all three very much in earnest about this bloody war. My best regards . . . to Mrs Colonel B . . . and I hope she gets some of the lemons I asked the boys to drape themselves in upon departure.'

Buckmaster's colourful reply, dated 6 October 1943, also survives on the files. 'Dearest Doodles,' it begins, 'What a wonder you are! I know you could learn radio in no time; I know the boys would love to have you in the field; I know all about the things you could do, and it is only because I honestly believe that the Gestapo would also know it in about a fortnight that I say no, dearest Doodles, no. You are really too well-known in the country and it would be wishful thinking believing that you could escape detention for more than a few days.'

Little could Buckmaster know how wrong he was to be proved on this point but he continued in the same avuncular tone:

You do realize, don't you, that what was previously a picnic, comparatively speaking, is now real war, and that the Gestapo are pulling in everything they can? You will object I know, that it is your own neck – I agree, but we all know that it is not *only* your own neck, it is the necks of all with whom you come into contact because the Boche is good at patiently following trails, and sooner or later he will unravel the whole skein if he has a chance.

Having got this off his chest, Buckmaster proposed that instead Virginia should come back to London as 'a briefing officer for the boys'. Her tasks would be to meet them when they came back from the field, listen to and analyse their stories, ensure the clothing and equipment produced by F Section met their needs, and brief 'the new boys' on what she had learnt and picked up from the latest arrivals. Hardly an agenda to appeal to a seasoned front-line veteran like Virginia.

He also thanked her for the press cuttings: 'We get a hell of a lot of paper, but the particular snippets you sent us are far more to the point . . . Please continue the service . . . German clippings [are] also very acceptable.'

Happily, the very next day Virginia's release from Spain was on the way in the form of a letter from D/F Section, which read: 'F [Buckmaster] has shown me your letter . . . I quite appreciate your point of view. I feel certain you will be much happier doing F Section work and . . . I have agreed to release you . . . the work which I originally intended for you has . . . become less urgent. Will you, therefore, make the necessary plans to leave Spain in such a manner as will permit you to return there "clean" at some future date should it be desirable for you to do so.' The accompanying instruction note adds: 'I have other officers in Spain who, between them, can cope adequately with the work.'

Following her return to England, Virginia was sent to Thame Park in Oxfordshire (Special Training School 52), which specialised in wireless training. A memo of 13 January 1944 passes on the commandant's concerns about his charge: 'Miss Hall states that she wishes to go to London every Saturday. It is not known whether this is in order or whether it is necessary for S.T.S. 52 to be given any information as to where she is going and for what purpose. I should be grateful if you would clear up these points, if only because there may be a tendency for other students to claim the privileges accorded to Miss Hall.'

Virginia returned to France on the night of 21 March 1944, arriving by boat on the Brittany coast. The report on her mission, which she submitted to OSS six months later, dated 30 September 1944 is a vivid portrayal of the daily difficulties and dangers that Allied officers faced when working in enemy-occupied territory, especially as the area where she landed was effectively German territory, filled with German troops.

She landed with Peter Harratt, code name Aramis, about whom she was soon to have serious doubts. They went straight to Paris by rail where an old friend of hers, Madame Long of 59 rue de Babylone, found a room for Aramis in a nearby *pension* with a Gaullist landlady. This ensured that he did not need to fill in registration forms. Madame Long placed her flat at Virginia's disposal but, after talking to Aramis for a while, Madame Long decided he was so talkative and indiscreet that he should never go to the flat again.

The next day Virginia set off to the Creuse with Aramis, who was suffering from a very painful knee, which he had sprained during the landing on the coast. On their arrival at Maidons near Crozant, Virginia met a farmer, Eugène Lepinat, who found her a little house with one room, without water or electricity, by the roadside. She was to eat at his house at the far end of the village. Aramis returned to Paris to start his own work and arrange couriers to Maidons.

Virginia started work on the farm, taking the cows to pasture and cooking for Lepinat, his old mother and his hired farmhand. This was done on an open fire as there was no stove in the house. 'I found a few good fields for receptions and farmers and farm hands willing and eager to help,' she wrote. Aramis returned twice, having found a flat he could use as a safe house. However, he did not seem to understand how to use couriers and fiercely resented advice. He was also exhausted by the travelling. 'In spite of his robust appearance he is not very strong, cannot carry parcels or packages of any weight, because he has no strength in his arms,' she said. Invariably, he was ill for a few days after each trip.

Very soon Virginia had once again established a wide range of contacts. On 26 April Montaigne and the W/T operator Pierre appeared with a biscuit box that she had asked for. They told her the grim news that their contact, Louis, and his cousins, Doctors François and Laurence Leccia, had gone to Tours with their radio equipment only to find that a W/T operator had been arrested nearby the day before and the whole place was teeming with Gestapo. Everyone was scared and they were not welcome at all. Leaving the sets, they returned to La Châtre while Louis went to Paris to try to make other arrangements.

On 1 May, Virginia received a telegram from OSS, saying that Pierre had come up without his true checks and was feared arrested. Virginia promptly packed her bags and returned to Madame Long in Paris. 'I left no address behind, of course,' she added.

In Paris she happened to meet an old acquaintance from Marseilles, a man whose speciality was arranging prison escapes. Without telling him what she had in mind, she arranged to see him again. The next day she went to Cosne with Madame Rabut, Aramis's friend, who had become a very devoted and useful companion. As an added precaution Virginia never travelled alone in France, but always with a French chaperone.

In Cosne she went to see Colonel Vessereau, the father-in-law of Louis's sister, Mimi. He and his wife had been told about Virginia's work by Louis and they immediately offered her a home, with permission to work in their attic. By now Virginia had become even more worried by Aramis's talkative tendencies and made Madame Rabut promise to keep the address of the Vessereaus a secret. She or her son Pierre were in future to act as liaison between Aramis and Virginia.

Two days later came news of a devastating betrayal. Pierre and Montaigne had been arrested and taken to the Cherché Midi prison in Paris. It transpired that Colonel Vessereau's son, Fernand, a Capitaine de l'École de Gendarmerie at Courbevoie, had put Louis in touch with Robert, otherwise known as Dr Lane, of 103 Boulevarde St Michel, who in turn had introduced him to one Filias.

Filias had successfully posed as an SOE agent, providing details about SOE officers and giving addresses that convinced Louis of his bona fides. Louis then explained his own mission, and his desire for a safe house and contacts in the Tours district. Filias said, 'Can do,' and sent him off by car to collect Montaigne and Pierre, together with the radio equipment. As soon as they had been picked up, all three agents were taken straight to the Cherché Midi prison. With the help of a friendly guard, Louis managed to smuggle a note out to a colleague, who soon got in touch with Fernand, Vessereau's son. Fernand himself was now in trouble, as he had filched the German plan for the defence of Paris from his colonel and had had it copied. Hoping to get it to the Allies, he had agreed to send the plan to the wretched Filias and entrusted it to two officers in plain clothes. When they duly failed to return, he had to disappear himself.

Now all of them had to go into hiding. Madame Vessereau arranged a room in town for Fernand, and Virginia went to live in the garret at the farmhouse of Jules Juttry at Sury-en-Lere. Père Jules, being eighty-four, was suspicious, fearing that Virginia was German. So, shortly after, Père Jules's widowed daughter, Madame Estelle Bertrand, took her in. Estelle she describes 'as a marvelous *paysanne* of fifty eight who aided and abetted me in every way, even going out and doing receptions with me. She deserves some special mention because after all, we were very much in German territory there.'

Once all were safely installed, Virginia went back to Paris and saw her Marseilles friend again; she found a German guard at the prison who passed a message to the boys. The answer came back, 'We are eight, not three.' Eight was too large a number to try a break-out, and the three, feeling themselves responsible for the others, would not attempt a break-out alone. Within weeks they were in prison in Weimar, in Germany.

As Aramis was making no progress, Virginia decided to start work on her own. Soon, she reported, she had a 'small very close mouthed group for reception work and three or four safe houses'.

Colonel Vessereau (who had been *chef de protocol* in the Daladier cabinet) was now working as her second-in-command in the Nièvre. He had won the confidence of the gendarmes in Cosne and had found about a hundred unattached men willing to work in the Nièvre. The new Maquis was split in four groups of twenty-five each.

Meanwhile Virginia's roving mission continued and in mid-June she went to the Haute-Loire at OSS's request, reporting that they had 150 men but no arms and no direction. A month later, on 14 July, she was back there, having firmly dismissed the suggestion that she should make use of Aramis, who had completely failed to keep in contact or, indeed, reply to her messages.

Irritatingly, nothing had been done about finding a place where she could live or work in the Haute-Loire. She had left, she said, a sound set-up in June but since then the group had quarrelled over the money she had left them. The five men who had taken control – with the 'fake names' of Fayolle, Gevold, Hulot, André and Maudet – were despised by the men or boys in their companies. But these recruits could not return to civilian life and wanted in any case to take action against the Germans.

Virginia stayed with Fayolle and his wife for a couple of days, explaining to him a new form of threat – 'planes with detection apparatus which come along and paste the place where a radio has been detected with bombs'. Soon after she went to live with a Madame Lebrat, who was busy running a farm near Chambron-sur-Lignon while her husband was a prisoner in Germany. 'Madame Lebrat has always kept open house for boys of the Maquis and has given refuge and food to many of them. She took me and my apparatus in without question – anything to help. I stayed with her two weeks and took over an abandoned house of the Salvation Army which I tidied up and lived in. It had three bedrooms and a very large barn which was excellent as a work room.' Madame Lebrat supplied her with food and sent her a hot meal every day when she could not go down to the farm.

Here she set out, as agreed with OSS, to work with Fayolle and the others, financing them and giving them arms on the basis that they would take orders from OSS through her. However, the five men were very jealous of their prerogatives and prestige, causing constant problems. Virginia reported: 'there were a couple [of] thousand men already in the mountains and I had hoped to be able to arm them and to do in most of the several thousand Germans then in Le Puy.'

When Gevold and Fayolle opposed the idea of officers from England as instructors, she asked for sergeants, hoping to avoid friction. Her position was made more difficult by delays in sending material but when three planes came at the end of July they enabled the Maquis to wreck many bridges and tunnels. Eventually by sheer bluff the Germans were forced out of Le Puy, some 500 or 600 of them surrendering.

A Jedburgh team, code-named Jeremy, finally arrived from Algiers in the middle of August 1944. They set about organising three battalions, 1,500 men in all, which Virginia financed and armed. 'I got three surprise planes from Algiers which helped a lot.' As soon as the battalions were formed, she was told they were going off to Alsace under the command of Gevold, by this time a colonel. When Hall demanded they should obtain the approval of the regional military delegate, the French Captain Fonteroise replied, 'Who the hell are you to give me orders?' Virginia expressed her anger to her superiors. 'You send people out ostensibly to work with me and for me but you do not give me the necessary authority. That does not bother me, but I thought going to the Belfort gap with Gevold as Colonel and fifteen hundred ill-trained men a stupid act and I refuse responsibility for the same.' Worse came when Gevold took 957,000 francs to finance the operation. 'I put myself on record as refusing to take further responsibility for this sum.'

Matters got worse when on 4 September two new agents, Raphael and Homon, were dropped thirty kilometres from the field where she was waiting, calling the plane on her Eureka. 'I do not know whether American planes are equipped with a Rebecca, if so such a performance is inexcusable – but then

I find American planes abominable, nonchalant and careless in their work . . . You had finally sent me the two officers I needed so badly when everything was over,' she wrote. As the Jeds were leaving with the battalions, Raphael, Homon and a French officer trained the sixteen boys that they had decided to take with them, giving them fire practice. The men evidently liked the officers and they set off for Clermont-Ferrand on a truck with a machine-gun mounted over the cab.

Here they were advised to head east and see what the 7th Army at Bourg might want them to do. On arrival, they had an immediate and keen reaction from Special Forces to their proposal to do ambush and intelligence work in the Vosges. Raphael and Homon found a small abandoned château near Bourg, which they ordered the boys to clean up and make habitable. 'These two officers are extraordinarily efficient at getting things done – just the sort I might have wished for from the beginning. Valérien (Captain Cowburn) was the most satisfactory person I have ever known to work with but those two run him a very close second.'

All too soon, with the Germans in headlong retreat, their orders were countermanded and the group had to be dissolved. Some were taken up to the recruiting centre of the 9th Colonial Division. Virginia gave each man 3,000 francs 'as something to start on, for most of them had been in the mountains for over a year'. She returned with the officers to Paris, continuing on to London on 26 September.

Looking back, Virginia explained that, when the Jedburgh team arrived, all the local 'officers' had added a stripe or two to their sleeves. The Jedburghs were captains and 'although they found it rather difficult at times directing Majors and Colonels, they made a very good tactful job of it'. By contrast Raphael and Homon were only second lieutenants, which caused serious problems. Virginia explains:

The French FFI and regular military authorities place a great deal of emphasis – and rightly so – on rank and it is hardly normal that a Lieutenant should direct the activities of superior officers, and it is doubtful that when traveling his requests be always honored. During the days when everyone was in civilian clothes, rank did not matter, except to cast a halo around the head of the agent who could honestly say he was a Captain. Later, when everyone was in uniform it was distinctly unfair to send men into the field without giving them the rank necessary to enable them to work efficiently, for by not doing so you gave them great responsibility without sufficient authority. Raphael and Homon have done excellent work for me and if I go out again I want them and no one else to go with me, but if they are to be in uniform I request that their grades be upped, otherwise we shall be very heavily handicapped again. This applies whether we go to China – where face is of great importance – or to Austria or Germany where rank is most highly respected.

Hall summed up her work modestly:

My life in the Creuse consisted of taking the cows to pasture, cooking for the farmers on an open fire and doing my WT work. In the Cher and the Nièvre I was again the milkmaid, took the cows to pasture, milked them and the goats and distributed the milk and was able thus to talk with a lot of people in the very normal course of my activities. Life in the Haute Loire was very different in that I spent my time looking for fields for receptions, spent my day bicycling up and down mountains, seeing fields, visiting various people, doing my WT work and then spending the nights out waiting, for the most part in vain, for deliveries.

The list of her sabotage activities (excerpted from telegrams between 27 July and 12 August) is impressive. It included a bridge blown at Montaigne, cutting the Langogne–Le Puy road; four cuts on the Langogne–Brassac railway; a freight train derailed in a tunnel at Brassac; a bridge blown on the railway between Brioude and Le Puy; a freight train derailed in a tunnel at Monistrol d'Allier and fifteen metres of track blown up behind the train that had gone into the tunnel to clear the wreckage. Other items include telephone lines rendered useless by felling posts and rolling up wires; a lorry full of German soldiers knocked out by bazooka; nineteen of the hated Milice arrested and German lorries destroyed.

During this time, a convoy from Le Puy surrendered after it was trapped between Chamelix and Pigeyre by a succession of bridges blown. Some 500 Germans were taken prisoner and 150 killed, while Resistance losses were negligible. Le Puy itself was taken on 19 August with thirty Germans killed to five Free French.

Like other SOE and OSS officers, Virginia 'took great care never to discuss politics' although the friction between various political groups was a constant frustration. 'I seemed to leave a seething salad behind me, but I don't consider that my affair,' she wrote.

For her work for OSS, Virginia became the first woman to be awarded the Distinguished Service Cross, the army's highest military award after the Medal of Honour. General Donovan, head of OSS, wrote to President Truman on 12 May 1945, suggesting that he might like to make the presentation personally. Remarkably, but perhaps not surprisingly, it was Virginia who declined, refusing any publicity on the grounds that she was 'still operational and most anxious to get busy'.

After the war, Virginia continued in intelligence with the CIA, but desk jobs did not suit her and she was ill at ease with a new generation of officers who had no war experience. In 1950, she married fellow OSS agent Paul Goillot. After her retirement in 1966, aged 60, they settled on a farm in Maryland where she planted thousands of bulbs, went bird-watching and surrounded herself with animals, using her experience in France to make an excellent goat's cheese.

Chapter 5

LISE DE BAISSAC

A very courageous, very diplomatic woman. Loved by all the members of my groups, she was known everywhere. She did all types of work, sabotage, receptions, sheltering of airmen and radio operators, even guerrilla attacks . . . she has been the inspiration of all those who met her and played a large role in the liberation.

Colonel Maurice Buckmaster, 21 April 1945

Lise de Baissac has no doubts as to the worst moment of her war. She was cycling from Normandy to Paris in the summer of 1944, carrying spare parts of radio sets concealed around her waist in her clothing. Stopped at a German checkpoint, she was given a thorough frisking by a young German soldier. 'He searched me very carefully. I knew he could feel the things I was carrying. But he said nothing.' To this day she does not know why. 'Perhaps he was looking for a weapon like a revolver, maybe he thought it was a belt. I do not know.'

It is only when you meet Lise de Baissac that you have an inkling of why a young soldier might hesitate to cross-question her without very good reason. She is one of those petite Latin ladies found in Italy, France and Spain, who despite their slim build convey a sense of calm self-assurance that turns quickly to fiery indignation if they feel they are being treated unreasonably – or being put upon in any way.

Even in advanced old age – she was ninety-six when I met

139

her – Lise retained extraordinary grace and poise, looking a full fifteen years younger than her actual age, still mobile and leading a full social life. Her beautiful features, perfectly *coiffée* black hair with hints of grey, her trim figure, were all testimony to a continuing zest for life and a strong independent nature.

These were the qualities that impressed her SOE instructors. The commandant of the Special Training School 31, at Beaulieu, reported:

Intelligent, extremely conscientious, reliable and sound in every way. Is quite imperturbable and would remain cool and collected in any situation. In both practical exercises and theoretical problems she has shown a capacity to sum up a situation, make a decision and stick to it without becoming flustered. A considerable experience of the world has built up for her a very high degree of self-confidence. A pleasant and quiet personality. She was very much ahead of her fellow-students and, had she been with others as mentally mature as herself, she would have shown herself even more capable. We would certainly recommend her for employment in the field.

This was strong praise indeed and significant, as Lise was one of the first two SOE women agents to parachute into France; Yvonne Rudellat, who arrived two months earlier, had been taken in by felucca.

Lise belonged to an important group of very capable and successful SOE agents who came from the island of Mauritius. These included the young Amédée Maingard, who was awarded the DSO for his services; France Antelme; and the Mayer brothers, who appear in the story of Paddy O'Sullivan. Lise's younger brother Claude also served in SOE, as did her future sister-in-law, Mary Herbert.

Lise was born in Mauritius on 11 May 1905. Both her father and mother came from old French families long settled in the island but Lise's mother had determined to bring the family back to Europe and they arrived in Paris when she was fourteen. 'Mauritius was very isolated. Before the war there were no planes. It took a month by steamer to reach Europe. My mother wanted us to become Europeans again,' she says. Her father, whose business was insurance, followed as soon as he was able.

Mauritius, named in honour of the Dutch Prince Maurice, had been taken by France in 1715 after the Dutch had abandoned it, but was seized by the British in 1810, becoming an important staging post on the way to India. Although French was the mother tongue of Lise and her whole family, they were British subjects and like many Mauritians were bilingual. When the Germans poured into France in 1940 Lise and her family had to leave Paris. Her elder brother Jean enlisted in the British army, going on to fight in North Africa. Lise went to the South of France where she had friends and was able to obtain help with travel arrangements to England from the American consulate.

This involved crossing into Spain and going on to Lisbon. Her brother Claude chose a clandestine route, crossing the Pyrenees on foot, only to be arrested (like so many) and thrown into gaol. Lise was able to visit him in prison in Barcelona.

In Lisbon she waited for five tedious months before receiving approval to proceed to Gibraltar, where a liner was waiting to take a large number of British refugees back to Britain. Here, to her immense delight, she was reunited with Claude. 'The boat was packed, the younger men all sleeping in the lower decks while I shared a very good first class cabin with another girl. We were given permission for my brother to come and sleep on the floor.'

When the ship docked in Scotland she made her way to London, where she was able initially to stay with friends who then helped her to find a cheap little room to rent. She went to the labour exchange and got a job in a shop. Soon after, she

made contact with Lady Kemsley whom she knew – this led
to a brief job at the *Daily Sketch*. A cousin provided Claude
with an introduction to SOE, and as soon as the organisation
began recruiting women Lise was determined to join him. Her
first interview with the legendary Selwyn Jepson led to speedy
acceptance.

Lise trained with the second group of SOE women
agents, including Odette Sansom, Jacqueline Nearne and
Mary Herbert. They did not go to Scotland, she says, but
trained principally at Beaulieu in a house in the woods. This
was part of Special Training School 31, which comprised
three substantial houses, one actually named The House
in the Woods, built in 1910. When requisitioned, it had
belonged to Vivian Drury, who had gone to the Bahamas as
first equerry to the Duke of Windsor. 'It was very pleasant.
We had a very good time,' she recalls. She remembers the
exercise when they were sent to a local town, almost certainly
Southampton, to deliver a letter. By contrast to later agents
for whom the ninety-six-hour exercises were a major testing
point, she does not recall it as being of any special use, but
speaks highly of the security lectures. 'We were very well
trained,' she says.

The accolades from her instructors meant that Lise was
dispatched not as a courier, but to organise her own circuit.
'I was asked if I wanted a wireless operator but said I wanted
to be on my own.' She was given a commission in the FANYs
in July 1942 and when the day came for her to fly to France,
it was Colonel Buckmaster himself, the head of F Section, who
came with her to the aerodrome, giving her dinner before they
set off. (Later it was usually his assistant, Vera Atkins, who
accompanied women agents.)

The plane, a Whitley bomber, flew out over Bognor late
on the evening of 24 September 1942 and climbed to over
750 metres, as they reached the French coast at Pointe de la
Percée, crossing the Loire at Orléans. They were now flying

in low broken cumulus with a ceiling of 150 metres. When they arrived at the dropping ground the pilot was puzzled to see white lights rather than the red ones he expected, but the flashing light gave the correct Morse code letter. Her companion, 22-year-old Andrée Borrel, jumped first. Lise, mindful of her training, followed quickly afterwards, with her luggage hurtling out so fast that they all landed together.

Lise's mission is most succinctly put in a briefing note to the Queen, dated 28 March 1945, stating that it 'was to form a new circuit and provide a centre where agents could go with complete security for material help and information on local details'. Lise was in effect to fulfil a role similar to Virginia Hall in Lyons, who in the previous eighteen months had been the first port of call for many agents sent to south-east France. Poitiers, situated close to the growing number of dropping grounds south of the Loire, was the perfect place for a similar mission to the south-west. She was not a courier, but was to form her own small circuit, Artist.

Poitiers she described as 'a quiet town with an ecclesiastical air' with many priests and nuns about. On her return, she told her SOE interrogator in August 1943 that people in Poitiers were 'neither collaborators nor frightened. They are interested, and there are lots of de Gaullist groups. There had been a big political organisation there, but two months before [my] arrival, it was blown and some of the members were shot and the rest were in jail.' Her brother Claude added that prisoners were 'extraordinarily well-treated there for some reason or other. A man he knew had been arrested, but was allowed to have lunch in town and live in a hotel. He had been suspected, but there was no proof against him.' As happened elsewhere, this may have been because the Germans were hoping he would lead them to other members of the Resistance.

Lise arrived in Poitiers with the cover story that she was

a widow, Madame Irène Brisse, seeking refuge from the tension of life in the capital. A member of her reception committee at Mer-sur-Loire had told her of an auctioneer (*commissaire-priseur*) in Poitiers, Monsieur Gâteau, who was well disposed to local Resistance groups. Lise stayed with Monsieur Gâteau and his wife for two months, then took the flat of a woman who was going to North Africa. 'This was an apartment on the ground floor where people could visit me without attracting attention, and I could live the life of an ordinary citizen.'

When she returned to Poitiers after the war her friends and contacts were astounded to learn that the quiet little lady they knew had been a British secret agent, leading a double life. One of them was a Spanish teacher who came to give her lessons two or three times a week. 'He was flabbergasted when I told him,' says Lise.

With characteristic nonchalance Lise had moved in next door to the Gestapo headquarters. She became personally acquainted with the Gestapo chief – Grabowski – who came from Cracow and had been a prisoner in the last war. He had remained in France and had a farm there. He was hated by everyone, she said. A few days before she left, the Germans came to requisition her flat, saying it was the best in the block. They promised nonetheless to find her another flat before ejecting her.

The Germans, she said, had been given strict orders to be polite to the population. 'They are never seen drunk in the streets. If they do behave badly in town, they are sometimes shot the next morning.' Lise said that she made as many friends as possible, asking them to meals at her flat. Her object was to ensure that visiting agents would not be noticed in the regular stream of comings and goings. Even the charwoman who was there all morning suspected nothing. An added advantage was that there was no concierge to notice visitors. As the flat was in a busy street leading to the station there were always plenty of people about, even at night. It was possible, she added, to obtain a pass from the station, although not to it, during the hours of curfew.

Collaborators, she added, were found in Poitiers but these were often shot, not by the Resistance proper but by ordinary citizens. This was the fate of a newspaper seller who had been informing for the Germans. He was shot near her flat one evening a few minutes after curfew began.

Lise described the black market in Poitiers, where the Germans were among the main buyers.

Only the poor people are starving because they have not the money to deal in the black market and have to exist on their rations which are insufficient. The soil is rich round Poitiers and most people have a small plot of ground for vegetable growing, but meat is very scarce. In the country districts everyone is killing his animals because he cannot feed them, and this year is especially bad because of the dryness and consequent shortage of fodder. Next winter will be bad everywhere because not only meat but also potatoes and beans will be scarce. Only wine and wheat will be plentiful.

There were, she said, only two or three good restaurants in Poitiers but, in the country, for example La Vendée, an excellent black market meal could be had for about 60 francs with six or seven varieties of hors d'oeuvre, omelette, lamb or roast pork. The workers all bought in the black market, even though their homes were poor. Their motto was 'tout pour la bouche'. The people working in shops and the little employers she said are 'the ones who are starving, and they are very unhappy in consequence'.

The Germans, said Lise, were afraid of air raids and also feared being killed in the streets. 'They never go about alone. They have orders to go to the shelters when the warning sounds.' Ironically it proved so expensive to sound the warnings every time a raid was imminent that the practice was stopped.

Being without a wireless or wireless operator, Lise had to go to Paris or to her brother in Bordeaux to receive and send messages and to collect fresh supplies of cash. Much of her travel was by train. The carriages were overcrowded and often she had to stand in the corridor. In Paris, her contact was with the ill-fated Prosper network but she only once saw the circuit leader, Francis Suttill, and dealt mainly with his courier, Andrée Borrel, with whom she had parachuted into France. 'We had orders as far as possible to avoid meeting with agents from other circuits,' she says. After a year in the field Lise had strong views on the clothes issued to agents. One agent, Oscar, had been two months in the field with only one suitcase and just one suit. 'It is difficult to convince people of one's cover story when one is shabbily dressed,' she said.

Another of Lise's visitors was Mary Herbert, whom she had trained with. Mary arrived in France at the end of October to work as courier to Lise's brother Claude in Bordeaux. Mary brought radio messages for Lise, they liked and trusted one another, and Lise introduced her to the Gâteau family. Mary and Claude, flung together by the tensions of war, had embarked on a love affair and Mary, in Lise's words, had asked Claude to let her have his child, 'a very dangerous thing to do,' she says. This indeed it proved when Claude was summoned back to London in August 1943 with Lise. Mary gave birth at the very end of 1943 to a girl. She was staying with friends in Bordeaux, but within weeks the friends heard that she and others were being hunted. Mary left for Poitiers to stay in Lise's old flat, but in February 1944 the Gestapo raided the flat and also arrested the Gâteaus. Mary was sent to prison, and the girl to whom she had entrusted the baby put it in a children's home. Mary was able to secure her own release, the Germans perhaps being ready to accept that a woman who had just had a baby was hardly likely to be an Allied agent.

Lise played an important role in receiving a series of new agents and helping them to acclimatise to local conditions. One was the Mauritian agent, France Antelme, who was dropped eight kilometres from Chambord on the night of 18 November 1942. He spent a night at Tours in a hotel before travelling on by train to Poitiers, where he met Henri Gâteau and Lise at the Café de la Paix. Antelme, nervous because he had never been to France before, was carefully schooled by Lise. She also gave him an introduction in Paris to Maître William Savy (Alcide), an international lawyer whom she had known before the war and had met by chance on a train. Savy arranged a loan of up to 1 million francs for Claude de Baissac and Francis Suttill of Prosper, both of whom had been out of radio touch with London for six weeks and were desperately in need of money. The loan was confirmed by Baker Street in the BBC *messages personnels* – 'Alcide est en bonne santé' – and Claude de Baissac and Suttill each received 250,000 francs.

Lise attended four or five reception committees, two of which were successful in receiving drops. After that she felt it was rather incongruous for an apparently ordinary, quiet citizen to be rushing about in the middle of the night.

On 17 March 1943, Lise's team arranged the landing ground for a double Lysander operation, bringing in four agents, three men and a woman, and taking back another group, including her brother Claude and France Antelme. The woman who arrived was Francine Agazarian, on her way to join her husband Jack and other members of Prosper. Others whom Lise helped were a group of SOE agents dropped blind on 23 March 1943 to the Butler circuit at Dissay-sous-Courcillon. One broke his ankle on landing and was taken in at a nearby farm. The two others (one a Mauritian, Rousset) had lost their baggage and radio set.

Lise put them in touch with Suttill's Prosper circuit in Paris, enabling them to contact London about their arrival and obtain the delivery of a new radio set.

Claude parachuted back into France some four weeks later on 14 April. By May he was reporting rapid progress – 700 men in the Basses-Pyrénées, 2,000 in the Landes, 11,000 in Gironde, 500 in Charente-Maritime, 1,500 in Charente and 5,000 in Poitou, Vendée, Vienne and Deux-Sèvres. He said that, if arms were sent, these men could be armed, trained and organised militarily. Attacks were made on railway lines. Distilled water destined for the batteries of German submarines was doctored and rendered useless or worse. Claude also provided such copious reports on submarines and shipping moving out of the Garonne that the Admiralty were able to stop blockade-running between Europe and Japan. This denied vital war supplies to the Japanese.

On 16 August 1943, Claude was again called to London for consultations and this time Lise returned with him, as her circuit in Poitiers had been penetrated by the Gestapo. However, a second one that she had established in Ruffec remained intact. Here she was assisted by Colonel Gua and a Monsieur Denivelle.

Over the previous ten months Claude's circuit had received 121 drops, consisting of 1,600 containers and 350 packages, including an impressive 7,500 Stens, 300 Brens, 1,500 rifles, 17,200 hand grenades and 18,000 pounds (9,000 kilos) of explosive. Back in London, Claude confirmed that his men were ready to deny the Germans use of all railway lines south of Angoulême and Périgord by repeated cutting of the rails. This would be done by the *cheminots* themselves, ensuring the lines were closed for four to seven days. A little army was ready to go into action, he said. This is important in prefiguring almost a year ahead of D-Day the strategy adopted by Allied High Command. Claude told London that, if arms deliveries continued, 20,000 men could go into action by 1 September. He warned nonetheless that his organisation could not survive more than two or three months if the Allied landings did not take place.

And this was just what happened. One of Claude's chief assistants, Monsieur Grandclément (Gérard), was arrested by the Gestapo in Paris on 19 September. They succeeded in turning him, and within a few days he was back in Bordeaux, indicating to the Gestapo the location of arms dumps and the whereabouts of his former associates. As a result of this one arrest, the Scientist circuit was practically wiped out in Bordeaux. A further result was that Claude was not allowed to return there but was sent instead to Normandy. Disaster as this was, it is a testimony to the resilience of SOE that Bordeaux was built up once again as a focal point of resistance. By D-Day Charles Corbin, a police inspector in Bordeaux and friend of Claude de Baissac, had been trained by SOE and parachuted back into France late in April 1944 to set up the Carver circuit between Angoulême and the coast at Rochefort. Roger Landes, Claude's former radio operator, also went back to France in March 1944 to establish the Actor circuit on the ruins of Scientist, even though Grandclément was still actively working for the Germans. By D-Day the buccaneering Landes had managed to muster 2,000 armed men ready to embark on sabotage. He achieved all this while the Gestapo were actively searching for him, making hundreds of arrests.

Lise left England again for the field on the night of 9 April 1944. Originally she had been intended for an earlier drop, but early in 1944, partly because she enjoyed parachuting, she had been sent to Ringway as conducting officer to two new women agents, Yvonne Baseden and Violette Szabo. In the event the two trainees jumped well and Lise broke her leg.

Lise's new mission was to join the active and successful Pimento circuit, established in the Toulouse area by SOE's Anthony Brooks (Alphonse). Brooks had pioneered the use of abrasive grease guns to disable the bearings of German railway wagons. Not long after Lise arrived, two French schoolgirls working for him had helped cripple eighty-two tank carriers belonging to the Das Reich, Deutschland and Der Führer divisions concealed in and around Montauban, depriving the Germans of vital reinforcements against the D-Day landings. But in one of those seismic quarrels that occasionally broke out between agents, Lise found herself completely at odds with her new colleagues.

Flown in by Hugh Verity in a Lysander, Lise was met by Pimento's Hector and Shaw. Eager to start work immediately, she spent the next day waiting for the first train to Montauban, where she arrived at eleven o'clock the following morning. 'I went to Michel and gave the agreed password for Alphonse.' No one was expecting her and Michel seemed very surprised to see her; he 'made me understand at once that I was not at all the person he needed'.

Alphonse, when he arrived, proved friendly and took her to Toulouse where, chez Gilbert, she 'found the same expressionless and hostile faces as with Michel'. Two days later Alphonse took her to Chambéry to meet Julien. Here she was cordially received, although effectively as a stranger, and was left alone the whole morning. Faced with more coldness, she demanded a conversation 'between four eyes' with Alphonse. He explained his groups and methods. Her job, he said, was to do the rounds of the groups each week, collecting papers for Julien, which he would send on to Switzerland. 'I was in effect postman and that was all . . . I told Alphonse that the work he was proposing for me did not please me at all.'

That evening he told her that she could start work in eight days' time with a rendezvous in Toulouse. In frustration Lise promptly decided to go to Paris and to seek help, alas, without success. She arrived back in Toulouse after spending twenty-four hours in the corridor of a packed train that suffered three sabotage attacks. She had had to change trains and walk 500 metres along the track without having eaten or slept. Failing to find Alphonse, she went on to Montauban, where she arrived at 10 p.m. exhausted. There Alphonse told her that Julien had formed the worst impression of her, claiming that she was asking indiscreet questions. Julien, he said, was refusing to work with her and was sending a highly equivocal report to London.

Lise told SOE: 'I was in a black rage and . . . told him that despite the reports . . . I would be very surprised if London took me for a double agent (which he indicated was the view of Julien) and that I was delighted to quit this circuit of which the ends and methods were in no way mine.' Lise's view was that the circuit was composed of militant socialists whose principal aims were political. She was also very critical of their means of communication. In her view, the wish to pass all messages via Switzerland was not because it allowed them to be more detailed than if sent by wireless, but because the political chief was in Switzerland and wanted to be kept au courant with everything.

Her thoughts now turned to joining her brother Claude, who had been dropped far south near Auch in Gers on 10 February 1944 with a radio operator, Lieutenant Maurice Louis Larcher (Vladimir). His mission was to work his way north to Normandy and reconnoitre large landing grounds that could be held for forty-eight hours while airborne troops established themselves. Lise obtained permission to join him in April, just as he was embarking on a period of intense activity, organising thirty receptions, and receiving 777 containers and over 300 packages.

Just before D-Day, Claude reported that his new organisation was complete and ready to receive paratroops on five controllable grounds. To safeguard this vital operation he split his circuit into two, sending his assistant, Captain Jean Marie Renaud-Dandicolle, and Larcher, the wireless operator, to work close to the coast in Calvados and Manche, where they could be in direct contact with the Allied bridgehead. He remained in the rear in the Orne and the Eure-et-Loir, ready to assist the Allied forces from behind German lines. Dandicolle and his men embarked energetically on a round of sabotage and guerrilla attacks. When the Germans counter-attacked, they concentrated on providing intelligence on enemy troop movements, sending details of valuable targets to the RAF.

On D-Day, Claude de Baissac's men went into action. During the following weeks over 500 German vehicles were put out of action, mostly with the aid of tyre bursters. The railway line between Caen and Vire was cut continually. Faced with repeated German counter-attacks, Claude broke down some Maquis groups to between four and ten men. He also organised massive receptions at Lessay and distributed arms to groups operating up to fifty miles (seventy-five kilometres) away. By 30 June all telephone lines and underground cables south of the Cotentin peninsula were cut.

It was dangerous work. Dandicolle and Larcher were denounced and five SS soldiers walked into their headquarters in a house near Pierrefitte-en-Cinglias. Dandicolle promptly killed one German with a silent pistol. Larcher and another man killed three more, but the fifth was only wounded and started shouting for help. The respite gained by their fast reflexes ended as the Germans in a camp just 400 metres away heard the cries and rushed to the rescue of their comrades. In the ensuing fight Larcher was killed outright and Dandicolle was wounded in the jaw. He was taken away and was never heard of again.

Elsewhere, while Claude's men were receiving a supply drop, the Germans suddenly appeared. As the arms were of vital importance to the Maquis, Claude and his men, although heavily outnumbered, did not retreat but immediately engaged the enemy patrol, inflicting heavy casualties and forcing the

Germans to withdraw after a twenty-minute gun battle. As a result, all the arms and material were safely spirited away. Claude was finally reached by the advancing Americans at Alençon. He was awarded the DSO and Bar.

Lise meanwhile was equally close to the enemy, using the code name Marguerite. 'We lived in a village beside the Germans. I had rented the first floor of a house where an old lady lay bedridden below. There was no furniture, just a mattress on the floor. One day the Germans arrived and threw me out of my room. I arrived to take my clothes and found they had opened up the parachute I had made into a sleeping bag and were sitting on it. Fortunately they had no idea of what it was.' On another occasion her group met in a school to receive instructions while the Germans were receiving their own orders in the next room. 'It was as if we were in the kitchen and they in the drawing room,' she says.

One night they received a massive drop of sixty containers. The number of planes involved in such a large drop naturally did not escape the notice of the Germans. Fortunately, she says, 'Bombers flying over from England were so frequent that they did not suspect an arms drop.'

Captain Blackman, the leader of an SAS party that parachuted behind the lines in July 1944, wrote strongly in praise of Lise's work, recommending her for an OBE rather than the usual MBE awarded to women agents.

Every day she would bicycle sixty or seventy kilometres. She often carried much compromising material on her person and bicycle, such as wireless material and secret documents. If she had been discovered carrying such things she would have been undoubtedly shot on the spot without trial or formal enquiry. Consequently she risked her life daily.

Lise, he said, did much 'to facilitate the Maquis preparations and resistance prior to the American breakthrough in the area of Mayenne'.

In his official report Claude wrote:

Marguerite [Lise] as usual was the most efficient assistant. She handled delicate contacts which I could not make myself, and took my place, as head of the circuit, when I was away 'en tournée'. When in need of officers, I twice sent her to Paris, where each time she was forced to cycle through thick enemy formations. Her missions were always of a very dangerous nature, because of the difficulties of moving around, and the danger of contacting people active in the resistance, and who were therefore always under Gestapo observation, particularly in the Paris area. On several occasions she personally took charge of the transport of Genevieve's W/T material. Once carrying plans and crystals, she was arrested and searched by the Germans and only got out of this hole by her great calm and sang-froid. Because of this my circuit was able to keep in touch with home station at a very crucial moment.

On another occasion a retreating German soldier, without any means of transport, demanded to requisition her bicycle. 'Go and see your senior officer,' she replied, vanishing before he could take any action.

She organised several groups in Normandy and continued her liaison until the Liberation, contributing with zeal to the provision of military information for the Allied forces. 'She was the inspiration of groups in the Orne and by her initiative caused heavy losses to the Germans with tyre bursters on the roads near St Aubin-le-Desert, St Mars as far as Laval, Le Mans and Rennes. She also took part in several armed attacks on enemy columns.' So runs a resumé on her file.

Before the war, Lise had fallen in love with a dashing young painter, Henri Villameur, but her parents had refused to give their blessing to the match. After the war he married another girl. Then no sooner had she heard that they had separated than he asked her to come on holiday with him. Shortly after, they were married. By this time Henri had become a fashionable decorator, providing interiors for shops, hotels and even oil tankers for Onassis – although not the oil tycoon's famous yacht, the *Christina*. Today Lise lives on in the apartment and studio he made beneath the eaves of a warehouse in the old port of Marseilles.

Chapter 6

NOOR INAYAT KHAN

There is one, however, above all the others remembered more often and vividly, and with her own name, not only in the dark hours of solitude with which we must all contend but at unexpected moments in daytime activity; it is as though a shutter opens in a familiar wall which I know has no shutter in it, and she is there, briefly, the light filling my eyes. She does not haunt me as do some of the others who but for me, that 'me' of the war, might still be alive. She is simply with me, now and again, for a little moment. And she is Inayat Khan.

Selwyn Jepson, recruiting officer for SOE, in the Foreword to *Madeleine* by Jean Overton Fuller

No woman agent has been the subject of such divided views as Noor Inayat Khan. To some she was a girl of extraordinary courage, even saintliness, and the calm and determined repose she showed during imprisonment impressed even her captors. These were the qualities that were to earn her a posthumous George Cross in 1949, following those awarded to Odette Sansom and Violette Szabo. The citation states that she was the first woman wireless operator to be infiltrated into enemy-occupied France. 'During the weeks immediately following her arrival the Gestapo made mass arrests in the Paris Resistance groups to which she had been detailed. She refused, however, to abandon what had become the principal and most dangerous post in France, although given the opportunity to return to England, because she did not wish to leave her French comrades without communications.'

Yet at repeated stages of her training and work in the field, there were those who had the most serious doubts about her suitability as an agent. Her naivety, her frequent lapses in basic security, her supposed inability to tell a lie, repeatedly caused acute concern, as they were a potential threat not just to her own safety but to all those who worked with her.

So indeed it proved when she was arrested. 'With Noor Inayat were captured not only the transmitter she had by her in the flat, but also – from the drawer of her bedside table – a school exercise book in which she had recorded in full, in cipher and in clear, every message she had ever received or sent since reaching France,' wrote M.R.D. Foot in his authoritative *SOE in France*.

In Paris, her fellow agents repeatedly reprimanded her for small lapses: for leaving a portfolio with her codes in an entrance hall; for handing over messages in a public place, where agents or informers were likely to be watching; for revisiting the house in the suburbs of Paris where she had lived before the war and where many people knew her; and for leaving her notebook with all her decoded messages open on the kitchen table overnight.

Noor's other-worldliness was a matter of both birth and upbringing. Her father, Hasra Inayat Khan, was a leading Sufi mystic who wrote a great many books. He had come to Europe in the entourage of the Maharaja of Bagoda and had a large following by the time the family settled in Paris. Noor grew up in a world of lofty idealism and self-sacrifice in which the spirit and the imagination had precedence over material concerns. Her father would sing sacred Sufi songs to Noor and her brother Vilayat when they could not sleep, and would never allow them to be awakened abruptly. If necessary he would sit down by the pillow and sing them out of their sleep.

These and many other details of Noor's upbringing, education and life are provided in a brilliantly researched biography written by a friend of Noor's, Jean Overton Fuller, as early as 1952 when virtually no official papers were available. Fuller assiduously tracked down and talked to many of those who knew Noor in Paris, as well as some of her captors. Noor's personal file both confirms and amplifies the amazing story she told.

Noor was the great-great-great-granddaughter of the Tiger of Mysore, Tipu Sultan, the last Muslim ruler of southern India. Her father, Hasra Inayat Khan, was born in 1882 and was a musician as well as a mystic, a pupil of a leading Sufi teacher who appointed him as his successor, charging him to make Sufism known in the West and to marry a Western woman who would give him children combining the virtues of both worlds. In September 1910, Hasra Inayat Khan sailed to New York. In America he met Miss Ora Ray Baker at the house of her guardian where he had been invited to give a talk. She was a relation of Mrs Mary Baker Eddy, the founder of the Christian Science Church. They fell in love, but the guardian would not approve the marriage and Hasra Inayat Khan sailed to France. Shortly after, Miss Baker followed and they were married on 20 March 1913. In London, the Begum, as she now was, adopted Indian dress. In December, the family moved to Moscow where Hasra Inayat Khan had been invited to teach at the Conservatoire. So it happened that Noor was born in the Kremlin on New Year's Day, 1914.

Noor's own breathless summary of her life as submitted to SOE survives. Written in a fluent spidery hand, it describes how the family left Moscow after six months, travelling first to Paris, then to London where they lived at 1 Gordon Square. Over the next six years, two brothers and a sister were added to the family. Then they went to Paris where Hasra Inayat Khan took a house near the racecourse at Longchamps. Later they moved to a house with a large walled garden at Suresnes.

Noor went to the Lycée de St Cloud, doing best at French and English literature, as well as studying German and Spanish. During these years her father travelled widely, establishing groups of disciples in England, Germany, Switzerland,

Belgium, Holland, Scandinavia and the United States. In the summer of 1926 he made preparations to go to India, from whence his family soon understood he would not return. He died in Delhi on 5 February 1927 of pneumonia aged just forty-four. Noor was thirteen.

'We went three years later to India to erect his tomb. Next followed travels in Switzerland – Geneva – Zurich – lakes – climbing and skiing,' she wrote. Not long after, two of her father's oldest disciples, the Baron and Baroness van Tuyll, invited Noor to spend a holiday with them in The Hague. Here she remembered riding in the dunes on the Van Tuylls' horses. 'Our friends in this country were very, very numerous,' she said. It was probably these friends who helped finance a lengthy trip across Europe. Noor gives the itinerary as: 'Italy. Milan, Padua and Venice and the mountains of the north. Spain. Barcelona – my brother and I visited Pablo Casals at San Salvador. France. We explored the Massif Central, the Alps and the Côte d'Azur from Monte Carlo to Marseilles – Royan – Rochefort. Deauville – Trouville – Le Havre – Dieppe. All these travels in a sports car.' By this time Noor was largely Europeanised, wearing Western clothes and using light make-up.

Her education continued at the Sorbonne where she studied child psychology.

Then I wrote for children. My collaboration with Willbeck le Mair provided the illustrations. I was engaged by Radio Paris for children's programmes, on *Figaro* for a children's page. In particular I adapted legends and folklore, French, Nordic. My books began to be published (Harrap, London, McKay, Philadelphia and Hachette, France). I worked with Alexis Danan at *Paris-Soir* on a plan for a children's newspaper but the war intervened and the plan was put aside.

Noor and her sister became nurses in the Union des Femmes de France (the French Red Cross). As the Germans approached Paris, they remained at work until the hospital was evacuated and they were cut off from their unit. The two girls rejoined their mother and brothers and set off in two cars for the South. At Bordeaux they searched in vain for their evacuated hospital unit. The British consul directed Noor and her sister to St Nazaire to join the British Red Cross but when they arrived the hospital ship had already left. 'We returned to Bordeaux where we were reunited with my mother and one of my brothers and found a Belgian cargo [ship] which took us to England. My brother became a pilot in the RAF and I joined the same service as a "wireless operator",' wrote Noor.

Now after several years of living and travelling in style and comfort, the family found themselves almost penniless, cut off from their father's supporters on the Continent. Noor formally enlisted in the WAAF on 19 November 1940 and rose steadily through a series of postings. First she was sent, as Aircraftwoman 2nd Class, to Harrogate to be trained as a wireless operator. A month later she was posted to No. 34 (Balloon Barrage) Group, RAF Balloon Command, and then, in April 1941, to No. 929 Balloon Squadron, Forth and Medhill.

In June she was remustered as a wireless operator and posted to HQ No. 6 Group, RAF Bomber Command. Her advance continued with promotion to Aircraftwoman 1st Class. In June 1942 she was sent on an advanced wireless course at No. 3 Signals School, being posted back to Bomber Command on 12 August and promoted to Leading Aircraftwoman on 1 December.

By the time she arrived at RAF Abingdon she had earned the nickname of Bang Away Lulu, thanks to the loud clackety-clack of her Morse key tapping – said to be the result of fingers swollen from chilblains. Noor's first interview about work with SOE took place on Tuesday, 10 October 1943 with Selwyn Jepson in Room 238 of the Hotel Victoria in Northumberland Avenue. Later he recalled that 'in spite of a great gentleness of manner' she seemed 'to have an intuitive sense of what might be in my mind for her to do. Also, I realized it would be safe to be frank with her, that "her security", as we called it, would be good, that if she felt herself unable to take it on, she would not talk about the reason she had been called to the War Office – which, as a W.A.A.F., was in itself rather odd.'

Jepson drew a picture of life in France, explaining the work of a W/T operator working clandestinely with British officers engaged in sabotage operations.

To my mind she stood out as almost perfect for this aspect of the work; she was obviously careful, tidy, painstaking by nature, and would have all the patience in the world . . . As usual, I stressed immediately the extreme danger, that in the event of capture she would be interrogated by the Gestapo – a thing no human being could face with anything but terror – that since she would not be in uniform she would have no protection under the international laws of warfare – in short that she might not return . . . She listened to me quietly . . . and I had scarcely finished when she said, with the same simplicity of manner which had characterized her from the outset of our talk, that she would like to undertake it.

Normally Jepson would have been uneasy at so prompt a response, but, with Noor, he felt she had thought about it as deeply and finally as a less direct-minded person might have spent days in doing. As a writer himself he evidently felt a kinship with her, and even suggested her talents could be more valuably employed helping children in the partially destroyed world after the war. 'She shook her head. She was sure and confident. She would like to try to become an agent for us, if I thought she could make it. I had not the slightest doubt that she could, and said so, and with rather more of the bleak distress which I never failed to feel at this point in these interviews, I agreed to take her on.'

Noor had, however, raised two concerns. These, she had

resolved in her own mind after speaking to her mother, when she wrote the next day from Abingdon, formally accepting his offer: 'Firstly, I realise that in time my mother will get used to the idea of my going overseas. Secondly, I may be able to provide her with more efficient financial help which would relieve me tremendously, as my war time writing income is quite inadequate. Besides, I realise how petty our family ties are when something like winning this war is at stake.' Her field salary was to be £350 a year, paid quarterly.

Noor went first to Special Training School 5 at Wanborough, where she trained with two other agents, Yvonne Beekman and Cecily Lefort. From here comes a brief two-line note on 23 February from Lieutenant Tongue: 'Has been doing arthritis [SOE for radio work] for two years, is in good physical condition.' Further sharply varying reports followed rapidly. On 10 March 1943 the preliminary report from Wanborough observes: 'Can run very well.' This was pertinent, as on at least two occasions Noor was to escape on foot from her German pursuers. It also observed that she was unsuitable for jumping. There are several references to her lack of coordination. On fieldcraft, it is noted: 'Can't help being clumsy though she tries very hard and is very keen and interested.' On weapons training, the comment is: 'Pretty scared of weapons but tries hard to get over it.' The instructor observed that she 'lacked confidence to begin with but has come on very well and shows considerable promise. Active, plenty of spirit and could be relied on to come up to scratch when the occasion arose.'

Just a day later, on 11 March 1943, came a glowing report from Lance Corporal Gordon, far more enthusiastic than the others. She 'is a person for whom I have the greatest admiration. Completely self-effacing and unselfish. The last person whose absence would be noticed, extremely modest even humble and shy, always thought everyone better than herself . . . very polite. Has written books for children.

Takes everything very literally, is not quick, studious rather than clever. Extremely conscientious.'

Five weeks later, on 19 April 1943, Lieutenant Holland was still more smitten.

This student, like her two FANY companions of the 27X party, has thrown herself heart and soul into the life of the school. She has any amount of energy, and spends a lot of it on voluntary P.T. with the object of overcoming as far as possible feminine disabilities in the physical sense. She is, also, very feminine in character, very eager to please, very ready to adapt herself to the mood of the company, or the tone of the conversation, interested in personalities, capable of strong attachments, kindhearted, emotional and imaginative. She is very fond of her family (mother, brother in the Fleet Air Arm and sister) and was engaged for about five years, but broke it off. The motive for her accepting the present task is, apparently, idealism. She felt that she had come to a dead end as a WAAF, and was longing to do something more active in the prosecution of the war, something which would make more call on her capabilities and perhaps, demand more sacrifice. This appears to be the only motive; the broken off engagement is old history, nor does she appear to have any romantic ideas of the Mata-Hari variety. In fact she confesses that she would not like to do anything 'two-faced', by which she means deliberately cultivating friendly relations with malice aforethought. The fact that she has already given some thought to preparing her mother for the inevitable separation and cessation of correspondence shows that she has faced some, at any rate, of the implications of the job. It is the emotional side of her character, coupled with a vivid imagination, which will most test her steadfastness of purpose in the later stages of her training.

A month later, serious reservations were again expressed about Noor in a report of 21 May 1943 from Boarmans, one of the large houses at Beaulieu, where many women agents for the French Section were trained. 'Not over-burdened with brains but has worked hard and shown keenness, apart from some dislike of the security side of the course. She has an unstable and temperamental personality and it is very doubtful whether she is really suited to work in the field.' By this time Buckmaster's mind was all but made up and he scribbled across the memo: 'We don't want them overburdened with brains. Makes me cross,' adding 'nonsense' to the comments about her temperamental personality.

A memo of 24 May 1943 adds: 'I suggest that care be taken that she be not given any task which might set up a mental conflict with her idealism. This might render her unstable from our point of view.'

By this time Noor was being carefully watched. The progress report from the radio school at Thame for 31 May 1943 reads: 'In the ninth week of training. Morse. Sending 18 words per minute. Receiving 22 words per minute. Codes. Understands the theory quite well, but needs more actual practical working to become fully proficient. Conduct. Good. Highly temperamental. Inclined to give in when confronted with difficulties rather than attempt to overcome.' A further report for the week ending 5 June 1943 notes: 'Has now completed a shortened course at the request of the Country Section. Her scheme [training exercise] was curtailed through a technical fault, but she gained some useful experience and is now more confident of her operating.'

Even at Chorley Wood, a large country house in Hertfordshire where agents were held on standby awaiting infiltration, there were renewed doubts. Two other women there felt impelled to write to Vera Atkins, saying that they did not think Noor was the type to be sent into the field. Miss Atkins took Noor out to lunch and put the matter to her. Noor understandably was shocked and hurt. By the end of the meal Vera Atkins was convinced that it was only the pain of recently saying goodbye to her family that had temporarily clouded her spirits.

A note describing Noor's mission instructions, which she

had to commit to memory, survive on her file. Her operational name was to be Nurse, her Christian name in the field Madeleine, the cover name on her papers Jeanne Marie Renier. As was often the case, details in the cover story resembled Noor's own life. Jeanne's American mother, like Noor's, had the name of Ray Baker and had married a Frenchman, Auguste Renier, who had been Professor of Philosophy at Princeton before he had been killed on the Marne in the Great War. Jeanne's mother had emigrated to America when France collapsed. Jeanne, like Noor, had studied child psychology at the Sorbonne, going on to look after children in various families. When the Germans broke through, Jeanne had stayed for a while in the Bordeaux area where she had been employed with a family named Jourden in Royan.

Noor was told: 'On arrival you will be taken to Paris, where the chief of your Reception Committee will give you instructions for contacting your organiser, Cinema. In case of any accident occurring, you will contact Henri Garry at 40 rue Erlanger, Paris 16e (8th floor opposite lift door).' This is a little confusing as Garry was her organiser. Noor's password was also awkwardly long: 'Je viens de la part de votre ami Antoine pour des nouvelles au sujet de la Société en Bâtiment,' to which the reply was: 'L'affaire est en cours.'

The paper continued:

You will receive and send messages for Cinema's circuit. Although you are under his command and will take your instructions from him, you are the ultimate judge as regards the technicalities of W/T and W/T security. We should like to point out here that you must be extremely careful with the filing of your messages. Cinema will give you as much assistance as he can, but at the same time you are expected to be as self-reliant as possible. You will encode the messages yourself and will accept none but those which are passed to you by Cinema, unless he gives you instructions to the contrary.

Noor was also given an address in neutral Portugal for postcards – Sr Luis Alberto Peres, Rua da Liberatade 220/20, Oporto. A further instruction concerned her code. Headed 'Nurse', it runs:

Instead of giving you a poem, we have chosen the phrases and done the numbering for you. All you need do is to start at the top of your list of keys and use the keys already worked out. You use the key on the left for your first transposition and the key on the right for your second. To decode, it is exactly the same. You write our message first under the key on the left hand side and then under the key on the right hand side, and the message will decode. Remember to use each indicator in sequence, and to make telegrams 100% safe, cut off each key after you have finished using it.

Noor, now known as Jeanne, was flown by Lysander from Tangmere on 16 June 1943 to a point 5¼ kilometres south of Tierce and 3¼ kilometres west-north-west of Villeveque. With her was another French Section woman agent, Diana Rowden. The pilot of the little aircraft was the famous Hugh Verity. By the next afternoon, Noor had arrived safely in Paris where she made swift contact with Garry, whose circuit had been named Cinema on account of his close likeness to the film star Gary Cooper. (Baker Street later decided this was a mistake and changed the circuit name to Phono.) Garry introduced Noor to his fiancée, Mademoiselle Nadaud. With impressive speed Noor came on air on 22 June.

It was Noor's misfortune to arrive in Paris barely a week before a major wave of arrests in which the Germans captured Francis Suttill, the head of the large Prosper network, and hundreds of those working with him. After the war Ernst Vogt, a member of the Sicherheitsdienst or SD (about whom more later), attested in writing:

Nearly all the letters sent by 'Prosper' and Archambaud [the radio operator, H.G. Norman] to the London Head Office were intercepted by our service and photostats made, after which they were forwarded. Through these letters (containing detailed accounts of the activity of the Prosper Sector and the parachuting grounds together with the BBC messages indicating the parachuting due) we learned the addresses of Prosper, Archambaud, Denise [their courier, Andrée Borrel] and their principal (French) collaborators and their letter boxes. This allowed us to arrest nearly all the members of their organization at one stroke.

Dr Josef Goetz, a radio expert for the SD, added in a statement made to Vera Atkins on 20 November 1946: 'I was recalled from . . . leave . . . at the end of June in order to take up the transmission of Archambaud. Before this time the organisation of the French Section was unknown but following the details supplied by Archambaud, we obtained a precise insight into the whole organisation. Archambaud helped me to carry on transmissions after he had noticed that London had failed to observe the security checks.'

Noor, waiting with Garry at his flat, was able to warn another key SOE circuit leader, France Antelme (of Bricklayer circuit), of Suttill's arrest. Antelme was due to meet Suttill at 11.30 on 25 July. Another arrest averted was that of brave Claude de Baissac, brother of Lise. He was due to meet Suttill on the 24th but found no one at the rendezvous and was warned by the concierge at Andrée Borrel's apartment that the Germans were upstairs. This same gallant lady had also given a warning to Noor.

The next arrests swept up the very members of the circuit whom Noor had first been taken to meet. These were a group operating from the École Nationale d'Agriculture at Grignon, north-west of Versailles. Here Professor Alfred Serge Balachowski had chided Noor for leaving a portfolio with her codes in the entrance hall. On 1 July about sixty German police, mostly in civilian clothes, descended on Grignon and reproached the director, Monsieur Vanderwynckt, for his anti-German sentiments. They posed him a list of questions, but he dealt with them all. They then presented him with a long list of names. He declared that he was acquainted with only two of them, Professor Balachowski and two pupils, De Gannay and Walter.

His son-in-law, Robert Douillet, was also interrogated. Following these interrogations, German officers arrested Vanderwynckt and called on him to reveal everything he knew. They made him step into a bus along with six former pupils and the gardener, Maillard, in which they were driven to a little wood near the school. Here, the Germans simulated a firing squad for each individual and in front of all the others, demanding that every man tell everything he knew to save his own life. This procedure yielded nothing. At one o'clock in the morning the police took Vanderwynckt back to his office and declared: 'We know you are not a Germanophile, that is your right, but you must not spread your ideas if you don't wish to be troubled.'

The next day the Germans returned and arrested Balachowski. On 10 July at 5 p.m. they were back again and, after unearthing a radio set, arrested Vanderwynckt. As he left, the director said to his wife: 'Do not worry on my behalf. I have only sought to serve my country.' The Germans pretended that they had been betrayed by British officers arrested in Paris.

All too little detail survives of Noor's hectic months of activity in Paris. An official note states that she 'sent about 20 messages for Phono [Garry], giving information about the circuit and pin-points for dropping-grounds'. Other entries indicate she was much more active than this suggests, transmitting messages for a whole range of agents, as well as sending important information back by Lysander and Hudson aircraft, which flew in to drop off and collect agents. On her file is a report headed 'Claire' and dated 18 August 1943. This informs Baker Street that 'two American airmen who jumped by parachute on the 16th are to be found at the

following address: Henri Kléroux, rue de Pontoise, Bagnolles.'
It continues: 'Madeleine saw Octave today. She lunched with
him.' After lunch Noor had gone back with Octave only to
find the Gestapo waiting. She obviously managed to give them
the slip, as the report goes on: 'I met Madeleine this evening
at 21 hours in the metro. She was not followed.' Further
evidence of an involvement with escape lines comes with
the brief tantalising statement (in a memo of 24 February
1944) that Noor 'has also been instrumental in facilitating
the escape of thirty Allied airmen shot down in France'.

Another note, brought back by Lysander on 19 September,
concerns what appear to be a series of automobile factories
'working for Germany in violation of the terms of the Armistice', adding, 'within eight days very complete information
on Orly'. These were presumably targets for sabotage or air
strikes. These details had been provided by Verlaine – 'shall
confirm identity by wireless', says a hasty note in Noor's hand.
Here she is following SOE procedure of spreading names and
addresses over two messages so that they are less vulnerable
to interception.

A breathless manuscript note (undated) from Noor runs:
'Please arrange everyday scheds, also using 3407 – if sched is
missed possible recontact at 1800 GMT, same day – Please
send another 3408 [frequency] crystal, one already u/s –
Suggest when message is sent blind, AB 10 is repeated after
message – have not yet found suitable operational site for
night work – Someday, if possible, please send white mac
F.A.N.Y. style. Thanks a lot! It's grand working you – the
best moments I have had yet – Kindly send one more Mark
II [type radio], as one is u/s – am trying to repair.'

A memo from Buckmaster to HQ Signals Office, dated 15
August 1943, states: 'Please will you listen every day at 15.00
hours for Nurse until further notice.' Another message from
Buckmaster to the Signals Office that same day adds: 'If Nurse
does not take Message No. 6 on her QRX at 17.30 today will

you please ensure that it is sent on the first possible occasion as it is extremely urgent. It will be remembered that she will be listening at 15.00 hours G.M.T. daily but the message is so important that I particularly want to get it to her *before* 15.00 hours tomorrow August 16th.'

Noor, working alone, had to take tremendous risks. Later, radio operators rarely travelled with their sets. These were transported separately by other members of the circuit. Since they did not know the vital codes and checks that would enable the Germans to play back the sets, they could not betray them, even under torture. Fuller relates one terrifyingly close escape that Noor had on the metro. Two German officers in the same carriage became suspicious of her suitcase and demanded to know what was in it. 'A cinematograph projector,' Noor replied brusquely. Opening the case to allow a glimpse inside, she continued: 'There are the little bulbs. Haven't you seen one before?' Noor's self-possession paid off. Fearing a loss of face the officers politely apologised and withdrew.

As Baker Street recognised, Noor was now within the sights of the all-too-capable Germans in the headquarters of the Sicherheitsdienst at 84 Avenue Foch, the broad boulevard leading from the Arc de Triomphe to the Bois de Boulogne. The SD occupied the fourth and fifth floors of the building and were under the command of SS Sturmbannführer (Major) Hans Josef Kieffer. Formerly a policeman from Karlsruhe, he directed the SD counter-espionage office in Vienna after the occupation of Austria in 1938, transferring to Paris in 1940.

Kieffer did not simply resort to brutality when trying to obtain information from Allied agents. Sometimes he relied on patient and long-drawn-out interrogation. By adopting a gentle line of questioning rather than aggressive bullying or torture, his men obtained innocuous-seeming details, which they were able to turn to devastating advantage. Repeatedly the SD then used such information to undermine the morale of captured agents, saying they knew all about SOE and many of its agents and even had a mole in London. Among those who carried out interrogations at the Avenue Foch were Ernst Vogt (sometimes referred to as Ernest). He was employed by Kieffer as an interpreter thanks to his fluency in English and French. From June 1943 Vogt was conducting interrogations by himself from his own office as it was found he obtained better results.

Wireless operators were also interrogated by Dr Josef Goetz, a radio service specialist who spoke good French and English. Kieffer and Goetz both made statements to Vera Atkins after the war when she was collecting evidence on the fate of missing SOE agents. These are on Noor's file. Vogt was also interviewed at length by Jean Overton Fuller on his release after a lengthy internment in March 1950.

Unusually, therefore, the story of Noor's betrayal and arrest can be told through accounts left by her captors. Goetz says:

I first learnt of the existence of Madeleine at the time of Archambaud's arrest. We then had a personal description of her and knew that she was a W.T. operator of the *réseau* Prosper. It was, naturally, of the greatest interest to us to arrest her as we suspected she carried on W.T. traffic with London. For this purpose we required a wireless detection station to observe carefully all W.T. traffic for checks of the French section. The wireless detection station had such a sender under observation but could not close in on it as the place of transmission was constantly changing. In October or about this time it was thought that one was closing in on it, but again it was impossible to effect an arrest.

The description fits Noor perfectly. Not only was she, at great risk, constantly changing her place of transmission, she was also, after the Prosper arrests, the only SOE radio operator still working.

The SOE memo of 24 February 1944, quoted above, continues: 'It was considered at the time that the risks she was taking were unjustified as the Gestapo knew enough to make her capture only a matter of days. She was, therefore, instructed to return to England, but pleaded to be allowed to remain and lie low for a month.' Hans Kieffer adds in another statement: 'We were pursuing her for months and as we had a personal description of her we arranged for all stations to be watched. She had several addresses and worked very carefully. All addresses were constantly watched for her, and through Bommelburg (head of the German Secret Police in Paris) we had an address of relations of Phono [Garry]. We had drawn into this enquiry a great many secret agents and eventually she was caught by Vogt at this later address.'

Werner Emil Ruehl, who made the arrest, takes up the story:

A Frenchwoman, about 30 years old, about 1.70m. with dark hair, fairly corpulent, came to the Avenue Foch and told Kieffer that she was prepared against a sum of money, to betray a female agent who was staying in her flat. It was arranged that the arrest should not take place in the flat . . . I remember that it was a corner house in a street parallel to the Avenue du General Serail which led off the Avenue Foch. The street was exactly opposite to No. 84, Avenue Foch [the SD headquarters] . . . We were distributed in small groups near the house in question when a young girl came out through the entrance and went into the baker's shop which was situated in the same house. After a short while she came out again and went away. I had a feeling that it might be Madeleine and Haug and I followed her. She was wearing a blue tailored dress trimmed with white, was about 1.60–65m., slim with dark hair, about 24 years old and wearing a dark hat. Madeleine turned suddenly and saw us. She quickly disappeared round a corner and we did not see her again. After a lengthy search we returned to the office. About two hours later I heard that Madeleine had, all the same, been arrested, I believe, by Capri. Kieffer and the whole office were obviously delighted.

By eluding Ruehl so promptly, Noor had once again put her

Beaulieu training to good use. Tragically, there were just too many German agents on her trail for her to succeed.

Noor was arrested in the middle of October, most probably on 13 October. Disastrously, her messages were quickly found by her captors. Professor Foot drew attention early on to the curious phrase in Noor's mission instructions, telling her 'to be extremely careful with the filing of your messages'. He suggested it may have arisen 'from a misuse of "filing" in the special sense it carries for journalists, of feeding a message into the communications system' as opposed to the more usual sense of keeping a copy for record purposes – which Noor understood it to be.

Noor was not alone in keeping copies of messages – as it was often necessary for agents to refer back to earlier ones. Usually these were kept well hidden away from the set, sometimes by the circuit organiser, not the W/T operator. For Noor's circuit, embattled after the Prosper arrests, there may have been no such opportunity. Beryl Escott in *Mission Improbable* (1991) adds a further layer of possible explanation – that, as Noor had received extensive radio training as a WAAF, she took only a shortened radio course with SOE and may therefore have been less fully briefed in SOE security procedures than other radio operators.

Goetz continues: 'I interrogated her with particular regard to her W.T. traffic ... We considered it was practically hopeless to take up this traffic but, on orders from Berlin, traffic was resumed after a break of three weeks. This was made possible by the fact that Madeleine, who felt we had been closing in on her, proposed in her last message to stop work for a short interval.'

A note on Noor's file states: 'In October 1943 we received reports that she and her organiser were arrested.' Tragically, these reports were discounted when the Germans came on air using her radio, and SOE did not begin to suspect that the Germans were controlling her set until early in 1944. Baker

Street then continued 'to exchange telegrams with her in order to find out where the controlled circuit was located'.

Indeed, Buckmaster was so convinced that Noor was operating freely and effectively that he recommended her for the George Medal on 24 February 1944. Ensign Inayat Khan, he wrote, had had several narrow escapes. 'Several times the house containing her W/T set became unsafe, but she was always able to save her set and re-establish it elsewhere . . . She was, therefore, instructed to return to England, but pleaded to be allowed to remain and lie low for a month. This was agreed to, and a month later she reported that she felt her security re-established as a result of arrangements she had made. Subsequent events have fully justified this course of action and ever since the reorganising of her circuit Ensign Inayat Khan's work and example has been beyond praise.' As late as 27 March 1944, Lord Selborne, head of SOE, proposed Noor for an MBE for playing 'a big part in maintaining a group in France which without her courageous leadership would undoubtedly have been permanently destroyed'. The attached citation says of the group that 'today it is in perfect order'.

The disastrous consequences of this were that on 29 February 1944, France Antelme (whom Noor had earlier saved from arrest) was dropped to a reception committee believed to be controlled by Garry thirty-one kilometres east of Chartres. With him were his wireless operator, Captain Lionel Lee (who had been awarded the Military Cross for a recent mission in Corsica), and his courier, Madeleine Damerment. Their mission was to organise a new circuit in Brittany but of course they walked straight into the hands of the Germans. The Germans maintained the pretence and SOE received W/T messages saying that Antelme had fractured his skull by landing on a container. Later he was reported to have died. Four other officers, dropped earlier on 8 February, also walked straight into a trap. One of them was intended to act as Garry's assistant and was carrying London's latest directive. Two others were destined for the Scientist circuit. A fourth was to approach contacts at Le Mans to investigate the Amédée Bollée piston ring works. If it proved important, he was to try to persuade the management to cooperate in sabotaging the works in preference to an RAF bombing raid. All seven agents were executed in German extermination camps.

Details of the so-called game (the *Englandspiel*) played by the Germans emerge from memos and telegrams on Noor's file. Indeed, the first telegram suggests that the playback began very soon after her arrest. From Nurse, it is dated 17 October 1943 (three or four days after her arrest) and states: 'From Madeleine my *cachette* unsafe new address Belliard repeat Belliard hundred fifty seven rue Vercingetorix . . . this perfectly safe goodbye.' Significantly the receiver added: 'True check present bluff check omitted.' Agents were given two checks: a bluff check he or she could reveal to the enemy and a true check they were to keep to themselves. It is also possible that Baker Street was being set up for the playback even before Noor's arrest. A telegram from Berne of 2 October states: 'Sonja returned from Paris 25th reports Ernest Maurice and Madeleine had "serious accident and in hospital". Madeleine is W/T operator.' The reply from London the next day states: 'Have had apparently genuine messages from Madeleine since twenty fifth therefore regard Sonja's news with some doubt.' Sonja was evidently a courier or contact working for SOE's Berne office with information that could be passed back to London.

A memo of 2 February 1944 reads: 'As you will remember one of your couriers is taking a set and other W/T equipment for our agent Madeleine to Belliard postbox in Paris. According to Madeleine, this equipment has not yet arrived and the Belliard address is no longer safe . . . Would you please let me know what steps can be taken to have the parcel delivered to their new postbox which is as follows: Monsieur Brousseau, Proprietor of My Bar, 44 rue Hamelin, Paris XVI.' Meanwhile Noor, still believed free, had been promoted with effect from 1 January 1944 to the rank of Ensign.

Noor was placed in one of the cells on the fifth floor of 84 Avenue Foch. An unusual feature of the SD regime was the long-term presence of an SOE agent, Bob Starr, who became a form of trusty, enjoying privileges that allowed him a certain freedom of movement. Some agents brought to the Avenue Foch were appalled to see Starr operating in this way. Starr, however, maintained that he was collecting important information about German tactics against SOE.

A statement on Noor's file, almost certainly by Kieffer, sets the scene. Starr had been dropped near Lyons as an organiser of the Acrobat circuit and had been arrested. He had made an immediate attempt to escape and had been wounded during the pursuit. When he had recovered, he was sent to the Avenue Foch. Kieffer continues: 'I very soon recognized "Bob's" great talent for drawing and I gave him more and more work to do.' These were mainly charts and lettering; Kieffer was careful not to give Starr anything that he could usefully divulge to London. But as Bob was in a cell next to the guard room, which had a permanent strength of four men, his escaping seemed to Kieffer out of the question. He continues: 'I gave him in course of time drawing tasks whose subject matter was to be kept secret. Since in the eventuality of an escape he posed a great risk to my office I impressed on the guards again and again that however affable and obliging "Bob" might be his lodging was to be carefully guarded and secured.'

Starr was even asked to check on the English of radio messages that were composed by the Germans and sent out on captured radios. 'It was by means of this activity that "Bob" gained a great insight into our counter-espionage work and got to know numerous arrested agents, W/T operators, and organizers of hostile intelligence services.' It was precisely at this time, in October 1943, Kieffer says, that 'Madeleine' was arrested.

Kieffer describes how, immediately after her arrest, Noor 'made an attempt at escape, when she got on the roof through a bathroom window situated on the 5th floor. She was re-arrested after the alarm had been given by Vogt.'

Taking pity on Noor, Starr devised a means of communicating with her. One day, he dropped a pencil of the round kind, which rolls easily, and managed to kick it near enough to her cell to slip a note unseen under the door. In this he proposed they exchange notes by leaving them in a crevice under the basin in the lavatory. On his next visit Starr found a reply from Noor, saying she was already in touch with a Colonel Faye, a Frenchman in the next cell to hers. For some time, like the Count of Monte Cristo, they had been tapping messages – in Morse. Like her, the colonel had obtained writing materials and would join in the exchange of messages. Their thoughts now turned to a daring triple escape. Instead of windows, their cells had rooflights that were set at the top of long shafts and protected by bars at the bottom.

Jean Overton Fuller relates how Starr ingeniously obtained the all-essential screwdriver to work on the bars. One day the cleaner knocked on the guard-room door to say the carpet sweeper was broken. Starr immediately volunteered to mend it and laboriously took it apart, taking care to spread a good deal of dust about. When the guards impatiently asked how much longer he was going to be, he replied it could all be done a great deal quicker if he had tools. A screwdriver duly arrived and Starr put the sweeper back together, ensuring the repair would not last too long. As the guards were watching him closely, he returned the screwdriver. But when the carpet sweeper duly collapsed again, and he was called to mend it, he was able to retain the screwdriver. By turns they used the screwdriver to loosen the bars of their cells, making good the damage done to the walls with plaster made from face cream and face powder, which Starr obtained from the girl in the cell next to his.

When the chosen night came, Starr and Faye emerged quickly on the roof. Unfortunately, it took Noor nearly two more hours to loosen the bars before she could be hoisted up onto the roof. Two minutes later, an air raid was sounded. As usual the cells were inspected by the SD and the alarm was raised.

Kieffer recalls his horror on learning of this second escape attempt:

One night about 3.00 am I was awakened in my room by the call of the guard that 'Bob' and 'Madeleine' had escaped . . . All three had broken through the iron bars in their cells leading to the windows of the ceiling and they had climbed up onto the flat roof and by means of strips of blankets and sheets knotted together they had let themselves down on to the balcony in the third storey of a neighbouring house and there smashed a window and entered the apartment. Faye had already left the house to continue his flight.

Faye was arrested on the street outside and, according to Kieffer, indicated in which house the other two could be found. For SOE, as well as the three prisoners, it was to be a ghastly tragedy. Kieffer continues: 'Had the three managed to escape then it is to be presumed that all the radio plays which were in full swing would have been finished.'

Few episodes illustrate more harrowingly the constant

tightrope that SOE agents walked between triumph and disaster. The escape had been brilliantly planned and prepared. Had the air raid alarm sounded just a few more minutes later, theirs might have been one of the war's great escapes.

Kieffer was incandescent. Yet he refrained from instantly beating or even executing them, and instead issued the surprising demand that each give their word of honour that they would not try to escape again. Noor and Faye refused and were subsequently sent off the same day to secure prisons in Germany. Starr, however, agreed, and Kieffer accepted his promise on the grounds that Starr 'had not broken his word of honour which he had given [earlier] . . . since at this time he had given it only for a quite specific case (namely transport to his flat in Paris to fetch his painting equipment)'. It was done ceremoniously with a handshake, Starr giving 'his explicit word of honour in the presence of witnesses that he would not undertake an attempt to escape again and that he would also not work against us. I then had confidence in him once more since in contrast to the French officers no English officer had broken the word of honour he had given me during my work in France.'

Although Kieffer now dispensed with Starr's assistance for some time, he talked with him about the reasons for the escape. Perhaps with a little ingenious dissembling, Starr told him that Noor 'had approached him with the escape plan and that if as a woman she had the courage to escape and had succeeded in doing so she would have made life impossible for him in England had he not displayed the same courage as a man.'

Noor's story is now taken up by Wilhelm Krauss, governor of the prison to which she was sent – in a deposition sworn before a War Crimes Investigation Unit in November 1946.

I remember that in November 1943 an English woman was delivered into Pforzheim prison. I was told that she was to be treated in accordance with regulations for 'Nacht und Nebel' prisoners (Note: 'Nacht und Nebel' means night and fog. It was the expression used for people who 'disappeared' and once in custody were kept on the lowest rations, in solitary confinement etc.) and moreover, that she was to be chained hand and foot. This order was carried through.

After some time, I decided to remove the chains from her hands, because I felt sorry for the English girl. Very shortly afterwards the Gestapo H.Q. from Karlsruhe telephoned and reprimanded me for not observing the regulations about chains which had to be strictly adhered to.

A harrowing description of Noor's appalling treatment was provided by a fellow inmate, Yolande Lagrave, who wrote to Noor's brother Vilayat after the war.

As for myself I was deported to Pforzheim and had the luck to return. I am the only survivor, all the others of my group have been murdered . . . At Pforzheim I lived in solitary confinement. There I could correspond with an English *parachutiste* who was interned and very unhappy. Her hands and feet were manacled, she was never taken out and I heard the blows which she received. She left Pforzheim in September 1944. Before that she was able to pass a message to me – Not her real name, that was too dangerous, but a pseudonym . . . I took note of this as Nora Baker, Radio Centre Officers, Service RAF, 4 Taviston Street London.

She wrote to this address to inquire about Noor but the letter was returned, marked 'Not known at this address'.

Vilayat wrote to the War Office on 12 February 1947, saying: 'The other informer is a German lady by the name of Elsa Findling (Widow Kitner) . . . who communicated the message through the kind services of Mr. D. McFarlin of U.N.R.A.', who was based at Pforzheim at the time the

Allies were taking Strasbourg. She had told him that 'all the internees were taken by the Germans to be executed,' and that 'the jail-keeper who is said to have beaten up my sister, has been maintained in his post as jail-keeper to this day'.

At one point it was thought that Noor had been taken with Diana Rowden, Vera Leigh and Denise Borrel from Karlsruhe City Gaol to Natzweiler concentration camp on 6 July 1944 – and had been killed with them by lethal injection. An official announcement was made to this effect.

It was only two years after the war had ended that the true circumstances of Noor's death finally emerged. On 26 June 1947, Major N.G. Mott of the War Office wrote to the Air Ministry, as follows:

It is now known that on 12th September, 1944, A.S.O. Inayat-Khan, together with three other specially employed women, Mrs Plewman, FANY, Miss Damerment and S/O Beekman, W.A.A.F., were removed to Dachau concentration camp, accompanied by three officials of the Karlsruhe Gestapo. They arrived at Dachau after dark and had to walk to the camp, which they reached about midnight. They spent the night in the cells and between 8 and 10 the following morning, 13th September, they were taken to the crematorium compound and shot through the back of the head and immediately cremated. The Gestapo officials and the prison director have been interrogated by the War Crimes Section of the J.A.G's branch and confess to their part in this wretched business. As will readily be realized, there is great difficulty in *proving* death in these cases, but it has now been possible to obtain documentary proof which leaves no reason for doubt.

More than a year earlier Noor had been awarded the Croix de Guerre with Gold Star. The citation, dated 16 January 1946 and signed by de Gaulle, mentions yet another tantalising episode about which more should be known. 'Falling into an ambush at Grignon, in July 1943, her comrades and she managed to escape after having killed or wounded the

Germans who tried to stop them.' The citation for her George Cross, issued over three years later on 5 April 1949, commended Noor for her most conspicuous courage, both moral and physical, over a period of more than twelve months. Buckmaster said simply: 'A most brave and touchingly keen girl. She was determined to do her bit to hit the Germans, and, poor girl, she has.'

Chapter 7

PEARL WITHERINGTON

Successful agents needed luck. Some also had a sixth sense that helped protect them. 'My antennae are always out. I can feel anything that happens around me,' says Pearl Witherington, who now lives in a wing of a château close to the fields and woods where she once personally headed a Resistance force that grew to be 2,700 strong.

'She was a very pretty girl ... *très sympathique*,' said Henri Diacono, a radio operator who trained with her at Wanborough Manor. When I met her, Pearl was aged eighty-four. She was still mobile, still alert, yet calm, composed and with an extraordinary recollection of her adventures in France. Recently she played a key role in setting up the SOE memorial at Valençay. She meets regularly with her Resistance colleagues who knew her as Pauline. 'Life then was so intense. Everything is imprinted on the memory. When we meet we are carried back immediately,' she says.

Looking back on her life, she remarks, 'Everything that happened to me was an accident, except that I wanted to get into SOE. In certain things destiny works for you.' Pearl was born in Paris on 24 June 1916. Her great-grandfather was a chemist and the man who introduced the recipe for Worcester Sauce to Lea & Perrins. Her grandfather was an architect in London, whilst her father travelled the world, working for a Swede who supplied paper for banknotes. He was also a spendthrift. When he returned home to Paris he would be out with his friends until two in the morning. In her memoir, *Pauline*, published in 1996, Pearl recalls: 'I would be sent to the bar which he frequented to collect 20 francs to buy food for the day. It would be handed to me by the barman who would give me a box of biscuits at the same time.'

One day she returned home to see all their furniture on the pavement. Her father had failed to pay the rent for the duration of the 1914–18 war. Fortunately, her uncle, her mother's brother, arrived in Paris and, realising the situation, helped to pay the rent. Pearl started work at the age of seventeen, giving all her earnings to her mother and making pocket money by giving English lessons in the evenings.

When the Germans invaded France in 1940, Pearl was working for the air attaché at the British Embassy. However, as 'locally engaged' staff, she was not included in the embassy's evacuation plans. On the ambassador's instructions, she took her family to Normandy but arrived too late to catch a boat. Here she had her first taste of resistance – helping two escaped British soldiers to make their way to unoccupied southern France. Returning to Paris in July with her family, she stayed there until December, living on advances from the American Embassy, until a boyfriend of her sister told them there was to be a round-up of all the English in the sixteenth arrondissement.

The family left Paris on 9 December 1940. Pearl had heard a man talking about taking horses over the demarcation line. 'I thought, if he can get horses across, he can get us across too.' Gallantly, the man undertook to pay for everything, and the family travelled first class. This sense of luxury did not last: when they left the train shortly before crossing into the Unoccupied Zone, they had to take shelter in a ditch while a patrol went past, and were quickly covered in mud. Once safely inside the zone, they took a bus to Mâcon, going on to the American Embassy in Vichy, where they received an unexpectedly frosty reception. 'We left the next day for Marseilles, hoping to board a ship taking refugees to England, but though the Italians gave permission, the Germans refused.'

Now they had to start all over again, obtaining papers for travel to Spain and Portugal. In Lisbon they had a further delay of three months. Here Pearl was able to find work with the air attaché at the British Embassy. Finally, she says, 'We secured a passage in a banana boat that took us in territorial waters as far as Gibraltar.' Here they found the Cunard liner *Scythia*, although they had to wait for the banana boat to return with another load of refugees before setting out again. They travelled 'very very fast across the Atlantic turning back towards Glasgow, to be escorted in by a Cruiser', arriving in England on 13 July 1941. The family took a train to London. Pearl settled her mother in a flat in Streatham and found a job in the Air Ministry while all three sisters enlisted as WAAFs. Now that she was confined to an office, Pearl's thoughts turned towards getting back to France. 'I could do more there to eject the Germans than I ever could occupied by paperwork in England,' she says. However, her boss, Air Commodore Douglas Collier, would not hear of it, strongly disapproving of what he saw as the amateurs now embarking on clandestine warfare. 'I don't want you mixed up with those people,' he said sternly.

Pearl was propelled by a sense of burning anger at the occupation of France. When she had arrived back in Paris shortly after 14 July 1940, Bastille Day, she had been incensed to read posters announcing the death of Parisians shot the night before. 'These unlucky people had often been arrested after curfew and if there was an incident during the night, they would be shot as hostages.' She was equally irate to see hundreds of Germans strutting in every direction and huge Nazi banners all along the rue de Rivoli. 'I still have trouble making people understand that the war in France and England was completely different. Imagine someone arriving chez vous, whom you do not like, giving you orders,' she says.

Now, outraged at her boss's attitude, she promptly rang a Parisian friend at the Foreign Office in London. Little did she know that this friend was now working for the Foreign Secretary himself. 'Years later she told me all she had to do was to ring and arrange an appointment with Colonel Buckmaster,' Pearl recalls.

She joined SOE on 8 June 1943 and began with three weeks' training at Wanborough where she received glowing reports. 'Outstanding. Probably the best shot (male or female) we have yet had,' ran one, while another on explosive and demolitions states: 'Very good indeed. Extremely keen on this and would like to specialise.' Her final report includes the following instructor's remarks: 'This student, though a woman, has definitely got leader's qualities. Cool and resourceful and extremely determined. Particularly interested in and suited for active work. She has had a good influence on the course and has been a pleasure to instruct.' The commandant added: 'Very capable, completely brave.'

For Pearl, nonetheless, there were difficult moments. 'I just couldn't get the hang of Morse code. I had been a Girl Guide and learnt semaphore but though I could see letters I couldn't hear them. I was getting into a state and went to see the commandant.' He told her not to worry – evidently she was not radio operator material. She also remembers problems with physical training. 'I was the laughing stock of the class. I just could not do a somersault. It took me three weeks to achieve one.'

When Pearl went to Beaulieu for seven weeks for security training, she suffered a further setback. She recalls: 'It was murder. All that cramming with theory and PT at seven in the morning. I said, "I can't run at seven." The instructor naturally asked how I would manage a quick getaway in France. "I'll deal with that when it happens," I replied.'

Her first ninety-six-hour exercise in Birmingham during August 1943 was not a success. She had to play the part of a Miss Pearl Wimsey on sick leave from the Air Ministry. According to the training report, she allowed herself to be 'put

off by an unfortunate remark on the part of her contact . . .
She is cautious by nature and this hesitation to act probably
accounts for the paucity of ground covered.' Pearl recalls it
rather differently. 'The man I was supposed to meet never
turned up. We had been told never to wait more than five
minutes so I left.'

The man, however, insisted that he had put in an appearance
with the result that it was Pearl who was in trouble. She also
remembers an interrogation by Scotland Yard; a woman and
a man arrived in plain clothes at her hotel bedroom, unaware,
it seemed to her, that this was simply a training exercise.
Pearl explained that she worked as a secretary, whereupon
the woman detective barked out, 'Take this down.' When
they looked at her shorthand they were still more angry and
perplexed, thinking she was writing in some kind of code. 'It's
a French system. I have told you I have lived in France,' said
Pearl vigorously.

The subsequent forty-eight-hour exercise in Portsmouth
later in August went better, with Pearl displaying 'more confidence in getting in touch with people'. In view of what she
was to achieve later, Pearl's final report from the commandant
is strangely pessimistic: 'Loyal and reliable but has not the
personality to act as a leader, nor is she temperamentally suited
to work alone . . . would be best employed as a subordinate
under a strong leader in whom she had confidence.' A doctor's
report of 26 August 1943 may provide an explanation. Pearl
had lost 8.5 kilos, was suffering from a troublesome skin rash
and 'appears very fatigued'.

The parachute course at Dunham Massey from 29 August
to 3 September went even better. Pearl did three jumps and was
classified first class. She 'had the fastest landing that anyone
of her sex has had here and took the shock extremely well',
noted the commandant, adding that she was 'physically much
stronger than she looks'.

SOE now gave Pearl her mission – dated 13 September

1943: 'To work as courier for an organiser, Hector, who is in control of a circuit in the region of Tarbes, Châteauroux and Bergerac'. Hector was Maurice Southgate, head of SOE's large and growing Stationer circuit. Her field name was Marie. With this came a false identity, with papers in the name of Geneviève Touzalin, secretary in the Société Allumetière Française [French Match Company]. Shortly before she left she was also granted an honorary commission in the WAAF of assistant section officer.

The mission instructions continue: 'Through Hector [Southgate] you are to make contact with a French Colonel . . . who has been described to us as having under his command a considerable number of men in the "maquis". You are to explain our requirements to him and if satisfied with his reaction . . . to arrange for the receipt by him of the materials and finance of which he stands in need.'

She was told that she would be parachuted to a reception committee eighteen kilometres south-west of Châteauroux and four kilometres north of Tendu. If she missed it, she was to contact Southgate through a postbox at the Café du Cygne, in the rue Diderot at Châteauroux, where she should give a message to the waitress Simone for Monsieur Maigrot. 'There is no password and the waitress knows nothing about the work we do,' she was told. As courier to Southgate, she was to 'take all instructions concerning your duties from him. He will help you in every possible way, but at the same time you are expected to be as self reliant as possible.' Southgate was to put her in touch with the French colonel. She was to tell him that 'our need is for resolute men who will take their orders from us and nobody else, and who will attack those targets given them by us. We should contemplate financing such a group on the basis of something under 1000 francs a head per month, and that we envisage an expenditure in the neighbourhood of 750,000 francs a month.'

Southgate's password was, 'Eh bien! Vous êtes allés vous

promener dernièrement?' and the reply was, 'Un peu, mais on use les semelles par le temps qui court.' Pearl was to be given 150,000 francs for her personal use and was told to try to keep an account of her expenses. To the amazement of Baker Street she duly produced this on her return, together with a substantial sum of cash.

Pearl was dropped on the night of 22/23 September, at her third attempt. On the first attempt no lights were picked up and the aircraft returned to base; the same happened the second time when two Frenchmen were with her. 'The weather was dreadful, they didn't even let out the pigeons,' she says, referring to the racing pigeons that were dropped in small boxes with parachutes for messages to be sent back to the Secret Intelligence Service.

Pearl finally jumped alone, in a high wind, and was blown off course, landing between two lakes. By contrast to the large turnouts that greeted some agents, Southgate, always security conscious, came with just one other, a farmer called Octave Chantraine, known as Octraine, a contact that was to prove her salvation later on.

Within hours, Pearl was reunited with her French fiancé Henri Cornioley, who had previously escaped from a German prison camp and who had joined Southgate in the Resistance. Less fortunate was the fact that her two suitcases of luggage had landed in the water and proved impossible to retrieve until much later. This was a serious setback, as clothing was hard to obtain in wartime France. Being without a change of underclothes presented problems, particularly when she briefly took refuge with her radio officer, who had rented a room from a milliner with very strict rules about visitors. 'He was terrified she would walk in and see my pants hanging up to dry,' she says.

After a brief stay at Limoges she went on to Riom where she remained in a safe house in the rue de l'Amiral Goubeyre. During this time she remembers inviting Francis Cammaerts (to whom Christina Granville was later sent) up to her room, 'against all regulations', where they sat on the floor trying to keep warm in the winter sunlight streaming through the window.

Just three weeks later Southgate was recalled to London for a fortnight's consultation, being picked up on the night of 16 October from a field near Amboise. He was away for three months, leaving Pearl to run the Stationer circuit with the Mauritian radio operator, Amédée Maingard (Samuel) and another courageous young courier, Jacqueline Nearne.

While Southgate was away, Pearl gave sabotage instructions to Jacques Dufour (Anastasie) at Salon-la-Tour; he appears in the story of Violette Szabo. Pearl also made contact with the Maquis through which a sabotage attack was made on the Michelin tyre works in Clermont-Ferrand. Although 40,000 tyres destined for German use were destroyed, the attack was not the complete success that had been hoped. Pearl reported that this was 'solely due to the lack of sabotage instruction at the time in that region. The sabotage parties were exceedingly keen . . . if they had been trained they would certainly have done much better.'

Infuriatingly, it took three months for her to find a room. In the interim she had to spend the nights in unheated trains, mainly between Clermont-Ferrand, Toulouse and Châteauroux, which were far too full of people to allow any chance of stretching out to sleep. 'Maurice Southgate had discovered a form of season ticket that allowed unlimited travel, first class, within a specified region. It was expensive but we avoided queuing for tickets and were able to travel in trains reserved for those with special tickets,' she says.

At night there were fewer German checks. She surrounded herself with pro-German magazines such as *Signal* and *Carrefour*, and wore her hair with a plait in Teutonic fashion. A number of times, the train was so full that the only option was to sleep in the corridor. After weeks of acute discomfort, she was stricken with an attack of neuralgic rheumatism and was forced to rest for three weeks.

Rationing, says Pearl, was worse than in England – no tea, no coffee, no milk. This was made up for, thanks to her SOE allowance, by one good meal a day in a black market restaurant. She had managed to obtain, through the *mairie* of Montant-les-Crémaux in the Gers, an authentic identity card showing her as Mademoiselle Marie Jeanne Marthe Verges, a travelling rep for a cosmetics firm, Isabelle Lancrey, that had been set up by her future father-in-law. The firm had her on their books and knew her position.

Her closest brush with death, she says, came not with the Germans but another Resistance group. Agents relied on passwords and checks to provide assurances when they made contacts with members of other groups. 'Maurice had sent me from Montluçon to Loches to collect a sum of money from a Gaston Langlois, saying, "There's no password and they know neither you nor me."' Arriving at the house, she was told that Gaston would not be back till the next day. This meant going all the way back to Montluçon and returning at a later date.

When she returned, she was beckoned inside to the frostiest of receptions. Her attempts to establish her bona fides by citing the code names of other agents met a complete blank. Her host became increasingly hostile.

'Finally I asked if he knew Octave. No, came the reply. In desperation, I gave the real name, Monsieur Chantraine, on whose farm I had been dropped. Suddenly they smiled and moments later several burly men tumbled out of the next-door room. They had been lying in wait to pounce on me in case I was an agent of the Milice,' she says.

Southgate recalls his return to France on 28 January 1944 'in a non moon period with the help of S-phone and Eureka . . . Good landing . . . Plenty to do and how! During the first week after my arrival London instructed me to organize a reception for about 20 agents.' However, he was soon having trouble with an agent called Gaëtan who he had sent to Poitiers with an introduction to the Treasurer of the Lycée. Gaëtan had returned from Poitiers to Montluçon, telling Southgate that he had had no success in finding any landing grounds. 'Sent him back to Poitiers with a raspberry,' says Southgate. Next a letter arrived from Gaëtan, asking Southgate or Pearl to come to Poitiers and fixing an appointment at the main railway station with a "mot de passe". 'The whole letter and story seemed phoney,' Southgate recalled. 'Eventually I sent Marie [Pearl] to Poitiers to see the *économe* du Lycée de Garçons de Poitiers. She returned very excited, saying the *économe* [treasurer] and his wife had been arrested. This information was given her by the concierge of the Lycée de Poitiers, who said: "Madame, clear out quickly. I don't know who you are, but I trust you had personal affairs to do with the *économe*. His house is full of Gestapo and the *économe* and his wife have been arrested."' Southgate never heard any more of Gaëtan.

Pearl was forced into effective command of her Maquis when, just over a month before D-Day, Southgate was arrested in Montluçon on going to see his new radio operator, the newly arrived René Mathieu (Aimé).

In his report, written after his return from Buchenwald, Southgate recalled that he had 'returned by car to Montluçon at approximately 1600 hours' and been dropped off

in a little back street owing to Milice and Gestapo patrols and activity in the streets . . . I must admit that I was pretty tired as a result of all my movements during the past fortnight, and I can honestly say that for the first time I did not take any elementary precautions . . . When I had knocked and the door eventually opened I found half a dozen guns pushed into my tummy, and at the same time saw in my mind four obvious Gestapo civilians walking up and down in the Rue de Rimard with hands in their pockets, just waiting for an eventual visitor to walk into that house.

Fortunately, a doctor who later came to the house insisted that the Germans should allow him in to see his patient. Afterwards he was able to get a warning to Pearl, who was out on a picnic with Maingard, her fiancé Henri and other members of the circuit. 'When we came back the town was surrounded by German troops, but we found a man who drove us out by a little back road,' she says. With Henri she escaped to Montluçon.

Southgate continues: 'I was immediately taken to Gestapo headquarters at Montluçon. I was robbed of everything I had, watch, wallet and all personal belongings.' Here he was handcuffed and badly beaten on the head, passing out at one stage. Aimé, who had been caught surrounded by three transmission sets, was soon receiving the same 'entertainment'.

That evening Aimé, in shocking condition, was dragged in and handcuffed to Southgate. They were then driven to Montluçon barracks and thrown into the same cell – 'a very foolish thing to do,' said Southgate. Before talking to each other, they made a thorough search for microphones. As an extra precaution, they wrapped their heads in their coats and a blanket that had been given them by the Wehrmacht. All through the night they planned the line that they would take with the Gestapo – that they did not know each other. The next afternoon Aimé was taken off by the Gestapo and returned four hours later, his back running with blood after a very severe beating. After a few moments' rest, he told Southgate the story he had spun to the Gestapo: that he was a poor fellow in need of money and that he had met someone in Paris who had offered to pay him 5,000 francs a month to sit in a room and look after valuable suitcases, letting no one near them.

Southgate continues: 'Strange as it may seem, this story was swallowed by the Gestapo men, mostly because of Aimé's very good bearing under severe treatment, when he never flinched.' Four days later it was Southgate's turn to be dragged out and interrogated. 'I made out that I was a stranger to the house, and that I had just called on . . . the proprietor . . . but this did not quite satisfy them.' Unfortunately they had found a second identity card of his in another false name, as well as one for Pearl, with her photograph, in the name of Madame Cornioley.

The Gestapo chief got hold of a stick and gave me the beating of my life across my back and legs. His interpreter, who spoke much better French, turned round to me with flaming eyes and called me 'a swine, and a son of a bitch'. I felt like kicking him, but just smiled innocently at him. He then got quite upset with me, and I realised it would be quite impossible for me to carry on on these lines, for they had far too many documents against me . . . so I remembered Beaulieu schooling, where they always used to say: 'Stick to the truth as nearly as you possibly can,' so I made out I was going to speak and started the following story.

Knowing the importance of the documents they had found, Southgate thought the best thing was to put them on a false trail, thus gaining as much time as possible to enable the May moon operations to take place. Having so many people to remember, he described Jacqueline as a courier in Toulouse and Pearl as a courier in Limoges, adding that he was introduced to the gang by a Monsieur Jean Mercier. As Jean was the Christian name of a very old friend of his, and Mercier was a big firm dealing in furniture in Paris, which he knew well, he would not contradict himself in further interrogation.

As soon as he mentioned the name of Jean Mercier, the two Gestapo inspectors were open-mouthed, saying 'How did you meet him?' This perturbed Southgate, but fortunately his interrogators went on to give a full description, asking if it corresponded. Southgate readily agreed, and it turned out that Mercier was a French captain, 'tall, dark and handsome' and head of a big Deuxième Bureau. He had met Mercier, he said, in the Quartier Latin and he spun out the story, saying that Mercier was often with a beautiful woman, a platinum blonde, and that Mercier often gave him sealed envelopes to take from place to place. This story, says Southgate, was thoroughly believed by the two Gestapo inspectors, and eventually they sent him back to his cell. Better still, they never mentioned Aimé, his radio operator, with whom he had been taken, neither asking if he knew him nor if he knew anything about his activities.

When asked if he knew that he was involved in espionage, Southgate swore blind that he had had no idea and promised not to get drawn in again. 'Incredible as it may seem, they believed every word I told them,' he said. To back up his story he gave them an address for Jacqueline Nearne in Toulouse, knowing that her hosts were not going to return till after the occupation was over.

After Southgate's arrest, the circuit was split into two parts. Maingard took the southern area across the Haute Creuse, renamed Shipwright by Baker Street, and Pearl took over the network of Resistance groups to the north, renamed Wrestler. She now worked directly with four good-sized Resistance groups – each with its own commander – distributing arms and giving weapon training.

Pearl and Henri found refuge with the tenants of the gate lodge of the Château des Souches, near Villefranche-sur-Cher, where the Nord Indre Maquis were encamped in the adjoining woods. The owners of the château, strong Pétainistes, had no idea of their presence nor of the munitions stored in their outbuildings.

On receipt of the D-Day action messages over the BBC, Pearl's Maquis started to fell trees across roads and cut telephone wires.

At dawn on 11 June, five days after D-Day, some 2,000 German troops mounted a pre-emptive strike against the Resistance groups centred on Les Souches, which had probably been located by low-level aerial reconnaissance. Pearl's official report in November 1944 states that the small Maquis,

comprising approximately forty men, badly armed and untrained, put up a terrific fight, with the neighbouring communist maquis ... which numbered approximately one hundred men. The German attack was fairly violent, they had guns and artillery, but considering the large number and the length of the battle (it lasted until 10 o'clock at night), the maquis losses were far less than those of the Germans, the latter having lost 86 and the maquis 24, including civilians who were shot and the injured, who were finished off.

As Henri started shooting, Pearl's own priority had to be to evade capture and protect a large sum of cash dropped by SOE for future operations. She plunged into a field of corn, just as the Germans torched a nearby barn, momentarily threatening to set the whole field ablaze with her in it. Keeping out of sight of German patrols, she crept across the field a few feet at a time towards a nearby copse. Fortunately the Germans on this occasion showed little inclination to pursue the Maquis into the woods; some of the more war-weary Germans simply settled down in nearby farmhouses, including the lodge where Pearl and Henri had been sleeping, and demanded to be fed.

Pearl's Maquis was now largely without either weapons or a radio. They found refuge further east at Doulçay with a brave local farming couple, Monsieur and Madame Trochet. 'There was an almost perpetual stream of people coming round, some staying with us, and quite apart from this they had received and hidden a considerable amount of arms parachuted. After a while we narrowly escaped the visit of 45 German soldiers to the farm, but fortunately the name given was not correct and the Germans went to the wrong people. From that time on, we slept in the woods and had our meals at the farm.'

It was not until the night of 24 June, her birthday, that she received a much-needed parachute drop from three planes, supplying weapons, ammunition, food and clothing. The dropping ground, recalls Pearl, was named Baleine, French for whale. 'All our parachute grounds were named after fish or crustaceans.'

These drops, Pearl reported, 'were exceedingly difficult', owing to the presence of lookout posts manned by Germans. 'It was quite impossible to have daylight operations and also to light fires in non-moon periods.' Even so she received some twenty-three drops, losing only one (at ground Rouget) when a container of hand grenades burst on impact and continued to explode for some time. This alerted the Germans, who found the ground and killed four *maquisards*.

Pearl chose as dropping grounds 'the biggest fields away from roads', which were not difficult to locate, although 'German look out posts and the guards on the demarcation line were a nuisance'. She wrote: 'After D-Day containers were put into prepared pits and camouflaged with greenery . . . It was absolutely essential to have everything cleared off the grounds before daybreak as reconnaissance planes were always scouring the countryside from 5 o'clock onwards.'

She had strong opinions on the weapons sent, particularly the Stens, which had a tendency to go off on their own. Pearl said she would have liked more personal weapons. She had also asked for Thompson sub-machine guns but never received any. Bren guns proved difficult to clean because of the amount of protective grease they carried. As well as bazookas Pearl received Piats, which stands for projector, infantry, anti-tank. This was a cumbersome, spring-powered device, which fired a bomb looking rather like a bazooka rocket. It worked on the HEAT principle (high-explosive, anti-tank) and generated a jet of hot gas, which burnt into the tank like a blowtorch. Pearl preferred the longer range of the bazooka. On one occasion, in James Bond style, a Piat was fired into a house to liquidate a Gestapo agent, but not surprisingly it embedded itself in the wall without exploding. Four-prong tyre bursters were found to be very efficient. The explosives and 'time pencils', used to detonate railway lines, would be placed on curves to derail the train more thoroughly. Pylons in woods were attacked so that the lines caught in trees.

Pearl put her SOE training to use by giving her Maquis demolition instruction. She encountered 'no nervousness in handling explosives'. More difficult was finding the necessary technical terms as her own instruction in England had been in English. With rather more sensitivity to the pride of French men than to that of women, the officer who debriefed Pearl back in England observed, 'The fact that informant was a woman was at times a handicap . . . The Clermont Ferrand group would have preferred a man to instruct them.'

Ambushes usually consisted of ten to twenty men, but when the 2nd SS Panzer division, Das Reich, was attacked on its way from Toulouse to the Normandy battle front, the whole Maquis turned out. From the beginning of July 1944, there were constant engagements with the enemy, including many successful attacks on convoys. In one attack on an SS convoy on the Route Nationale 20, the Germans admitted to losses of 76 killed and 125 wounded; Maquis losses were just 5 wounded. At Valençay, in September 1944, 800 Maquis went into battle against 4,000 Germans, liberating the town. They killed 180 Germans and wounded 300, against 21 losses of their own.

Agents communicated by radio with SOE in London, receiving instructions, requesting arms drops and, after D-Day, providing reports on clashes with German troops. Pearl's signals to and from headquarters, decoded on squared paper, are rare survivors. 'Tell us how many bogeys you see on all tanks coming through your region,' runs one message she received soon after D-Day. The explanation for this request was that Allied commanders badly wanted to know how many German Tigers were hastening towards the Normandy front.

Tigers were the new super-tanks, which completely outgunned Allied armour. Realising that eager Resistance fighters might call any tank a Tiger, they wanted a wheel count to be sure.

Another message read: 'We are happy to tell you that the RAF located 60 petrol wagons on the railway line between Vierzon and Bourges and bombed the target the next day with very good results. The Supreme Commander asks us to congratulate you on the information you sent.' Eisenhower's personal interest is evidence of the importance he attached to Resistance operations behind German lines and, in the daily situation reports issued after D-Day, key Resistance activity is listed after military and air-force action.

The signals sent back by Pearl give a sense of the drama and urgency of the situation. 'Our strength is now 2,000 men of whom 1,400 are armed. Between four and five hundred Boches have been killed since our part of the battle intensified.' Another signal reads: 'We cannot any longer hold this sector if you don't urgently send us the parachute drops which we were waiting for in the last moon period.'

Pearl's success in the field was recognised by promotion to the rank of section officer on 20 May, reflecting the fact that she had taken over control of the circuit after Southgate's arrest. On 1 September she was raised to the rank of flight officer, acknowledging that she had been in complete control of a Maquis region since D-Day.

The four sub-sectors of her Maquis carried out numerous attacks on the retreating Germans. On 18 August, one attacked a detachment of SS in Reuilly, 30 of them against 300 Germans. During a battle of an hour and a half, the Germans lost 20 men with numerous wounded. The Maquis lost just one, who was found two days later horribly mutilated, his face lacerated by bayonet wounds. Eight days later outside Valençay, another group held up a column of 128 German vehicles, forcing it to turn back, and inflicting 150 casualties for one Maquis dead and two wounded.

Pearl's summary of the achievements of the Wrestler circuit reads: 'German losses over five months 1,000; the wounded can be counted in thousands. We participated in the surrender of 18,000 Boches in the Issoudun sector, prisoners delivered to the Americans at Orléans.' When she arrived, the Stationer circuit had comprised a tight circuit of about twenty. At the end of the war, the *réseau* Marie (Pearl's circuit), with its four sub-sectors in the north Indre and the valley of the Cher, was 3,500 strong.

Pearl was very precise in her recommendations for decorations and recognition. She wanted a letter of appreciation and a French decoration for Monsieur and Madame Sabassier, who had housed Pearl and her comrades in the gate lodge at the Château des Souches. 'They lost everything they possessed on the 11th June during the attack by the Germans.' She also requested a letter of appreciation from the Prime Minister for the Trochets who 'received and hid armament for over a year'. She suggested a letter from Colonel Buckmaster for the Steegman family, Belgian farmers at Doulçay who 'received and hid large quantities of explosives and arms' and who sheltered Pearl's radio operator, Tutur, for two months.

She also proposed eleven officers for the Croix de Guerre, including 'Lieut. Henri Cornioley [who] was my second-in-command and took part in the battle of the 11th June, prepared an ambush for twelve Germans, killed one of them, but could not hold out, as the Germans approached the farm and set fire to it. He has now become my husband and I will refrain from any further comment.' Scribbled in the margin is 'Why?!' – a sad reflection on how SOE failed to comprehend Pearl's understandable modesty and to recommend Henri for the decoration that he richly deserved. But then 'No action' is also written across the top of all Pearl's recommendations for civilians, cited above, although she herself was ultimately the recipient of the MBE Military.

Pearl emphasises: 'It is important to remember that most

of France south of the Loire was liberated not by the Allies but by the Resistance.' For this reason she strongly objected when a large force of Germans was allowed to surrender to the Americans rather than the Free French, and 'were received by the American Red Cross with cigarettes, chocolates and oranges (things unknown to French civilians for the past five years), and were seen to walk arm in arm in French towns. This . . . was a heavy blow to FFI pride, and totally undeserved.' But this was something that was to happen many times. It was partly a matter of principle – German commanders would only surrender to a properly constituted army, be it American or British. Perhaps they were exercised even more by a fear that the FFI would exact reprisals for the brutal treatment the Germans had meted out to them.

Chapter 8

PADDY O'SULLIVAN

Many of her instructors thought Paddy O'Sullivan was quite unsuitable to be dropped into France at all. Her fiery temper, ungovernable nature and chaotic organisation prompted the most serious doubts at every stage in her training. When she arrived in France as a wireless operator, her circuit organiser was not only enraged because F Section had sent him a woman, but was astounded at her complete lack of security training and, worse still, her inability even to ride a bicycle. Yet it was he who was later to write:

I could not have wished for a better type, although she contained an explosive mixture of Irish and Breton blood. In spite of the fact that she was sent into the Field with inadequate training, she carried out her duties wonderfully well – courageous and hard-working, nothing was ever too difficult for her. She has had most of the time to live on farms, very often under atrociously unsanitary conditions, with never a grumble or complaint. She was really inspired by her job, and if any good work has been done by the Fireman Mission as a whole the greater part of the credit goes to her for her untiring efforts and great patience.

Maureen Patricia O'Sullivan was born in Dublin on 3 January 1918, the daughter of an Irish journalist and English mother who tragically died fifteen months after giving birth. She was sent to school at St Louis Convent in Dublin but when she was seven she went to live with an aunt in Belgium. Here she attended the Convent des Soeurs Paulines in Courtrai, moving at the age of eleven to the Athenée Royale in Ostend.

By the time she was fifteen, she spoke fluent French, albeit with a Belgian accent.

For the next few years she led an almost cosmopolitan existence, changing schools annually, first going back to Dublin to the Rathmines Commercial College, then moving to the Mesdemoiselles de France private school in Paris, then to an Ursuline convent in Bruges. At the age of eighteen she was transferred to a child welfare school, the École de Puériculture in Brussels. In January 1939 she started two years' nursing at Highgate Hospital in London.

Before war broke out her father appears to have moved back to Dublin and was living in a modest house at 2 Charleville Road, Rathmines. Paddy could have stayed in neutral Ireland. Instead she enlisted in British forces, joining the WAAFs on 7 July 1941. By 1943, when she came to SOE's notice, she was serving as acting corporal No. 450686 at RAF Compton Bassett. She was formally accepted for training at the end of May and started training in July.

Her SOE history sheet lists an unusual trio of hobbies – books, psychology and walking. Her languages are listed as French, English, Dutch and Flemish (fluent) with a knowledge of German.

Her first report from the training school at Winterfold in Surrey was positive: 'A pleasant intelligent Irish girl with a mind and will of her own. Purposeful and determined once she is convinced that what she is doing is right. Likes change, but could be relied upon to see any job through on which she has set her mind. Very independent and with good self-reliance which should increase with training.' A note of caution followed: 'No mechanical and little practical sense. Can manage men and would probably be excellent as keeper of a safe house. She would appear to be accident-prone and hence it is probably inadvisable to allow her to jump.'

A month later, the report dated 7 September from the paramilitary training school in Scotland describes her as 'intelligent, but very stubborn' and 'anxious to do the actual work'. Two weeks after that report was written, serious doubts were being expressed.

I had a very poor opinion of this student at the beginning of the course ... She did not give herself any trouble whatsoever to pick up the different subjects taught here, no keenness, no team spirit. In fact one would have thought that she had been ordered, compelled to choose this work. Most amazing attitude. I talked to her quite recently on this matter; I made it perfectly clear that unless she adopted immediately a different attitude she would be sent back to her unit. She says she is very keen to do the actual work and would like to become a W/T operator. There has been a very noticeable improvement in both her work and attitude since I had this talk with her.

Nonetheless, the next fortnightly report of 8 October again reveals very mixed feelings about her suitability as an agent.

Contrary to her childish appearance, this student is serious and earnest at bottom. Although bad tempered at times she is very kind hearted. She has an undisciplined character. She is definitely not the type of student which I would recommend for this work, but there is just a chance that she might improve with further training. She knows she has a violent temper, consequently she realises that in action it is absolutely vital that she should work with somebody with whom she gets on well.

In October 1943, Paddy was being considered for work as a courier and was sent on to the Wireless Training School at Thame Park from which Captain Clitheroe reported on 7 December: 'A tough type of woman ... seems to be popular with all the students. Is more of a boy than a girl.'

At one stage she was reprimanded for going on leave without authority and was told she could have no further leave. Characteristically she refused to accept the school commandant's ruling. In exasperation he wrote:

This student absented herself without leave over the week-end and returned to duty this morning at about 12 o'clock noon. When questioned about her absence she states that application was made to the security sergeant for leave on Thursday, 10th February, the day following her return from scheme. It would appear that as arrangements were not made to her satisfaction she proceeded on leave without pass or authority. I consider her conduct very unsatisfactory . . . she was trained in the WAAF, and accustomed to discipline, she has no excuse . . . She has been informed that she will not be granted any further leave while she is under instruction, but states that she is unwilling to accept my ruling in this matter and presumably intends to ignore these instructions. The report on her work is far from satisfactory in that she has now completed four months at this school. She would appear to treat her work too light-heartedly having no regard to her future responsibilities as an agent of the French Section.

Despite all this, by March 1944 F Section was keen to send Paddy to France during one of the next two moon periods, which meant she would not have a chance to attend the all-important security course at Beaulieu, planned for 12 March. Not surprisingly, when asked whether she was prepared to go into the field without further training, she leapt at the opportunity.

Although she had only done the standard Morse course attended by all SOE trainees, she was now dispatched as a W/T operator. Her mission was to join the newly formed Fireman circuit. Two seasoned SOE agents who had worked in Madagascar had already been sent in to start this circuit, the Mauritians Major Percy 'Teddy' Mayer, code name Barthelemy, and his brother Lieutenant, later Captain, E.R. 'Dicko' Mayer, code name Maurice, who established his headquarters at Prissac. Their intended radio operator, a

Canadian lieutenant, had cried off at the last minute and so the two brothers had been dropped at St Céré, near Angoulême, on the night of 6 March. The reception committee was on the point of leaving when the plane flew over, and they rushed back to shine their lights. However, the plane overshot the actual dropping ground and the agents were dropped too low, on rocky terrain.

The Mayers' task was to contact a Resistance group with the name of Veni in the Limoges area and to supply it with arms and equipment, helping to train and organise fighting units for guerrilla warfare. Major Mayer graphically explains the problems they encountered in an end-of-mission report of 6 November 1944. It was quickly evident that the Veni organisation had no substance at all. The nominal head was a Monsieur Tavet, a lieutenant in the Intendance Militaire in Limoges. His right-hand man was his brother-in-law, Monsieur Pariset; he too worked in the Intendance but in a civilian capacity. Their wives were two sisters who also took an active part in this Resistance work.

Mayer describes Tavet as 'an honest, straightforward, hard-working and courageous man who was trying his best to serve his country with, as far as I could see, no personal ambition. Pariset is a weak, chicken-hearted individual who was dragged into the resistance movement by his entourage and not through personal inclination or sense of duty.' Tavet had been a communist and had built up a loose network of contacts with various organisations, on the basis that he would help supply them with money, arms and equipment. The result, according to Mayer, was that when Tavet was arrested on 5 May, 'The supposed Veni organisation vanished into thin air as each group went back to its own recognised organisation.' Fortunately Tavet was arrested as a communist and not as a Resistance organiser. His flat was searched but nothing compromising was found and Madame Tavet was not taken. The 'chicken-hearted' Pariset was warned and went into hiding.

Limoges was a centre of Gestapo activity. Although it had a reputation in the rest of France as 'une ville rouge' (a communist stronghold), according to Lieutenant Mayer the inhabitants were badly demoralised by the constant seizing of hostages and there was little apparent resistance in the town. Snap controls and police 'raffles' (round-ups) were daily occurrences. The day before the Mayer brothers had arrived, there had been a disastrous round-up in which some of the best Resistance people had been taken. By contrast, in the country districts around Limoges it was a different story and resistance was strong.

Paddy's aircraft took off from England on the evening of 22 March 1944. Weather conditions were bad, and the pilot asked her if she would like to turn back as it meant jumping in thick fog. She decided to go through with it, landing heavily on her back and for a moment thinking she had broken her neck and was dying. Then she lost consciousness. Later she would say it was the 2 million francs strapped to her back that broke her fall. She awoke with something breathing in her face, freezing until she realised it was a friendly cow. Then she heard voices which at first she thought were German, until someone swore in French. The voice said, 'I think the poor Anglais has broken his neck.' Evidently they were not expecting a girl and momentarily their astonishment seems to have been as great as that of Siegfried as he removes the breastplate to discover Brünhilde.

Paddy had jumped at 11.20 p.m., followed rapidly by twenty-two containers packed with arms that arrived with two cases of personal belongings and two wireless sets. The twenty Maquis, who until then had had no more than two revolvers between them, were delighted. One of them took the pick and shovel, which were standard issue to SOE parachutists, and went to bury the tell-tale parachute. Quickly Paddy was taken to a farmhouse to rest and have a meal. She slept for twenty hours.

SOE had provided her with two tailored suits with no means of identification on them. Even so, Paddy had decided they looked too English to be safe, and so wore a skirt and old sweater until she was able to acquire some cotton frocks locally.

Next she was taken to a village where she met Barthelemy, Major 'Teddy' Mayer, who was furious that London had sent him a girl. Reluctantly he took her to spend a night in a 'grange' owned by the cowardly Pariset. However, he was so terrified of being found out that the next day Mayer was forced to take her on to stay with three men who, she said, would willingly have sheltered her indefinitely. But after ten days she moved on to Argenton where Mayer rejoined her and set about teaching her to ride a bicycle. He later recalled:

I was horrified when I found out that she could not even ride a bicycle. It was absolutely necessary . . . as for reasons of security she had to move from place to place and the only way it could be done without attracting undue attention was by cycling . . . she had at first to move about in taxis with all its obvious dangers and inconveniences. We had to teach her how to ride a cycle on public thoroughfares and this in itself went against the rules of security, as it attracted undue attention to us. As she had no inborn sense of balance she had most of the time a bandaged limb and narrowly escaped several bad accidents. It is all to her credit that she persevered and finally managed to cycle some fifty kilometres a day in a hilly country.

Had Paddy not been able to cycle she would never have been able to carry out her duties as after D-Day taxis were not allowed to run. Mayer vented his feelings in his report:

I feel very strongly that no one should be sent out in the field, specially on such delicate and dangerous work, without proper training. This is especially true for women. Miss O'Sullivan spent six weeks in Scotland on demolition and weapon training. I suggest that this time could have been more profitably spent at a security and radio school, or simply learning to ride a cycle. The requirements for a radio operator are not that she should be able to shoot straight or even shoot at all, but that she should know how to use a W/T set properly. Her means of defence should be to know how to use her wits to baffle the Gestapo rather than to know how to shoot them . . .

Her knowledge even in such simple matters as setting up a pool aerial, making a pool earth connection or changing a fuse was very scanty. She had not been trained to be orderly and systematic in her work . . . In the beginning she was continually losing or running after bits of paper, tearing up messages that had either not been transmitted or communicated to me.

Paddy was to be known in the field as Micheline and her false documents were in the name of Micheline Marcelle Simonet. The cover story she had been given in London was that she was a 'dame de compagnie' of a doctor in Paris, helping the doctor in his surgery and looking after his children. She had been given a month's leave to look for a Belgian parent supposed to have been lost in the Creuse area. She had all the necessary papers to substantiate the story, including a letter from the doctor recommending her to another, non-existent doctor, asking him to give all possible help to find her parent. She also had an identity card, issued in Vichy and restamped in Paris. This was certainly one of F Section's stranger cover stories, particularly in view of the date limitation imposed by the month's holiday leave, but Paddy never had to use it. Instead she characteristically resorted to one of her own – that she was an ex-pupil and friend of the school-teacher's wife whom she had met in Alsace while teaching there. This allowed her to stay in the area without arousing suspicion.

Paddy was constantly on the move between different safe houses. The risks incurred by the French families who knowingly offered safe haven to SOE agents are vividly illustrated by her movements. Almost all the houses belonged to relations of schoolmaster Monsieur Maldant. She was constantly on the move between Maldant's house in Fresselines, his parents' farm at La Forest, a farm at Puylandon, St Dizier (where she lived in a farm belonging to Georges, Maldant's brother-in-law), and Genouillat, where the mayor of the village had found her a house, which she rented to carry out her work. She would stay in each place for no longer than a fortnight, her moves always directed by Mayer.

Paddy was isolated from the rest of the group for security reasons and was kept in touch principally by courier. At first Mayer used one of his own girls, Gilberte. He then recruited a friend of Pariset's, Marie Louise Thomas, who had been working in Limoges as a bank clerk. She lived in the same house as Paddy, who said Marie Louise was always willing to take messages, sometimes cycling up to 140 kilometres a day when there were urgent messages to be delivered. Another courier was Maldant's brother, who owned a farm and could only act as a courier every other day. When Marie Louise's journey was too long, someone would meet her and take the message on to Mayer. Paddy always knew where he was and the couriers would take the newly received messages directly to him. Post, telephone and telegrams were never used, not least because identity cards had to be produced to send a telegram or make a call. Mayer always sent his messages to Paddy *en clair*. Marie Louise hid them in the tube or even the tyres of her bicycle. The security-conscious Mayer lived on a farm; as there were always plenty of visitors on a farm, the daily arrival of a courier did not arouse suspicion.

It is a measure of the success of SOE in dropping supplies by this stage of the war that Paddy had seven W/T sets in different houses. While she was away the set would be buried; while she was staying in a house it would be hidden under a pile of sticks in the yard.

When she was sending or receiving there was always some-one on watch. In Argenton, Dicko, Mayer's brother, acted as her bodyguard. In Fresselines, the owner of the house would keep watch and latch the garden gate so that she could hear when anyone arrived. Paddy said she always 'worked in a very tight key' so her transmission was not audible outside the room where she was working. As an extra precaution her host left the wireless on in the next room. In La Forest she made her transmissions from a barn in which the grain was stored. The daughter of the house was primed to warn her of any danger – or an enemy approach – by bursting into song. In St Dizier she worked over a grocer's shop where the attendant would sing 'J'attendrai' if there was any danger.

Paddy was not troubled by the direction-finding vans, which were regularly sent out to search for illicit broadcasts, but whenever there was any suspicion of German activity around La Forest the fourteen-year-old son of the house would be sent out on his bicycle to bring back information on any car cruising around.

After a month of working with her Leo Marks 'silk', she found that she had memorised the combination of letters and was able to destroy it, so that when she was travelling the only potentially incriminating item she had to carry was the latest page from her one-time pad. This she concealed in the false bottom of a bag provided by London. Before each 'sked' or scheduled radio contact, she would learn by heart the contents of the messages intended for transmission. She made a point of never moving the wireless set herself.

She had attempted her first contact with London on her second day but although she could hear the other side plainly, she received no answer. The problem, she thought, lay with the aerials. It was only a fortnight later that she made her first contact and from then on she was able to keep in touch regularly. Just before D-Day she often had as many as seven 'skeds' a day. Rarely did she have to ask for messages to be repeated, although she did gather that London was having some difficulty with her coding.

The coding and decoding she did herself with the help of Marie Louise in the house where she was transmitting. The one part she found very difficult was decoding by candlelight. Her practice was to have four envelopes – two incoming and two outgoing – one of coded, the other of uncoded messages, neither of which she kept for more than twenty-four hours. Mayer would retain copies of all messages.

One of the first things Major Mayer did was to look round for a W/T operator to serve as a standby for Paddy. He knew she had just left hospital in London where she had been laid up with 'lung trouble'. During her whole stay in France, she was to suffer from some form of chronic or active form of bronchitis. He wrote: 'This, fortunately, never prevented her from carrying out her duties, but I naturally feared complications. We tried . . . three operators . . . It goes to the credit of Miss O'Sullivan that in spite of the great amount of traffic she had to handle she . . . found time to train these three W/T operators.'

Paddy's workload involved handling the signals of both the Fireman circuit and those of the attached Warder circuit, run by Mayer's brother Dicko, who operated with the *nom de guerre* Maurice. Dicko had been anxious to have his own W/T operator but never received one. He was also unable to find anyone reliable or discreet enough to carry out regular work as a courier and was obliged to do the work himself, cycling many miles a day with messages and instructions to and from his brother's headquarters. One of his friends would deputise on occasion and then the message would be kept as short as possible with compromising words in veiled language – although definitely not ciphered.

He also made use of live *boîtes aux lettres* as opposed to dead drops. A courier would leave a message at a certain address and this would be collected and taken on either to his brother or back to himself. The people whose houses were used in this way were members of the Resistance. Lieutenant

Mayer started off trying to train an instructor in each Maquis camp in demolition and sabotage work. However, he was not satisfied with the result and preferred to spend two or three days in each camp, doing the training. In this way, he said, he personally trained about 800 men.

The Germans in the Creuse area at this time were Wehrmacht with a few Feldengendarmerie or military police. By contrast the local French Gendarmerie were friendly and would often turn a blind eye to Resistance activities. Before D-Day there were few road blocks and even if the gendarmes spotted something wrong with papers, they would often be overlooked. After the Normandy landings, controls became much stricter, carried out by the hated Milice and the Wehrmacht. As luck would have it, Paddy came to a road block on the one and only occasion that she was carrying her wireless set with her, strapped to her bicycle in a suitcase. She showed her papers, which brought no comment from the Wehrmacht guard. Then he asked the dreaded question: what was in her suitcase? Clothes, she replied. The guard was just about to open it when a German lieutenant appeared and interrupted, saying, 'Ah Mademoiselle, vous rassemblez à une Fräulein.' Seizing the moment, she said that her mother was German (not true at all) but had died when she was a baby. For the next half-hour, he in German, she in a mixture of Flemish and German, chatted on. Using just the right degree of flirtatiousness she was able to extricate herself by agreeing to a date the next day. The suitcase was forgotten.

The second time that Paddy was stopped was hardly less alarming. This time it was the Milice, who searched the bag containing her coding sheet with great thoroughness. Fortunately, as there was only a single sheet in the false side, he could not feel it and let her pass.

A more unexpected threat came when she and a female colleague were stopped by the Maquis while cycling in the country and were ordered to give up their bicycles. They had not bargained on a hot-tempered redhead. Paddy flatly refused to give up her bicycle and rode on with her friend, leaving the astonished Maquis open-mouthed.

Another time she was travelling with Percy Mayer from Argenton to Limoges. When they changed trains at Brieves they noticed that a man who had also joined the train at Argenton was still with them. He asked them if they were going to Limoges and Mayer said yes. Arriving at the town, they thought they had lost him, only to find another man following them. Fortunately on this occasion the wireless had travelled separately.

The need to be constantly alert is evident from the case of a Belgian who told a colleague of Mayer's that he had been in the Intelligence Service and that his father was an Englishman. This man took a great interest in Paddy – although not in her feminine charms, she said – and was constantly badgering her with questions. Once he started to talk to her in English; she immediately countered by replying in a broken accent. Another time when he started to speak in German, she replied quite genuinely in her halting accent. In August 1944 the man approached Major Mayer, who was by now in uniform, asking to join the Maquis. He was firmly told it was too late.

Dicko Mayer explained how informers would eavesdrop on conversations in cafés and hotels. 'They were generally of the bourgeois class and very few informers were from the working class people. Women would be sent from Limoges to try and find out the location of maquis camps and the names of the group chiefs.' Informers would often write to the Gestapo; according to Paddy, these were practically all women. In one village the mayor collected all the letters from informants and after the Liberation the women all had their heads shaved.

On her return to England, Paddy was very frank about her lack of security training. But for Major Mayer, she said, she would have slipped up many times. For example, she was a very heavy smoker and few French girls smoked or, indeed, could afford the very high price of cigarettes. Smoking in a public place instantly aroused notice and Mayer warned her against it. It was not a total ban, which would have perhaps been more than the tempestuous Paddy could bear, but a strong caution.

Paddy came back to England on 5 October 1944 and a year later, on 4 September 1945, was awarded an MBE Civil. Colin Gubbins had recommended an MBE Military. A cryptic F Section note runs: 'Stenographer was sent to the Field with imperfect knowledge of the technical side of wireless operation and handicapped by chest trouble . . . her willingness to learn made it possible to maintain satisfactory communications with HQ for her first efforts resulted in mutilated telegrams . . . She transmitted 332 messages.'

Well before she received her medal, Paddy was in the news, rather to the annoyance of her masters. It began when an MP, Sir Archibald Sinclair, spoke out in praise of brave WAAF officers who parachuted into France before D-Day. The next week the *Sunday Express* carried an article by Squadron Leader William Simpson, DFC, naming Paddy as one of the girls. Soon after, an article appeared in the *Daily Mail* on 'Paddy the Rebel': 'A vivacious personality, good looks, calculated daring, and a knowledge of foreign languages made 25 year old Miss Maureen O'Sullivan, WAAF officer, one of the most valuable pre D-Day parachutists.' Interviewing her in her Irish home, the reporter heard the story of the German officer who said she looked like a fräulein and added colourfully, 'Until the invasion she crawled through hedges and ditches watching the movements of German troops.'

In June 1945 she was posted to Force 136 in Calcutta as a liaison officer with the French, presumably in connection with operations into the French colonies in South-East Asia. Here she began to attract still more attention and a full story appeared in the local press, headed 'WAAF parachutist works in Calcutta: lived seven months in enemy territory', written from Headquarters Air Command South-East Asia. 'A WAAF officer now working in Calcutta as Liaison Officer to the French wears . . . the ribbons of the MBE and the Croix-de-Guerre,' it ran. Memories of problems during her training, not to mention her difficulties with the bicycle, were forgotten. The first step 'was a test for intelligence and resource to discover if she was temperamentally suited for the job, and included tree climbing, tight rope walking, trials in foxing the enemy, and even picking pockets. She and another girl were then sent to a lonely island off the coast of Scotland, where they learnt to handle mortars, stens and Tommy guns, worked with demolition parties, and went on night exercises.' The French peasants who sheltered her, it said, had refused to take more than a nominal sum for her board, and of the 100,000 francs she had been given for her personal use she returned 85,000 to headquarters. 'Almost daily came news that one or another member of the resistance group had been captured or shot. Paddy . . . worked on, tapping out her messages, asking for vital stores and directives, and pouring intelligence into the waiting ears of London . . . Not content with her incredible adventures in France, she immediately went into training with the hopes of being allowed to jump in Germany, but, as she said "Monty beat me to it".'

A telling glimpse of life as it might have been is provided by one of Paddy's SOE friends, Mrs Wrench, who helped prepare departing F Section agents for France. She describes how one evening shortly before the end of the war she had Paddy and the two Mayer brothers to dinner. 'The two brothers were so impressed with my cooking that they proposed that Paddy and I should both come out to Tananarivo (Madagascar's Capital) when the war was over, I to run a restaurant, good ones in the island being non-existent, and Paddy to manage an adjacent flower shop.'

In the event the brothers never returned to Madagascar but joined a company run by an uncle in Durban. She continues:

'Paddy was one of those who went to Burma after France's liberation. There she met an English engineer [Walter Eric Alvey] whom she married. They returned to England and set up home in Boston where I visited them years later by which time they had two boys.' The marriage did not survive and Paddy 'was living, not too happily, in London. This was not the first time I had been confronted by the sad fact that those who shine in times of crisis are not always adept at managing their lives in normal circumstances.'

Chapter 9

VIOLETTE SZABO

She was really beautiful, dark-haired and olive-skinned with that kind of porcelain clarity of face and purity of bone that one finds occasionally in the women of south-west France.

Colonel Maurice Buckmaster in *Specially Employed*

Violette Szabo still generates more interest and more column inches than any other woman agent. The 1958 J. Arthur Rank film, *Carve her Name with Pride*, based on the book by R.J. Minney, is a classic, with Virginia McKenna providing a sensitive portrayal of Violette. Transforming the story into a film inevitably meant adjustments to achieve the desired cinematic drama, as well as the usual gun battles in which no one ever pauses to reload, but by the standards of some modern Hollywood war films it was a model of historical rectitude, with both Odette Sansom and Leslie Fernandez, one of Violette's SOE instructors, serving as technical advisers. More recently a museum has opened near Hereford devoted to Violette.

Quite early on some SOE stalwarts became annoyed about the fictions being written about Violette. M.R.D. Foot, in *SOE in France* (1966), savages the Minney biography for its clearly invented tale of how Violette was supposedly tortured and its spurious fly-on-the-wall dialogue between her and her torturer. Yet Violette's is a harrowing and inspiring story, and she made an immediate and often indelible impression on many who met her. She was extremely pretty, fun and full of high spirits.

Her daughter Tania, who was two years and seven months old when her mother was killed, fiercely keeps alive her memory. She heard much about Violette from her grandparents who brought her up, as well as from Violette's four brothers and numerous friends. To this can be added material in Violette's personal file on her training, capture and imprisonment, and gripping details in SOE archives about the operations in which Violette took part, providing the dramatic background to her two missions to France in 1944.

Tania recalls: 'Violette was born of a French mother and an English father in the British Military Hospital in Paris. She grew up in both countries, travelling back and forth. She was not in any way masculine but a tomboy in the traditional sense. Her father was an excellent shot, and used to stand her under a tree and shoot apples off her head. This greatly distressed my grandmother who would say, "How can he do such a thing?"'

A *Daily Graphic* article of 18 December 1946 quotes Violette's father, Mr Bushell: 'She was always the tomboy ready for excitement and adventure.' Mrs Bushell added: 'She was a crack shot before joining up. They wouldn't let her shoot at the fun fairs after the first few times because she always knocked the cigarette packets down.'

Bushell, once a welterweight champion in the army, was now a taxi driver. He liked to be his own boss and set up a succession of taxi services, in both England and France, sometimes driving important clients long distances to Switzerland and the mountains. 'My grandmother was a first-class milliner and had trained in the French theatre where she did wonderful gowns,' says Tania. 'My mother looked after her brothers, did the washing up, prepared their lunches for school.'

By her own wish, Violette left school aged fourteen. While her elder brother Roy enrolled as a pageboy at the Savoy Hotel, she went to work at Woolworth's. One day, without telling her parents, she took her passport and set off to France,

THE WOMEN WHO LIVED FOR DANGER

the first of a series of episodes in which she determinedly asserted her independence. But she returned and in December 1939 Violette was assistant no. 437 in the perfume department of the Bon Marché store in Brixton.

Tania says: 'After the Fall of France in 1940 the Free French arrived in London and began to hold parades. My grandmother thought how nice it would be if we could invite one of these boys home on Bastille Day and give him a real French meal.' Violette was dispatched and returned with a captain from the French Foreign Legion. Churchill's memorable Bastille Day broadcast impressed them all: 'I proclaim my faith that some of us will live to see a Fourteenth of July when a liberated France will once again rejoice in her greatness and her glory, and once again stand forward as the champion of the freedom and the rights of man.'

Étienne Szabo was indeed a character from *Beau Geste*, not tall, at five foot six, just three inches above Violette, but good-looking, lively and full of charm. He also had a certain likeness to her father. Born in 1910, Étienne was eleven years older than Violette. His mother had died when he was eleven; his father, a gendarme in Marseilles, four years later. The Szabos were Hungarian but his mother had been determined he should be born in France. Étienne had entered the Legion and had risen through the ranks during action in Algiers, Tunis and Morocco as well as in Syria and Indo-China. Already much decorated, he wore the Légion d'Honneur and the Médaille Militaire with both star and palm – the equivalent of a medal with two bars in Britain.

When war with Germany was declared, he had been sent in bitter winter to Narvik in northern Norway, where 1,000 legionnaires had fought alongside the Chasseurs Alpins, as well as soldiers of the Scots and Irish Guards and the Welsh Borderers. As the evacuation from Dunkirk began, the Legion was brought back from Narvik, landing on the Clyde on 13 June 1940. Étienne promptly volunteered for service with de

Gaulle's Free French and was sent to Liverpool for training. On Bastille Day – 14 July 1940 – he had come with a group of legionnaires to join thousands of Free French marching proudly along Whitehall, with their new emblem, the Cross of Lorraine, on their uniform. Tania recalls: 'The whole family fell in love with Étienne,' and after a suitably whirlwind wartime romance he and Violette were married at Aldershot on 21 August 1940. General Koenig, one of the few senior French officers to rally to de Gaulle, kissed both the bride and the groom, and reporters wrote up the story of the Free French soldier who had married an English girl.

After a honeymoon of just a few days at an Aldershot hotel, Étienne sailed with the Legion, travelling round the Cape to East Africa and sending cards from Durban and Eritrea, before they landed in Asmara and set off south to confront the Italians in Abyssinia. Then, in 1941, a telegram arrived from Liverpool to announce that he was back. Violette jumped on a train to Liverpool and during their brief happy reunion, Tania was conceived. Soon after, Étienne sailed again with the Legion, this time to North Africa. Tania was born in June 1942, just as Étienne was taking part in the first great French feat of arms in the war.

In an attempt to turn the British flank, Rommel had switched tanks from his Panzer division in the north to the south, to attack the Legion at Bir Hakeim. Rommel told the Italians that it should take 'only fifteen minutes' to crush them, but the legionnaires were well protected by minefields and had burrowed no fewer than 1,200 separate dugouts for men, guns and vehicles. Heroically, the Legion held out through fifteen days of nightmare bombardment, before General Koenig successfully evacuated 2,500 men under cover of darkness – having set back the German advance and given a big boost to Allied morale. 'Seldom in Africa was I given such a hard-fought struggle,' Rommel conceded later. The story is enthrallingly told by the Legion's only woman legionnaire, the English girl Susan Travers, in *Tomorrow to be Brave*.

Étienne heard the news of his daughter's birth soon after, but this time there was no prospect of the hoped-for leave. On 23 October the long-awaited battle of El Alamein began, and four days later Étienne died from his wounds.

The news of her husband's death filled Violette with a burning anger, a very physical desire to take up arms against her husband's killers. Some months after, she received a letter from an E. Potter, asking her to attend a meeting at Sanctuary Buildings in Westminster. Potter was the cover name for the thriller writer, Selwyn Jepson, who was one of SOE's principal recruiting agents. Jepson was looking for candidates who spoke fluent French and he had heard about Violette from the War Office.

Violette was sent for training at a series of SOE schools. At Winterfold in Surrey in August 1943, she was described as 'a quiet, physically tough self-willed girl of average intelligence. Out for excitement and adventure but not entirely frivolous. Has plenty of confidence in herself and gets on well with others. Plucky and persistent in her endeavours. Not easily rattled.'

The next month in Scotland, doubts emerged. 'I seriously wonder whether this student is suitable for our purpose. She seems lacking in a sense of responsibility and although she works well in the company of others, does not appear to have any initiative or ideals.' Two weeks later, the doubts continued.

For this member of the party one's feelings are bound to be mixed. Character difficult to describe: Pleasant personality, sociable, likeable, painstaking, anxious to please, keen, mature for her age in certain ways but in others very childish. She is very anxious to carry on with the training but I am afraid it is not with the idea of improving her knowledge but simply because she enjoys the course, the spirit of competition, the novelty of the thing and being very fit – the physical side of the training.

Given that Violette was just twenty-two and had left school aged fourteen, this might nonetheless seem a positive balance sheet. She also had concerns about Tania, raised in an SOE memo of 4 September 1943. 'She has a one year old child and is very anxious to know, at once, what pension arrangements would be made for her in the event of her going to the field . . . I am sure she feels unsettled about her training and future until this question has been dealt with.'

Worried though her instructor in Scotland was, he concluded: 'She has proved to possess certain qualities which I never would have suspected her to have, and for this reason I consider it advisable for her to carry on with the training.' In the final report of 8 October things once again looked black.

I have come to the conclusion that this student is temperamentally unsuitable for this work. I consider that owing to her *too* fatalistic outlook in life and particularly in her work, [and] the fact that she lacks the ruse, stability and the finesse which is required and that she is too easily influenced, when operating in the field she might endanger the lives of others working with her. It is very regrettable to have to come to such a decision . . . with a student of this type, who during the whole course, has set an example to the whole party by her cheerfulness and eagerness to please.

With Noor Inayat Khan we have Buckmaster's angry comments on such criticisms; with Violette we can only guess at his reaction, but he must have decided to proceed as Violette was sent on to Dunham House in Cheshire for parachute training at Ringway.

Here she had a nasty accident, spraining her ankle so badly that she was sent to Bournemouth to recuperate. There is a photograph of her in a bath chair (an early form of wheelchair) in Minney's book. Next she went to Beaulieu for the security course, and by February she was back at Ringway to complete her parachute training. The instructor reported on 25 February 1944: 'On her return she still seemed to be as nervous as she was on her first visit, but after making her first descent she gained confidence and carried out the remaining descents with verve . . . On all three descents, one from aircraft and one from balloon by day and one by night . . . her exits were good.'

It was at Ringway that Violette met Major Staunton, who figures so prominently in the film. Staunton was not the professional British officer he might seem. His real name was Philippe Liewer and he was a French journalist. He had originally been recruited in Nice on 20 September 1941 by SOE's Ukelele (Captain G. Langelaan); they had met there by chance through a friend. Staunton had also established contact with another SOE stalwart, Commandant Bégué (code name Noble), at Châteauroux. Then on 11 October 1941 he had been arrested at his home in Antibes by the Vichy police – his address had been found in Langelaan's notebook when Langelaan had been arrested shortly before.

Staunton was taken to Périgueux prison and then sent on to Mauzac, from which he and a group of other officers escaped after nine months, on 16 July 1942. On 28 August he set off across the Pyrenees, arriving in Barcelona just three days later and avoiding capture by Spanish border guards – the fate of so many who later used this route. Travelling via Lisbon, Staunton reached London in little more than two weeks on 17 September.

As Violette's departure for France neared, Buckmaster sent her to Leo Marks, the SOE codemaster, for a special briefing. Violette, Marks noted, was having problems with her poem code, which seemed to be a nursery rhyme in French 'based on Three Blind Mice'. After watching her encode a message, which came out as indecipherable, Marks noticed she was missing the S off the end of *trois*. When he pointed this out Violette was in despair. He explained to her, 'Some agents who were otherwise good coders often made spelling mistakes in their key-phrases, and we'd found that they weren't really happy with their poems, though they didn't always know why.'

Marks says he then wrote out a new poem, the one that was to be made famous by the film. There it was used in a very different context, as if written by Étienne and filling Violette's mind as she struggled to resist her Gestapo tormenters.

The poem reads:

> The life that I have
> Is all that I have
> And the life that I have
> Is yours.
>
> The love that I have
> Of the life that I have
> Is yours and yours and yours.
>
> A sleep I shall have
> A rest I shall have
> Yet death will be but a pause.
>
> For the peace of my years
> In the long green grass
> Will be yours and yours and yours.

Marks relates that he had written the haunting words on hearing of the death of the girl he loved in an air raid. 'Who wrote this?' Violette promptly asked him.

'I'll check up,' replied Marks, just a touch unconvincingly.

Buckmaster also gives a vivid picture of Violette in the days before her departure, in the slim volume, *Specially Employed*, which he wrote on agents in 1952. It is worth bearing in mind Buckmaster's tendency to embroider and switch details.

He had arrived at the Orchard Street flat used for briefing purposes to be told by Park, the janitor who 'marshalled the agents with the smoothness of a Jeeves', that Violette was nervous. Buckmaster felt sure, when he sat down, that 'it was not due to nerves, but to that wholly admirable tension of the mind and the senses which causes people to overcome fear and hardship when there is a tough job to do'. He took her through her cover story, that she was Madame Villeret, the widow of an antiques dealer of Nantes whose shop had been destroyed by a bomb, giving her no love of the Allies. He watched in admiration as she acted out the part. 'The creature of our imagination had come to life in Violette's vivacious personality.' He showed her on the large-scale Michelin map the exact area where the drop was to take place. 'She carefully memorized the geographical features of the area, traced the path she would follow through the wood to the side-road which led to the farm cottages where she would spend the rest of the night and the whole of the next day'. The day after D plus two she was to walk to the cross roads, take the bus for Poitiers and go to a house where she was to ask for a Madame B 'de la part de Annie'. When the lady appeared, Violette was to give her password to which the reply would be: 'Vous voulez dire Annie de Bretagne' – a strangely jovial reference to the Duchesse Anne who married the French King Louis XII.

Buckmaster next told her of a warning signal – an empty canary cage hanging in the window. If Violette saw this, she was to walk straight past the house to the little bistro at the corner where she was to sit as near the door as she could and put her gloves on the table with a railway timetable. Buckmaster produced this with a flourish, saying: 'Yes, it's an up-to-date one, it was brought back last week on an operation.'

Her mission, said Buckmaster, was to go to Le Havre and circumspectly find if the circuit was 'brûlé'. 'I handed her a town map of Le Havre. I warned her that the bombing . . . might make recognition of the streets difficult.' Violette, he said, seemed to tuck the facts away carefully in a capacious memory and be able to produce them immediately, spontaneously.

As portrayed in the film, Violette's mission seems a desultory one, double-checking what, alas, was all too evident – that there had been numerous arrests in Rouen and Le Havre, and that Staunton's Salesman circuit was beyond rebuilding.

The real situation was both more complicated and more positive. After arriving in England, Staunton had received the usual SOE training and was sent to Rouen to build up a Resistance circuit. Despite the heavy presence of Germans he was able to initiate two circuits, which rapidly grew to impressive size. His initial contact was a Madame Micheline who had a dress shop in Paris with a branch in Rouen. Through her doughty Rouen manager, Jean Sueur, Staunton started to build up the organisation. He found lodgings in a small flat within a large block of ninety-six apartments with the Francheterre family until 5 February 1944.

In July 1943 he received a radio operator, Captain Isidore Newman (Pepe, Pierre), who was given shelter by a dressmaker, Madame Desvaux, under cover of being her nephew and assistant. Newman rapidly found several widely scattered houses from which he could transmit – one was a sixty-kilometre bicycle ride from Rouen. He was to send fifty-four messages before his arrest in March 1944. (He was executed at Mauthausen on 6 September 1944.)

On 23 August 1943 the circuit was joined by Lieutenant Robert Maloubier, who came to act as arms instructor. By virtue of his forceful personality, he was soon leading a series of attacks on industrial establishments that were working for the Germans. During one of these he was badly wounded. By this time, Staunton had formed a group of eighty men in

Rouen under Claude Malraux, brother of the famous writer André Malraux, and forty in Le Havre under Roger Mayer.

The next month they brought off a spectacular coup, the destruction of a German minesweeper of 850–900 tons, equipped with three pom-pom guns, two four-barrelled M-guns and a bigger gun for action at sea.

Staunton describes the incident in his report to SOE: 'It had been attacked, probably by Typhoons . . . and had been brought up to the yards of the Ateliers et Chantiers de Normandie, near Rouen.' After a thorough overhaul it was ready for trials in early September. These went well, champagne flowed and a handsome cheque for 5 million francs was handed over to the shipyard for the work. The ship was loaded with ammunition and supplies waiting on the quayside, sufficient for three months at sea, as well as Asdic equipment worth 12 million francs. It was due to sail the next morning at 4 a.m. The quayside was guarded by German sentries but, at five o'clock the evening before, Hugues Pacaud and two other members of the Salesman circuit succeeded in getting aboard under the pretext of carrying out a last-minute adjustment. Pacaud placed a 1.5-kilo plastic charge low on the inside of the hull. Staunton had made up the charge himself and fitted it with two six-hour 'time pencils.' As his report stated:

At 11 pm the charge exploded, making a very satisfactory hole, later ascertained to be 5 feet by 3 feet [1.5 metres x 0.9 metre], and the ship sank in six minutes . . .

The Gestapo arrived at 7 o'clock in the morning and very quickly decided that the charge had been placed internally. They found out that thirteen men had access to the ship and asked that each of these men be pointed out to them on arrival. Their method of questioning was ingenious. As each man arrived, they took him kindly but firmly by the arm and said, 'My poor friend, you forgot to press the pencils.' Achieving nothing by this method, however, they assembled the thirteen and told them that they would all be shot unless the man responsible confessed. In the meantime, the German Admiralty had acted. Hating the Gestapo quite as much as the Army does, they brought in their own experts, two of whom entered the water at 2 pm and pronounced that, by the size and characteristics of the hole, the charge could only have been an external one!

Baffled, the Gestapo were forced to release the thirteen workmen, and the sentry who had been on duty on the quay was arrested instead. Rather more unfortunate was the lot of the crew. On learning that their ship had no prospect of sailing, they visibly expressed their delight, only either to be shot with the unfortunate sentry or sent to the Russian front. The best part was that, for the moment, Staunton's circuit remained intact.

By February 1944, it was nonetheless becoming perilously large, with 150 men in Rouen and 200 in Le Havre. Staunton was recalled to England for talks. On 5 February he was flown back from a landing ground near Angers accompanied by the injured Maloubier. They brought with them vital information on the new V-weapons.

Immediately after his departure, mass arrests began, but not prompted by the explosion on the ship as is usually suggested. The leader of the Serquigny group had been arrested, probably for black market operations. Under pressure he may have given away names. Claude Malraux, Staunton's second-in-command, was arrested about 25 February. Then it was the turn of Roger Mayer, head of the Le Havre group, who was arrested and practically beaten to death by the Gestapo but he gave away nothing. He had derailed a German troop train and blown up the main lathes in a factory working on U-boat components. He had also been instrumental in burning German stocks of flax and oats. When he returned from Germany after the war, in appalling health, he was awarded the Military Cross. The radio operator, Newman, was arrested, as well as the landlady who had sheltered him for eight months, although thankfully she was released soon after. In all, ninety-eight members of the Rouen and Le Havre circuits were rounded up by the Gestapo and transported via Compiègne to Germany. But it was not the total disaster portrayed in the film. The separate circuits that Staunton had formed to go into action on D-Day were intact.

Nor was it persistent foggy weather that delayed Staunton's and Violette's return to France, as Buckmaster related, but a cable that arrived at the last minute on 12 March 1944:

FOLLOWING NEWS FROM ROUEN STOP CLAUDE MALRAUX DISAP-
PEARED BELIEVED ARRESTED STOP IF CLEMENT [Staunton] STILL
WITH YOU DO NOT SEND HIM STOP DOCTOR ARRESTED STOP
EIGHTEEN TONS ARMS REMOVED BY POLICE STOP BELIEVE THIS
DUE ARRESTATION OF A SECTION CHIEF WHO GAVE ADDRESSES
ADIEU

Staunton and Violette flew out on the night of 5/6 April in a double Lysander operation. The two pilots, Flight Lieutenant Taylor and Flight Lieutenant Whittaker, took off from Tempsford, returning to Tangmere on the coast, thus reducing the length of the journey to within the Lysander's range. Staunton and Violette landed not in Normandy but on a field 1.5 kilometres east-north-east of Azay-le-Rideau. One of the other passengers was Frager, who appears in the story of Peggy Knight.

They made their way to Paris. Violette had to proceed to Rouen on her own as Staunton was now known to the Germans and there were posters calling for his arrest. While there, Violette was able to do important work, attending to the wants of the families of the agents who had been rounded up by the Germans. Returning by Lysander to Tempsford on 30 April, Violette and Staunton brought back valuable details about the German Naval HQ in Rouen and German port installations at Le Havre. Violette brought back her fake identity card in the name of Corinne Reine Leroy, of which photographs survive. Shortly after, an internal F Section memo of 4 May 1944 states that Violette has 'just returned from an important mission in the field which she has performed admirably. It is desired to recognize this before she goes out again by commissioning her as an Ensign in the FANY.' This was approved on 24 May 1944.

Before she left Paris, Violette had walked boldly into Molyneux, the well-known couturier in the rue Royale, and had bought herself some clothes. Minney saw the bill, dated 28 April 1944. It was made out to Mademoiselle C. Leroy and itemises a dress of black crêpe de Chine with a lace neckline, costing 8,500 francs. Another dress 'en écossaise' was in red tartan or plaid. The third was of silk print. There is no record of anyone in SOE questioning these enterprising, and morale-boosting, items of expenditure – although there is of her wearing the dresses on her return. Mrs Wrench, who helped prepare agents for France, wrote: 'I had an extremely soft spot for Violette Szabo, a delightful and extremely beautiful young woman who, one day, brought to the Office her . . . little daughter who conjured up a picture of the prettiest doll in a toyshop. When Violette returned from her first Mission she was wearing a beautiful dress and told me that she bought it from one of the renowned couturiers in Paris – the first lovely dress she had ever possessed.'

The afternoon of 5 June found Violette at Hasell's Hall in Bedfordshire, a handsome red-brick Georgian country house belonging to the Pym family and set in a beautiful landscape park laid out by Humphry Repton. She was laughing and piecing jigsaws together with a 22-year-old SAS officer, John Tonkin, who had already fought in North Africa and Italy, and who made a remarkable escape from German hands to rejoin his regiment. Now he was to be parachuted into France to prepare a landing ground for forty men who would follow and attack German communications from a base south of Poitiers.

Hasell's, he wrote later to his mother,

was the 'last resting place' for all agents to enemy countries. We were very well looked after by ATS. The only operational people there were Richard and I and the Jedburgh team for Operation Bulbasket, two of our officers for Houndsworth, two for Titanic, and four agents, of whom two were surprisingly beautiful girls. We had checked and rechecked everything and packed our enormous rucksacks about fifty times. Finally, there was nothing more to do, so we spent the time very profitably with the girls, doing jigsaw puzzles.

The wait had been prolonged by a day, after the Normandy invasion had been postponed for twenty-four hours due to bad weather. Violette set off for the aerodrome at Tempsford on the evening of 7 June. Her accompanying officer was Vera Atkins, who said: 'I have never seen her look more beautiful. She had on a pair of white marguerite earrings which she had bought in Paris.' This time Staunton and Violette were flown in an American B-24 Liberator. With them jumped Robert Maloubier (Paco), who had served with Staunton in Normandy, and the American W/T operator, Jean-Claude Guiet.

Staunton's mission was to intensify resistance in the Haute-Vienne. This had been part of the large Stationer circuit built up by Maurice Southgate. Following Southgate's arrest on 1 May 1944, the northern part of his circuit had been divided into two; one part had been taken over by his capable courier, Pearl Witherington, and the other by the courageous young Mauritian, Amédée Maingard, with Staunton arriving to take command of the South.

Staunton was appalled by the situation he found.

When I left London I was given to understand that I would find on arrival a very well organised Maquis, strictly devoid of any political intrigues, which would constitute a very good base for extending a circuit throughout the area.

On arrival I did find a Maquis, which was roughly 600 strong, plus 200 gendarmes who had joined up on D-Day; but most of these men were strictly not trained, and commanded by the most incapable people I have ever met; also almost decided not to fight, as was overwhelmingly proved by the fact that: primo, none of the D-Day targets had been attended to; secundo: the following three weeks it each time took me several hours' discussions to get a small team out, either to the railway or the telephone lines.

The chief of this Maquis, Staunton continued scornfully, was 'by trade a saxophonist in a Bal Musette, and a *soldat 2ème classe*, with no war experience'. He called himself Major Charles. Later, Staunton was to do rather better with the local communist leader Georges Guingouin, who after some initial argument 'never failed to execute immediately all orders from London, as well as to attend to all targets'.

Meanwhile, it was Violette's ill luck to cross the path of the notorious SS Panzer division Das Reich as it was making its much-delayed push to the Normandy front, a journey that should have taken three days. Thanks to constant harrying, ambushes and guerrilla attacks, it was to take seventeen days, so depleting and enraging the battle-hardened division that it would commit numerous atrocities at virtually every stage of the advance. Their climax was the horrific massacre of an entire village of 642 men, women and children at Oradour-sur-Glane. The story is told in revealing detail in Max Hastings' book, *Das Reich: the March of the 2nd SS Panzer Division through France, June 1944.*

On 9 June, the night before Violette was to set off on her fateful journey, one of the stars of the division, Major

Kämpfe, was hurrying back in his open Talbot to headquarters at Limoges. Kämpfe was a 34-year-old former printer and Wehrmacht officer who had transferred to the SS in 1939. Tall, strong and a keen athlete, this Nazi ideal of German manhood had fought fiercely in Russia, winning the Knight's Cross.

At dusk, as his car approached a junction in the hamlet of La Bussière, twenty kilometres (fifteen miles) before Limoges, he saw a lorry approaching and flashed his lights in greeting before drawing to a halt. Far from being a German lorry as he thought, it proved to be full of *résistants*, returning to their camp after blowing up a bridge at Brignac. They were travelling by minor roads and were cautiously crossing the main D941 when they chanced upon Kämpfe. Accounts differ as to whether Kämpfe was alone, had a driver, or was escorted by outriders who had sped ahead. The Maquis was led by Sergeant Jean Canou, a miner from the nearby town of St Leonard, head of a group of FTP, the Francs-Tireurs et Partisans. These communist *résistants* took their title as freeshooters from the roving bands of French guerrillas who harassed the Prussian lines of communication during the war of 1870.

Canou, aware of his splendid catch, hustled Kämpfe in the lorry but had to leave the Talbot behind, as the only one of them who could drive was already at the wheel of the truck. Canou and his men turned up a narrow dirt road towards their camp at Cheissoux. Later they were to testify that they handed Kämpfe over to another Maquis and never saw him again. What happened next is unclear; all that is certain is that Kämpfe was at some stage killed by the Maquis.

Meanwhile Dr Muller, the battalion doctor, found Kämpfe's car with the engine running and doors open, a Schmeisser without a magazine lying beneath it, but no signs of blood or fighting. The SS were incensed. All night they swept the area, roaring up tracks to farms and woods. Two farmers from the hamlet of La Bussière, Pierre Mon Just and Pierre Malaguise, both in their forties and the fathers of five children, were shot beside the road and left in the ditch when they failed to provide any useful information.

Every available man of the Panzergrenadier brigade was combing the Limousin on the morning of 10 June for any trace of Major Kämpfe. Shortly after 10 a.m. at the village of Salon-la-Tour, some thirty kilometres south of Limoges, soldiers, probably from the first battalion of the Deutschland regiment, were approaching the village.

It was here that Violette was to cross their path. That morning, 10 June, the third morning after their arrival in France, Staunton sent Violette out with the young Jacques Dufour (Anastasie) on a mission to Jacques Poirier (Nestor). Poirier was a very brave young man, aged just twenty-two, who had taken over the Author and Digger circuits in the Corrèze and Dordogne after the leader, Harry Peulevé, had been arrested in March. Peulevé had reported having 2,500 men under his control, two-thirds in the Maquis and the remainder in the FTP.

Poirier was himself extremely vulnerable as the Gestapo had both his name and his photograph. But, by May, he had rebuilt his circuit with new groupings. He also worked with André Malraux, the brother of the Claude whose arrest had delayed Violette's first mission. By May, Poirier had marshalled some 10,000 men of all political groupings in the Dordogne, Corrèze and the Lot.

There have been many descriptions of Violette's capture and Dufour's escape. In the film he is shown as swimming across a river in a hail of bullets. Minney relates: 'Many Germans were seen to fall when they closed in on her, for they presented a wide semicircle which she raked with her gun. But no one can tell the exact number, as the entire village remained behind closed doors for the rest of the day. No bodies were found. The Germans were not likely to leave their dead and wounded on the fields.'

Staunton's own report, made on 12 October 1944 and covering his whole mission, makes rather brief mention of Violette. At the top of his recommendations for awards, it reads:

Highest possible decorations for holders of British commissions for: Mrs Zabo [*sic*], my courier. On 10th June, at 11 a.m. she came [up] against a German road block near Salon-la-Tour (Corrèze). She was riding in a car driven by Anastasie [Dufour]. With great coolness and gallantry she fought it out for 20 minutes with her Sten Gun, covering Anastasie while he was retreating, and being covered by him while she was retreating through fields. She only surrendered being completely exhausted and short of ammunition, and she is believed to have killed one German.

On Violette's file is a much fuller report by Staunton, dated 6 October 1946, vividly describing the odds Violette faced. 'On the morning of June 10th 1944, I sent out Szabo on a liaison mission to contact Nestor and to prepare a meeting between him and I [*sic*], as per instructions from my briefing in London.' As the distance was over 150 kilometres Staunton 'accepted Dufour's suggestion to drive her, with her bicycle in the car, as far as safety allowed, through Maquis controlled country . . . I saw them both off, made sure Dufour's Martin GMG [Gatling machine-gun] was in working order, and handed Szabo a Sten-gun, loaded with two magazines for her, as she specifically insisted on carrying a weapon for the car journey.'

The next part of the story is told in Dufour's words, as Staunton recollected them from the account Dufour had given him. Dufour began: 'We stopped at the first village on our way, namely La Croisille, to collect my friend Barriaud, who could thus keep me company on the way back, later. Barriaud climbed in the rear seat and I drove on, Szabo sitting beside me in front.'

He continues:

Nearing the village of Salon, we came, after a bend in the road, to a T-junction. At a distance of fifty yards [forty-five metres], I saw we were coming to a road block manned by German soldiers who waved me to stop. I instantly put out my arm and waved back, slowed down, and warned Szabo to get prepared to jump out and run. I stopped at thirty yards distance from the road block, jumped flat on the road surface by the car, and started shooting – I noticed Barriaud, who was unarmed, running away, but found out that Szabo had taken up a similar position to mine on the other side of the car, and was firing too.

By that time, though one of the three Germans had been hit, the other two were spraying us generously. I ordered Szabo to retreat through a wheat field, towards a wood four hundred yards away, under cover of my fire. As soon as she had reached the high wheat, she resumed firing and I took advantage of it to fall back. At first, the going was good, as we walked, bending so as not to show our heads over the top of the wheat, but soon we heard the rumble of armoured cars, and machine guns began spraying close to us, as they could follow our progress by the movement of the wheat. So we had to continue our progress towards the wood crawling flat and cautiously on the ground, an exhausting and awfully slow process. Then we heard the infantry running up the road and entering the wheat field while other armoured cars went driving around it. So we had to resume firing each in turn to cover the other's progress, to keep the infantrymen from running up to us. When we weren't more than thirty yards [twenty-seven metres] from the edge of the wood, Szabo, who, by then had [her] clothes all ripped to ribbons and was bleeding from numerous scratches all over her legs, told me she was exhausted and could not go one inch further. She insisted she wanted me to try and get away, that there was no point in my staying with her. So I went on while she kept on firing from time to time and managed to hide under a haystack in the courtyard of a small farm. Last I know was that, half an hour later, Szabo was brought to that very farm by Germans; I heard them questioning her as to my whereabouts, and heard her answering, laughing, 'You can run after him, he is far away by now.'

Staunton appended another statement from Barriaud who 'walked fifteen miles to come and give me warning, so that the local maquis could try and do something about freeing Szabo and Dufour. The only thing he was positive about, was that he had heard firing going on for over half an hour while he was escaping through the woods.' Violette had only two magazines for her Sten, each containing just thirty-two rounds, quite a few of which must have been spent even before she reached the wheat field. In making her ammunition last so long when faced with hopeless odds, Violette showed the courage and calculation of a true professional.

The Germans took Violette to Limoges, to the prison on the Place du Champs de Foire (now the Place Winston Churchill). Here she was interrogated by Major Kowatsch, assisted by the divisional interpreter, Dr Wache. The previous day, Kowatsch had presided over the gruesome mass hanging of ninety-nine hostages in the town of Tulle. The men, workers in the German-run arms factory, were killed in reprisal for a Maquis attack that had left forty German soldiers dead, their bodies badly mutilated and therefore an outrage to the Germans. Although only two of the four hundred hostages that they continued to hold were in fact *maquisards*, this was hardly an issue. Kowatsch, a big man of about thirty, had been in the police force before joining the SS. Contemptuously, he told the local Prefect that he was being merciful by not burning the town too. But the hangings only stopped when the Germans ran out of rope. When the bodies were cut down from the lamp-posts that had been used as gallows, Kowatsch was only dissuaded from throwing them into the river by French officials, who convinced him they might also be a health hazard to the German garrison. Instead, they were thrown on the town rubbish dump on the Brive road and were later buried there.

In a subsequent statement, traced by Max Hastings, Dr Wache the interpreter claimed that Violette 'was treated with great politeness and supplied with clean clothes. She was then passed to the SD in Limoges. I know nothing further of the treatment of this agent.'

Staunton now prepared a plan to spring Violette from the prison in Limoges on 16 June, but before the attempt could be made she was taken by road to the prison at Fresnes outside Paris, where so many SOE agents were held, including Alix d'Unienville. Here she shared cell 435 on the fourth floor with Madame G. Meunier, who wrote on 11 September 1947 to the Air Ministry with details of their imprisonment. She describes Violette as 'Very slim – Very dark hair and eyes – Gipsy type, very good looking. While in jail at Fresnes, had her hair parted, and she wore it in a plain long style.'

Madame Meunier relays a disconcerting story, suggesting that Violette's captors already had details of her mission and of others held with her. The Germans, she said, knew Violette's real name.

This fact made Violette think that the full information concerning the *parachutage* had been given to the Germans, with perfect and precise knowledge of the names, date of birth, place, date of the *parachutage*, and of the duty to be fulfilled. Young Violette, all these evidences being given to her, had to admit that she was in fact Violette Szabo, and not Louise X . . . Having been brought to Paris, avenue Foch [the SD headquarters], she was given a suit-case containing some effects, as her personal belongings had been stolen while she was in the country. However, when she arrived in the Fresnes jail, she was wearing the same dress as when she left London; a new one, in crêpe de chine, with blue and white flowers. Her shoes were of blue leather, wedge heel type . . . She was also wearing a shirt in black crêpe georgette, with yellow lace, this being one of her personal belongings.

Violette, she said, used to repeat: 'I know who has denounced us. He is a member of the French Section, he is at the moment in London, and he is the one who told the Germans about our real identity.' The immediate conclusion is that she was referring to Henri Déricourt, SOE's air movements officer, who had been ordered to return to London in February 1944 under suspicion of betraying SOE's Prosper network to the SD. An SOE tribunal found his treachery 'not proven'. When he returned to France after the war, he was again tried and again found not guilty, but it is now clear that he did indeed betray some of his colleagues. However, Déricourt was concerned with Lysander and Hudson landings rather than parachute drops, which were set up directly with individual circuits. In any case he must have been stood down from involvement with air operations, after he was recalled to London, although Buckmaster and others continued strongly to believe in his innocence. An alternative is that the names were provided, wittingly or otherwise, by a source in France. The SD was also expert at using their knowledge of SOE to sow doubts in the minds of captured agents.

Just over eight weeks after her capture, on 8 August, Violette was brought out into the prison yard for transport to Germany. Here she briefly saw the SOE agent Harry Peulevé, whom she had known in London. They were taken to the Gare de l'Est and put on a train. The prisoners were all packed into one coach; the other carriages were filled with German wounded. The girls, now chained in pairs by their ankles, were put in one compartment; the men, also in chains, in two barred compartments nearby. Guards patrolled the corridor outside.

On this train was another of SOE's greatest agents, 'Tommy' Yeo-Thomas, known as the White Rabbit, who was later to escape from Buchenwald. Before the war he had been a director of Molyneux in Paris – where Violette had bought her dresses. But such things were far from the minds of the prisoners as the train inched towards Germany. Twenty-two hours later, as they neared Châlons-sur-Marne, just eighty kilometres from Paris, two British planes began to strafe the train. The German guards leapt out to take cover, leaving their prisoners behind. In the confined compartments where the men were held, there was panic. Yeo-Thomas wrote: 'We all felt deeply ashamed when we saw Violette Szabo, while the raid was still on, come crawling towards us with a jug of water she had filled from the lavatory. She handed it to us through the iron bars. With her crawling, too, came the girl to whose ankle she was chained ... Through the din they shouted words of encouragement to us, and seemed quite unperturbed.'

The raid successfully disabled the train. After a very long wait the Germans, as determined as ever to take their prisoners back to Germany, commandeered two farm trucks, which ferried them to Metz where the prisoners spent the night in stables attached to the barracks. Here Violette was able to talk to Peulevé. Maurice Southgate, Pearl Witherington's organiser, had also been on the train.

From Metz they were taken to Strasbourg and then to Saarbrücken, from whence the women began their journey to Ravensbrück, where they arrived in the last week of August 1944. This was not an extermination camp equipped with gas chambers but a vast women's camp. Its inmates were, as a matter of deliberate SS policy, worked to death, dying as a result of exhaustion, malnutrition, indiscriminate brutality and lack of medical care – or were executed, mostly by hanging.

Survivors from Ravensbrück provide a few tantalising glimpses of Violette. Hortense Daman, who arrived a few days later, saw her there in Block 7. Marie Lecomte told her daughter Tania after the war that Violette endured the entire term of her imprisonment in the thin blue dress she was wearing when captured. 'She had no warm clothing at all.'

Violette was sent out on a working party with two other SOE agents, Denise Bloch and Lilian Rolfe, to a dependent camp at Torgau, where fitter prisoners went to work in local factories or on farms and roads, and where the food was marginally better. Returning to Ravensbrück, they heard of a second working party, which they joined, only to find the conditions there atrocious. As bitter winter descended they were made to labour outdoors, without any warm clothing, on clearing a site for the construction of a new airfield at Königsberg. It was exhausting work, lifting heavy weights, hewing out tree stumps, dragging boulders, digging in ice-cold water. Pneumonia, dysentery and tuberculosis took a steady toll, while others broke down from cold, exhaustion or random beatings. By the time they returned to Ravensbrück only Violette's stamina and determination kept the other two going at all.

A letter from Madame Solange Rousseau, dated 25 October 1945, reads: 'I knew Violette very well, we worked together in the forest of Könisberg s/oder ... I loved Violette very much, she always had so much pluck. She had changed little, her health was still good, much better than that of her companions.'

Vera Atkins, Buckmaster's assistant, obtained further details after the war.

Lilian [Rolfe] was befriended by Renée Corjon. Her health was failing and she spent some time in hospital. She was in hospital at the time of her recall to Ravensbrück. According to Mme Corjon, Lilian was warned at 10 pm on the night of the 20th Jan 1945 to be ready for departure at 5am the next morning ... As they were specially recalled to Ravensbrück there was some speculation as to the motive. The girls were hopeful that they might be repatriated via Sweden or Switzerland. When they arrived back at Ravensbrück they were put into the punishment block which meant they could not see or be seen by any of their former friends. However, an internee working as a policewoman in the Strafeblock (Mrs Julia Barry of Joyce Grove, Nettlebed, near Henley) saw them and helped with food and clothing. All three were in a pitiful state and Lilian [was] too weak to walk. After three or four days they were moved to the bunker (a block of cells).

Precise details of Violette's execution were obtained by Vera Atkins in a sworn statement from Obersturmführer Johann Schwarzhuber, the SS camp overseer of Ravensbrück.

I declare that I had delivered to me towards the end of January 1945 an order from the German Secret Police countersigned by the Camp Commandant Suhren instructing me to ascertain the location of the following persons: Lilian Rolfe, Danielle Williams [Denise Bloch] and Violette Szabo. These were at that time in the dependent camp of Königsberg on the Oder and were recalled by me ... One evening they were called out and taken to the courtyard by the crematorium. Camp Commandant Suhren made these arrangements. He read out the order for their shooting ... I was myself present. The shooting was done only by Schult with a small caliber gun through the back of the neck. They were brought forward singly by Cpl Schenk. Death was certified by Dr Trommer. The corpses were removed singly by internees who were employed in the crematorium and burnt. The clothes were burnt with the bodies ...

All three women were very brave and I was deeply moved. Suhren was also impressed by the bearing of these women. He was annoyed that the Gestapo did not themselves carry out these shootings.

Alas, there is a fraction of doubt as to whether even this grim, clinical account is wholly true or has just been provided in the all-too-familiar way to show that camp officials were only obeying orders from above. Mary Lindell, an escape line organiser who survived the hell of Ravensbrück, believed the three girls were simply hanged like the other unfortunates. Their clothes, she said, were handed in to the clothes store unsoiled and were not burnt as Schwarzhuber declared.

What is not in doubt is that, as with all the other SOE men and women killed in German concentration camps, the orders came directly from Berlin where, even as their thousand-year Reich collapsed around them, the SS still found time to send out execution orders for every single agent they could trace.

Chapter 10

MARGUERITE 'PEGGY' KNIGHT

Young girl of an altogether exceptional courage and good sense and very marked intelligence. She has rendered services of a remarkable nature without regard to the risks she ran. Courageous in front of the enemy she has shown a completely unexpected military sense and has been an inspiration to her comrades.

Colonel Maurice Buckmaster, 19 June 1945

In 1947, Marguerite 'Peggy' Knight was one of a group of 100 British service men and women, including the famous Group Captain Douglas Bader, who received decorations for bravery from the French ambassador in London. Less than three years before, at the age of twenty-four, she was working in a London office. So urgent was SOE's need for fluent French-speaking couriers in the weeks before D-Day that she was parachuted into France on the night of 6 May 1944, well before she had completed the usual exacting training.

Dropped to the wrong ground, where the head of the reception committee had the far from reassuring name of Breakneck (Casse-Cou), she was placed under the double agent, Roger Bardet. Amidst the constant feuding between members of the Donkeyman circuit, it was almost impossible for her to know whom to trust. During her time with the circuit, three of her colleagues would be shot as traitors; another would be the subject of a bungled assassination attempt by two comrades; and her circuit organiser would be betrayed.

Donkeyman had been born of the Carte circuit in which many of the early hopes of SOE had been placed. Carte was formed by André Girard, a painter who claimed to have good contacts among senior Vichy officers, and it appeared to have the makings of a military organisation, with potential members running into many hundreds. These hopes were dashed when a courier, André Marsac, fell asleep on the Marseilles–Paris train in November 1942. When he awoke his briefcase was missing; in it were over two hundred names, addresses and telephone numbers, complete with personal details and descriptions of the work the recruits could do, not even in code. They had been taken by a German Abwehr agent.

By December 1942 a furious quarrel was raging between Girard and his lieutenant, Henri Frager. Both demanded to go to London to put their case as to how the circuit should be run. Girard, who arrived first in late February 1943, did not make a good impression and SOE's Peter Churchill sided with Frager. SOE then decided to split Carte into smaller circuits. Girard, further shattered by news of the arrest of his wife and two of his daughters, eventually went to the USA, where his sense of security is illustrated by the lectures he gave to New England matrons, describing every detail of organising a network.

Frager was now placed in charge of the large new Donkeyman circuit, centred on Auxerre in Burgundy but with a remit that extended to Normandy and Nancy.

Marsac was the first to be arrested, shortly after Frager's departure to London. The notorious Sergeant Bleicher, posing as 'Colonel Henri', a German officer sympathetic to the Allied cause, persuaded Marsac to give him a note addressed to circuit members in Annecy. This led Bleicher to a hotel at St Jorioz where he arrested Odette Sansom and Peter Churchill. Bleicher was able to worm his way into the confidence of Frager's deputy, Roger Bardet.

Bardet himself should have come under suspicion, if only because he had been arrested on successive occasions by the

Germans and in each case was promptly released. He was also a frequent visitor to Bleicher's flat. Bardet later set out to implicate Frager in this double game but the evidence suggests that Frager, although gullible and impetuous, was completely loyal to the cause.

This was the situation into which young Peggy Knight was thrust. She was born in Paris on 19 April 1920 to a British father, Captain Alfred Rex Knight, and a Polish mother, Charlotte Beatrice Mary Ditkowski. She was given one French and two English first names – Marguerite Diana Frances. Nothing appears to be recorded of her education but she evidently grew up bilingual in English and French. By 1944 she was living in the East End of London at 88 James Lane, Leyton, and was working as a shorthand-typist for Asea Electric in Walthamstow. Without question it was her fluent French that attracted SOE.

The official record shows that she came to SOE's notice in March 1944, attended a Students' Assessment Board at Wanborough on 11 April, and was dispatched to the field less than a month later on the night of 6 May, which was almost certainly a record. The alias under which she was to be known was Nicole – her operational name, used in some of the documents, was Kennelmaid. Her story is told in her own words in two interrogations carried out after her return to England.

The initial Wanborough report of 14 April was encouraging. 'She has a very earnest attitude to the work and throughout her tests was determined, energetic, thorough and showed both imagination and a capacity for constructive thinking. Her leadership situation was a model of good planning, firm control and decisive action. She has good physical stamina and staying power and steady nerves. Her civilian record is excellent showing that she is efficient and adaptable. She has an excellent sense of security. She would make a good courier.'

Soon after, her instructors at Thame Park were understandably far from sure whether she was ready. The report read: 'This student is undoubtedly promising in many ways, but she is at the moment quite raw and untrained . . . She is tremendously keen . . . She needs further training in basic work, suitable to her role, together with further instruction in security, and above all, practical schemes . . . she needs further time. I could personally accept no responsibility for passing her out as fit for the field.'

The report from Saltmarsh, Hampshire, of 27 April 1944 is more optimistic.

She is well educated, well above the average intelligence, thoughtful, practical and quick. Indeed sometimes she jumps to conclusions and makes decisions too hastily. She seems reliable and trustworthy and although nervous about the work which she will have to do she has her emotions well under control. It is possible, however, that in time she will find the strain of working very exhausting. She has a very pleasant and amusing personality and should get on well with everyone. She does, however, find it difficult to keep control of herself when attacks are made on the British and British Policy.

This last comment is interesting for showing one of the many unexpected ways that agents were tested during training – to see whether they could maintain their cool in the face of violent and sustained anti-British comment. Her instructor certainly proved percipient, although in the event her fiery patriotism in just such a situation was to work to her advantage.

The instructor adds that Peggy did 'a very good scheme [training exercise] and seems well suited to act as a courier. Indeed she has the intelligence and initiative to take on even more responsible work.'

Most SOE girls did three practice jumps (in contrast to the four allowed to the men). Peggy did just one, owing to bad weather. Yet the report states that she showed 'no signs of nervousness in the aircraft and her descent was good'.

Peggy parachuted with a new radio operator, Noël, who was to work with her on the Donkeyman circuit. She provides a vivid account of her arrival in France.

We left the airport with an American crew on the 5th May 1944. The crew was very good. We were dropped near Marcenay in the Côte d'Or, where a local group under a man called Casse-Cou received us. The reception committee was very bad; they left us hanging about on the ground for more than an hour, asking us any amount of questions, taking away as much of our cigarettes, chewing gum, etc., as they could . . . parachute[s] as well, and finally when I reminded Casse-Cou that the Germans might be around, he decided to take us on foot to the nearest village.

By this stage in the war, all SOE agents were extremely conscious of the need not to draw attention to themselves in any way. Peggy continues: 'We stayed there two days, indoors, hoping to see nobody, instead of which the whole village came in to see us, to wish us the best of luck and ask how pleasant it was to be parachuted.'

She therefore determined that they must leave and asked Casse-Cou to find an isolated farm, to keep quiet and to get his chief to guide them out of the area. After a few more days, which they spent in the cramped conditions of a shed, Roger Bardet arrived to collect them, in a car without a permit – thereby adding to the potential risk. But they reached Aillant-sur-Tholon without incident, although without Noël's wireless sets, which remained in the Côte d'Or.

The Donkeyman circuit also operated in Normandy and Bardet wanted to send them both to Paris without delay. However, due to transport difficulties only Noël went and Peggy remained behind with another circuit member, Michel.

Her instinctive judgements were sharp and perceptive. 'The first time I met Roger I took an intense dislike to him. I did not like the look in his eyes, he never looked you straight in the face but always down.' She added that he 'looked to me like a hunted man very often, he never smiled, had big lines under his eyes and always looked as if he had something on his mind. I told him once that he ought to take more sleep and he muttered something about he could not sleep while this war was on.'

Peggy also felt intuitively distrustful of two other members of the group, Lieutenant Richard Armand Lansdell (Oscar) and Alain de Laroussilhe (Michel). Lansdell had been brought in by Lysander on 30 April, a week earlier than Peggy, to act as assistant to Frager. Frager, she said, never liked Lansdell, who had failed to go to the Côte d'Or when instructed by Frager and instead used the car to travel around with Michel, making themselves conspicuous. 'They used to stick to the same people's houses. It seems strange that the Gestapo did not get on to their track as they used to go to these same houses and bring all their pals there, make a lot of noise, drinking and eating and discussing their work, and always throwing plenty of money about.' Michel, she said, had a very bad attitude towards his men. 'He was always rude to them, gave them no definite work, except that he was very keen on their getting stocks of tobacco, food tickets and "perception money" [monies levied from locals in support of the resistance]. What he did with all that I did not know at the time, but later on it came out that the money was for him only; the tickets, tobacco, etc., he sold on the black market for his own profit.'

Nor did she form that high an opinion of Frager, her circuit organiser. He was, she said, 'the sort of man who would listen in to everything in a conversation, would not openly disagree while talking to the man but when he had gone would shrug his shoulders and say: "What a twerp"'. Roger Bardet did not endear himself to her by his attitude to his family. He 'detested his brother [Maurice] who was a very nice boy of about 21 years. His brother used to do every little job he was told to do in a quiet way but Roger would come down on him like a ton of bricks for any little slip he made.' Maurice, she said, was also 'very brave and would go through almost anything without turning a hair.' Once she set off with him on a motorcycle without a permit for a meeting. 'We went to a main road at a time when the Germans were stopping every vehicle in order to requisition them. We passed many Germans on the road who seemed on the point of stopping us, but Maurice just carried on driving and took no notice.'

Bardet would later take charge of the Burgundy area but never engaged 'the Germans in battle himself but always got others to go . . . He never did anything in the way of active sabotage but just picked up suitcases and took them from one place to another.'

Bardet was also at odds with Pierre, 'a very nice man of about 40', who led a small Maquis group in the Côte d'Or. Pierre 'wore glasses, was dark and going bald; had a pinched nose; talked like a lawyer; came of a very good family . . . and seemed a very good man . . . He was very efficient about looking after their arms, cleaning them, putting them out of the way. One very big job he did was to capture three big Gestapo chiefs who were walking about the town disguised as Canadians.'

Then Raymond, another in the group, was shot as a traitor.

He had been a P.O.W. in Germany. Jean Marie [Frager] suspected him as he was always trying to get out and go to the village so he was watched carefully and his papers were searched. It was found he was friendly with a girl from the village who had some association with the Gestapo. Amongst his papers was a description of how to get to our camp and a plan of it. He was shot on the 8th or 9th June just as we got there. He was very short, dark, little bit wrinkly, straight square forehead, small lips, with a leer on his face. Was about 35 years old.

The people most at risk in many ways were the French

families who gave shelter to agents. Peggy paid tribute to
Monsieur and Madame Guillet of Aillant-sur-Tholon, who
'for months on end, gave hospitality practically every day to
any member of the Resistance. They fed them, sheltered them
and provided them with all kinds of things. They were very
badly compromised and risked being visited by the Gestapo
more than once. They would never accept anything in return,
and merely said they did it because they were true French
people.' Peggy also stayed for six weeks with Monsieur and
Madame Cuffaut of Senan, who 'treated me like a daughter
and did anything I asked of them, in spite of the danger of
denunciation'. Violent German reprisals were indeed taken
against the Berthot family, who lived near Sommecaisse and
let the circuit use a farm just ninety metres from their own
house. When this came to the attention of the Germans, they
beat up the farmer's sons, took their stock and burned down
the building that Peggy and her comrades had been using.

Over the next week Peggy helped with parachute drops
and arms inventories, and ran a few errands for Michel. She
considered that Michel was the opposite of security minded,
publicising their activities so that soon everyone knew she was
a British parachutist. 'The whole security of the place was nil,'
she said.

Shortly after, the circuit organiser Frager arrived to survey
the region and give orders, telling Peggy to remain a little
longer with Michel. She was increasingly aware that Michel
did not like the idea of her going to Paris, fearing perhaps what
she might say about him. He was also becoming much closer
to Lansdell.

She now had a set-to with Bardet, manoeuvring him outside
and talking to him frankly. 'I told him that I had come to
do some work and that for one thing I did not like his
attitude to the British at table. He had several times run
them down in front of Lansdell and myself, for inefficiency.'
Her show of anger produced an immediate response. Bardet

not only promised to change his ways but he suddenly became extremely nice to her; he also began to be efficient and quiet, and got on with things.

Bardet, they understood, had escaped from a camp in Germany and had made contact with the Resistance in Annecy, offering to work with the British. Frager told Peggy that London had disapproved of his appointing Bardet as his second-in-command – people who had been in German custody were always suspect. There was the obvious risk that their escape was a pretence and that they had done a deal to secure their release, undertaking to report back. Frager insisted that Bardet was very much better than a lot of others and as an example cited the hair-raising case of a man who had attended their Lysander operations, taking a picture of them and giving it to the Gestapo. Peggy also mentions another case of a young Englishman, too lazy to walk eighteen kilometres, who stayed in his hotel and was caught.

During her first days at Marcenay, a 'coup dur' (a round-up of suspects involving systematic house-searches) occurred two kilometres away. At 6.30 a.m. the circuit members had to get away from their base, avoiding controls on the road. They succeeded in moving their material with them. By now Peggy was having serious trouble with Michel. She told SOE that he put her in some embarrassing situations – or, in her own words, 'awkward situations'. She was so fed up that she nearly decided to escape through Spain. She only relented when she was allowed to go to Paris and contact Frager there. These 'awkward situations' may simply have been of an amorous kind but Michel was also involved in a series of betrayals. According to SOE, he was not only selling arms to the Germans (arms that had been dropped by SOE) but also ration coupons, intended for agents, on the black market. 'He held up arms deliveries and misappropriated funds.'

When Lansdell joined the group, she told him, as a British officer, of her worries about Michel. At first he appeared to agree with her but after a few days his attitude alarmingly changed altogether. He lost all idea of security and started setting out on day-long drives in the car with Michel on so-called jobs, which in Peggy's view did not exist. From this time Lansdell hardly spoke to her so she was unable to make any further comment to him. 'During the few days that followed I realised for some reason or other Michel did not like the idea of my going to Paris. I carried on doing a few errands on a bicycle for him.'

Then a new assistant, Jean Delplace (Julien), arrived from Paris and told her that Frager would wait for her at 11 a.m. at the Gare de Lyon in Paris. Michel promptly tried to frustrate the plan, saying this meant catching the 7 a.m. train from Laroche twenty-eight kilometres away and claiming that he had no petrol. Determined to get to Paris, Peggy had a row with him and eventually was able to catch the slow train, which arrived in Paris at 5 p.m. Having missed her rendezvous at the station, she had to go to an address she had been given – that of Madame Lyon in Neuilly – to fix a new rendezvous, which was arranged at the house for the next day.

This time it was Frager who did not appear. Finally, at 11 p.m. two others arrived, Jean and Nadine, saying that everyone in the house had had to leave in the early hours of the morning as trouble was expected: they had heard that papers were going to be checked at dawn.

Peggy therefore moved to another house, staying with people who knew nothing of her clandestine work. Finally, she managed several meetings with Frager, in which she told him bluntly of her concerns about Michel and the lack of security and discipline. He agreed, saying mysteriously that he was already working on this.

Then came the serious news that Julien had been 'accidentally' wounded in the knee by Michel and Lansdell. This, it appears, was nothing less than a bungled attempt to eliminate him. The three of them had been in a café, sitting on high

(*above*) Born of an Irish father and an English mother, Paddy O'Sullivan grew up in Belgium. After joining the WAAFs, she parachuted into the northern Creuse as a wireless operator on the night of 22/3 March 1944. (*below*) An agent's wireless in its original case.

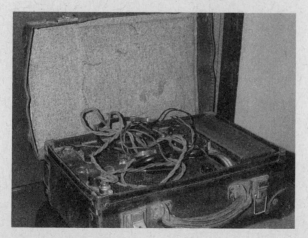

Paola Del Din was just twenty years old when she set
off from her home in northern Italy to find a way
through the German front line at Florence, taking
urgent messages from the partisans to No. 1 Special
Force – SOE's Italian arm.

(*above left*) Paola Del Din, determined to carry out her mission after her brother had been killed leading a partisan attack.

(*above right*) Paola Del Din (centre) with colleagues with whom she was to be dropped behind German lines in the spring of 1945.

(*below*) Peggy Knight was working as a secretary for the Electricity Company in Walthamstow when her fluent French came to the attention of SOE. Her training was cut short so that she could be rushed to France to serve as a courier, arriving by parachute in the Côte d'Or in early May 1944.

Lela Karayanni worked with five of her children,
organising sabotage and aiding escapes from Greece.

(*top*) Born in Mauritius, Alix d'Unienville grew up in France and escaped with her family to London when France fell. She was recruited by de Gaulle's RF Section and parachuted into France on 31 March 1944.

(*bottom left*) Hannah Senesh, a Hungarian Jewess, escaped to Israel and volunteered to return to Europe to help bring others to safety. After training with SOE in Palestine, she was arrested as she re-entered Hungary.

(*bottom right*) Born near Paris, Yvonne Rudellat settled in London in her late teens and was working in a hotel there when she came to the attention of SOE. She was the first of SOE's trained women agents to land in France, arriving by sea in July 1942.

During the war, the existence of SOE was never mentioned in the press and the exploits of its women agents first came to light when the deeds of WAAF parachutists were praised in the House of Commons in March 1945.

Accounts of Christina Granville's bravery and daring filled the press after her brutal murder in 1952.

Stories of Violette Szabo's heroism appeared in the *News of the World* early in 1946. She was awarded a posthumous George Cross at the end of the year.

CHRISTINE GRANVILLE was passionate, and compassionate. She flirted with men, and with death. She loved, and she hated, with a frightening intensity.

She was recognised by British and German Secret Service chiefs as being THE ACE GIRL SPY ON EITHER SIDE IN EITHER WORLD WAR.

Everyone who knew her considered her one of the most intriguing women who ever lived.

But when she was stabbed to death in a London hotel by a love-crazed man, none of them knew the full, strange story of Christine—British secret agent, Polish countess, and one of the great heroines of all time.

HE LIVED WITH HER 'GHOST'

TODAY one man knows. His name is W. Stanley Moss. He has lived with her ghost for four years since she was murdered.

He, too, was a secret agent—who once helped to kidnap a German general on Crete—and he was a close friend of Christine.

In France, Poland and Hungary he has spoken to her friends, enemies, relatives, colleagues, and men who loved her.

Moss has done all this because he is determined the world shall know the true story of a great woman. It is a story which will be told fully in a book and on the radio.

But in an exclusive interview with the *Sunday Pictorial* he has revealed these astonishing, inspiring facts about Christine, The Girl Spy.

Moss said: "I don't think anyone who knew her was surprised when she came to a violent end.

"She always lived dangerously and predicted she would die violently.

"She thrived on danger. She sought it out as a challenge to be met and defeated. It was the way she lived and the way she died."

Dennis George Muldowney, her murderer, made a statement to the police just after he was arrested. In this statement Muldowney said: "CHRISTINE HAD DARED ME TO KILL HER ON THREE SEPARATE OCCASIONS."

Muldowney had threatened to kill Christine for not taking sufficient notice of him.

Moss commented: "I can almost hear her mocking, contemptuous, self-confident reply: 'Go on . . . go on, then . . . you'd never dare !'"

BEAUTY

BUT that was the one time Christine over-estimated her power over men. He chose to hang for murder rather than let her go.

At the time of the murder—in June, 1952—Christine was forty-two.

When the war started she was twenty-nine, twice married, and at the height of her beauty.

But although she had once won a "Miss Poland" competition which she entered for fun, she was not of conventional Hollywood-type beauty.

Moss explained: "She had what one French underground fighter called 'the beauty of the devil.' [UN-]QUOTE DEVIL'S BEAUTY."

[FRE...] CHARM

CHRISTINE was 5ft. ..., Italian dark, with a slim figure.

She bothered little about clothes. ... wore a suit.....

... happiest in a ... wore ...

[left column fragments]
... when they set [off] the flat they ... Andrew ... with the full ... ment ... He was ... rain he would ... Gestapo H.Q. ...

... vivacity, flirtatiousness, charm and sheer personality.

"She could switch that personality on and off like a searchlight that could blind anyone in its beam."

Christine, a countess in her own right, was born in Russia. She was half-Jewish, and that was one of her main reasons for hating the Nazis.

While still in her teens [she...]

FOR A HEROINE... ALL THIS, THEN NEGLECT
An O.B.E., the George Medal, foreign awards—and two months' pay to live on.

AT WAR

BUT they travelled to [continued]

SHE ordered the Gestapo: 'Set agents free'

SHE flirted with men—and with death

January, 1942, Christine arrived in Budapest alone, with no helpers, but with authority to do what she wished.

"THE WAR BETWEEN CHRISTINE GRANVILLE AND THE GERMAN REICH WAS ON.

Soon she met a Polish cavalry officer named Andrew Kowerski.

He was organising mass escapes of Polish soldiers from internment camps all over Hungary.

PARTNERS

HE placed his underground resources at her disposal.

"This was the beginning of a partnership—in every sense of the word—which lasted until the day of her death," said Moss.

Christine's first mission was to Poland.

There she made contact with the underground cell in Warsaw and carried back microfilms and vital information.

On her second journey she was arrested, but escaped.

On her third she found that the Gestapo were offering a reward of 100,000 zlotys (£2,500) for her capture.

But she still obtained a job in a munitions factory, which she kept until she had gathered information on its output and war potential.

ESCAPES

AND she arrived back in Budapest again with information from the underground.

Then she started helping Andrew with his mass escape operations.

Almost at once she had again to prove her coolness and persuasive powers.

She was arrested on the Yugoslav frontier, just after she had smuggled four pilots across.

But Christine talked the guards into believing she was on a picnic.

She also got them to push her car, which had stalled, until it started again.

With Gestapo pressure in Budapest increasing, Christine decided to take one last ski trip into Poland, this time to rescue British P.O.W.s

BULLETS

THE British prisoners did not arrive at the mountain rendezvous. Christine had to return alone.

On a long slope in the snow-covered Tatras she was spotted by a German reconnaissance plane.

She was trapped like an ant on a tablecloth.

With machine-gun bullets spattering all round her, she flashed down the slope on her skis.

She dived into the shelter of some rocks with such [speed that she seriously in-]

At last: The startling facts about Christine

BRITISH FORCES
IDENTIFICATION CARD

captured by the Gestapo and were in the dreaded jail of Digne.

In the Gestapo prison the three officers were subjected to brutal interrogation for three days and nights.

One night they were summoned from their cells and marched out into the courtyard, where prisoners were usually shot. They expected death.

But instead of being stood against a wall they were marched through [...]

Colonel Cammaerts added: "SHE WAS PERHAPS THE GREATEST PERSON I HAVE EVER KNOWN."

Moss echoed: "No one could have done more.

"After the war in the Secret Service expected the highest honours for her.

"But everyone forgot. The greatest heroine produced by either war re-[ceived...]

...ceived only the George Medal and an O.B.E.

"And she was paid off by the British Government with two months' salary—£100."

The cash didn't last long. Christine had to find work.

She was a shop assistant and a hotel receptionist.

Then the girl who had the "Devil's beauty" got [...]

After the end of the war, Vera Atkins, personal assistant to
Maurice Buckmaster, head of SOE's French Section, went to
Germany to determine the fate of women agents who had not
returned from their missions.

stools. Lansdell and Michel had gone out for few minutes and on their return one of them had drawn out a gun. They began to discuss the gun and examine it when, as Lansdell took hold of it, a shot went off, wounding Julien. Fortunately, at that moment he had been clasping his knee in front of his chest, protecting him from mortal injury. The others, Peggy heard, had not been too helpful, carrying him roughly upstairs and messing about for some time before they called a doctor.

The next day she was asked to return to the Yonne and collect Noël's messages. She got to Cézy and waited several hours for Michel. Eventually he turned up with Lansdell, both of them slightly drunk. Michel was very rude, refusing to give her the wireless set. Noël, he said, was miles away, and he could not be bothered to fetch the messages himself. Peggy continues: 'He *asked* me to go to a *parachutage* that night – the tone of his voice was such that I thought I had better go. We didn't return from the *parachutage* until 8 a.m. next morning – again I missed my train [to Paris].'

That evening Roger Bardet arrived and there was a major row. Bardet said that Frager was coming the next day and asked Peggy to remain where she was, adding pointedly that things would no doubt alter very soon. Meanwhile Michel and Lansdell appeared to be on very bad terms with Bardet, talking in hushed tones and lapsing into silence whenever anyone entered the room.

Next morning, full of apprehension, she went to find Frager, only to learn that he had not arrived. 'I was told by Michel I couldn't come in, and ordered to return to my billet.' After an interminable wait of two hours, Michel, Lansdell and André Remu drew up in a car and told her to jump in. They drove to a country farm where Frager, Roger Bardet and several others whom she did not know were waiting. A discussion started in the farmyard over maps. Peggy quickly realised she wasn't wanted and went to wait inside the house.

'A few minutes later I heard shots and wondered whether

Germans were surrounding the place. I walked to the window and saw Michel running up the yard pursued by the others; no sign of Germans.' When she went out to see what was happening, Frager appeared and took her behind the house, explaining that a very painful job had to be done. 'I then understood there must have been a traitor amongst us but still didn't realise who it might be. When it was all over they told me it had been Michel and Lansdell. I had a shock. The two men were buried there by the farmer's sons.' Peggy said later that just before he was shot, Michel had said to Bardet, 'If you hadn't got me I would have got you eventually.' She saw this as an expression simply of their fierce mutual hatred but it could suggest that Michel was suspicious about Bardet's earlier dealings with the Germans. After Michel was shot his suitcases were found at his apartment. In them, says Peggy, 'was found a photograph of Hitler and several Russians, letters from women and a lot of money'.

Returning to Aillant, she was suddenly told to undertake a liaison with Switzerland the next day. Somewhat disturbingly, she was to be accompanied by Henri, whom she had not even met. 'Then at 6 p.m. I was told I wasn't going after all. The next day Jean-Marie [Frager] said there had been some doubt about me, and they had decided to have me interned in Switzerland; on evidence from everyone, however, they had realised they had made a mistake. They now hoped we would all work together, and forget the incident.' Over the next few days, said Peggy, discipline became quite good, security measures were taken and, as D-Day came, plans were made to form a small Maquis, training men to use arms and carrying out sabotage.

Her days continued to be full of incident. One morning while they were poring over maps in a private house a boy rushed in, shouting: 'Alert – Germans are outside.' 'We quickly collected our things, rushed out at the back and finally had to cross the river Tholon, [up] to our waists in water.' They emerged in a large clump of stinging nettles and, dripping wet, walked to another safe house two kilometres away. Eventually a car came for them and although there were still Germans in Aillant, they braved their way through the village and formed a new headquarters four kilometres away at Villiers.

That night they walked thirty kilometres to Cézy to blow up the railway line. The following day she had to cycle there twice, on the second occasion bringing back a group of fellow resisters from Nancy who had come to collect arms.

Here she met Captain I.P. Thomson for the first time and struck up a rapport with him. Following his escape from Germany, he had reached Cézy in the Yonne and joined their group. He trained the Maquis in the use of arms, making an excellent impression on the French. Whenever there were ambushes to be laid or reconnaissance to be carried out, he was always the first to go, often on 'very risky expeditions'.

The next day they set off to form their own Maquis on an empty farm between Sommecaisse and Perreux. The men were trained there and sent out on expeditions. Noël, the radio operator, worked in the open, some ten kilometres away, always guarded by armed men. 'For myself, there was no courier work to do at this time, so I filled in time peeling potatoes, cleaning arms,' doing sentry duty and going out on armed escorts.

One Saturday they mounted an operation, setting an ambush. Noël was to lay the bait by broadcasting for three hours at the chosen spot. Frustratingly, the Germans did not appear although, Peggy says, 'As a manoeuvre it was a very good show.' Walking back to the camp, they found a British airman brought from Sens. He was in a bad state, having been shot in the head while sheltering with another Maquis. They bandaged him and, an hour after midnight, were able to settle down to sleep. Peggy continues: 'At 5 a.m. I went on sentry duty with Capt. Thomson. Five minutes later we heard a shot. Capt. Thomson with great calm took a bicycle and went on a reconnaissance while I gave the alarm.' More shots were heard and Captain Thomson returned, saying he had been shot at. Henri then set out on patrol, working his way through the woods and returning two hours later to warn that they were surrounded by 700 Germans. The rumour, said Peggy, was that the Germans had been prompted by a butcher in Pinelle, who had been caught, tortured and then shot.

Like Robin Hood and his men, they prepared to move deeper into the forest, fearing their camp would soon be discovered. Frager asked Peggy to carry all the arms she could manage to a safe place. With eight other men she made her way into the heart of the forest. Suddenly they heard shots. The men in front dropped the equipment and rushed forward, desperate to see some action. She and Robert stayed behind to try to hide the equipment rather better, deciding they should remain concealed in the woods and await events. 'We lay there from approximately 8.30 a.m. to 7 p.m., hearing the Germans searching parts of the wood.' This was an unusually thorough operation. Often at this stage in the war the Germans would remain outside wooded areas for fear of being shot at.

Peggy and Robert had no food or drink. However, they managed to tidy themselves a little, to avoid looking conspicuous, before emerging from the woods without being seen by the Germans, who still lay in wait. They then embarked on a twenty-two-kilometre walk back to Aillant. They spotted German lorries outside the village and hid in a field for half an hour until they were able to enter Aillant and find a secure house. Over the next two days they gradually heard that everyone was safe.

Frager and Bardet went to Paris for new instructions, and the following week Bardet returned alone, convening the circuit at Aillant to be briefed. The decision had been taken to maintain a mobile HQ in the future. This was to be staffed by Bardet, Peggy and four others. Initially just a few men would live in a camp in the country, carrying out sabotage. Such was the continuing possibility of betrayal, even as the Allies advanced, that it was now agreed Frager would not return to the region.

Peggy moved to a safe house in Senan and began a series of regular liaisons around the Côte d'Or to Sens, Toucy, Joigny, Villefranche St Phal and Courlon, on a bicycle that she had boldly stolen from a collaborator. Bardet distributed arms and gave orders for sabotage to be carried out on railway lines, bridges and telephone lines.

Then came the news of the American breakthrough under Patton. On 16 or 17 August, Peggy's Maquis went to Sommecaisse and occupied it, followed by the neighbouring village of Les Ormes. They now had several hundred men, more and more of them armed, who began to attack the retreating Germans.

A Jedburgh team, consisting of Major William Colby, Lieutenant Jacques Favel and Second Lieutenant Louis Giry, had been dropped early on the morning of 15 August to join them on the outskirts of Montargis. With remarkable cool, wearing full uniform, the three had reached Peggy's Maquis thirty-three kilometres away.

Colby provides details of their journey in his report: 'Landing was made in the gardens amidst houses and adjacent to a main street. There were luckily no injuries to members of the team.' Despite the difficulty of landing in a town in the dark, they rapidly found each other and were soon surrounded by civilians who had been aroused by the noise of containers falling among the buildings. They quickly learnt that they were some thirty kilometres from the intended dropping zone – the pilot had been confused by fire from a village burnt out by the Germans. Worse still, there was a German garrison in Montargis. 'It was obvious from the scattered positions of the containers that we could not locate the radio nor our equipment without spending at least an hour or two searching, in which time a large crowd would be gathered and the Germans alerted, so we proceeded off to the south-east through the fields.' As the Germans combed the town and surrounding villages, they hid all day in a ditch by a wood, moving off as night came on a compass bearing towards the safe house whose details they had been given.

A heavy storm broke and they had to use their pistol lanyards to link themselves together as they slithered blindly through the mud. The lightning flashes revealed a lone house so they decided to make an approach in the hope of receiving aid. Favel knocked on the door while the others covered him. Their luck could not have been better – they had arrived at a Resistance radio post with an operator dropped from London eight days before. The cottage was La Fourmilloire, north of Château Renard. The next day a telegram was sent announcing their position and they were given a ride in comfort to their safe house. From there they were passed on to Bardet at Sommecaisse, who, they found, could command some 500 armed men. 'The tactical situation in the area was that the Germans had garrisons of about 500 in two or three large towns and were moving convoys through the department with very light guards,' wrote Colby.

The Jedburgh team now occupied themselves with weapons training and assisted in small operations against the enemy. On 22 August they heard reports that American armoured units had arrived at Courtenay. When they made contact, the Americans immediately requested that the Resistance provide information about German troop concentrations. Seeking out German positions was exceptionally hazardous; the best people to do it were often innocent-looking young women on bicycles. Colby reported: 'Ensign Peggy Knight, F.A.N.Y. and Mme Raymond did some very fine and very hazardous work in connection with this, pushing alone into heavily occupied towns such as Montargis. Large amounts of information were given to the American forces by the F.F.I. of the area.' Madame Raymonde was the wife, not of the traitor who had been shot, but of another man in the Resistance who had been arrested. According to Peggy she then began to do courier work, which involved a great deal of cycling.

Peggy, posing innocently as a local girl, was sent to Montargis on a bicycle and managed to enter the town despite stiff German controls. No Americans had been sighted, although rumours suggested that they were just twenty to thirty kilometres away. It was evident that the Germans were planning to withdraw; they were blowing 'one or two things up' and looking panicky.

As the Americans pressed east, General Patton gave the Resistance the task of protecting the American right flank and pushing the Germans as far away to the south as possible. Harassing actions were increased; towns were occupied and posts established to give warning of any German troop movements towards the north. Colby describes a typical incident. A strong German column of over 1,000 men, equipped with artillery and fleeing from Montargis to Auxerre, had stopped during the day near Sommecaisse. He requested that the 2nd US Cavalry make the main attack with the FFI holding the flanks, 'to some extent out of sight so that the Germans could surrender to the American troops and . . . not fight to the end as they would if they saw the FFI'.

Excitement grew as the first American patrol arrived at Aillant, followed by the news of the fall of Montargis and then Courtenay. Groups of Germans remained in various positions and fights took place in the woods. At Moneteau the Resistance played a key role in occupying the town to prevent the Germans returning to use – or destroy – a large petrol store. The Germans had attacked the town with 200–300 White Russian troops, mortars and machine-guns. The FFI, armed only with lighter Brens, were pushed back but later regained Moneteau. Peggy had gone there by car with Colby at the beginning, sending in the first men to collect the petrol, which ran FFI transport for the next month. By occupying numerous small towns and setting up road blocks, the Resistance forced the Germans to waste time in detours and also prevented many demolitions.

Intrepid as always, Peggy now started carrying out reconnaissance for the American commanding officer on the roads between St Florentin Tonnerre, Chablis and Auxerre. The next day she carried out an extensive recce along the Loire by bicycle to find out how many bridges had been blown, where the Germans were and how free the district was. This took her on a journey that would have been impressive in times of peace. From Gien she cycled past Briare and Cosne – some forty kilometres. Thomson said these recces were 'carried out cleverly and fearlessly', providing the Americans with 'urgent news of the precise whereabouts of the enemy'.

After this she went on to Auxerre for a few days with Major Colby and his team. Then she joined an SAS group in search of an American convoy and returned with them to Avallon 'through the so-called German lines', finding her way back to Auxerre in an SAS convoy. Next she joined Bardet, who had now moved with all his men to occupy the banks of the Loire. Finally, on 12 September, Bardet released her and she went to Paris. Four days later she was en route to London by plane.

It was during this period that Frager was betrayed by Bleicher and arrested. He was taken to Fresnes and then on to Buchenwald, where he was executed on 6 September 1944. In all this there was to be a final twist, when Bardet, recognising that he was in mortal danger as the Allied landings were consolidated, did what any double agent can be expected to do: he threw himself back into service for SOE, seeking to ensure that his record would protect him from any future charges.

The reports Peggy made on her return about her comrades provide fascinating detail about life in the Resistance. For Bardet, she had in the end only praise. Evidently setting his days as a double agent firmly behind him, he had done the work of three people. 'He was liked and respected by all his men because he was just. He did his work solely for the purpose of getting the Germans out of France and never mentioned politics to anyone,' she said. In the Yonne, Bardet had had 'to begin from scratch at a very late hour, because of Michel's inefficiency' and the German 'coup dur of June 25'. In a very short time he 'managed to get various groups together, had arms distributed, got plans made for various sabotage operations'. When the Americans pushed through to Orléans he prepared the whole area for military action in just three days, repeatedly ambushing the Germans and taking five villages within a week.

The end of Peggy's career in SOE was almost as sudden as the beginning. A note of 18 November 1944 states: 'Agent has completed a successful mission in the field and it is regretted that no further employment can be offered to her by F. Section or the F.A.N.Y.'s. She herself has requested that she be outposted, in order that she can get married. She realises that on outposting she will be subject to normal call-up regulations in force in this country.'

Her return to civilian life was complete and immediate. In December 1944 she married Sub-Lieutenant Eric Smith of the Royal Navy. Her first son, Peter, was born in September 1945 while her husband was still in the navy. Her second, David, arrived a year later when she was living in a new house that she and her husband had bought in Waltham Cross. According to an article in the *Sunday Express* of 19 January 1947, headed 'Mrs Smith: Train-wrecker, spy, and Nazi-killer', she had entered into domestic life with the same zest and commitment as that of a special agent.

'You would not suspect that the prim little woman who comes out of the newly built house, 61 Eastfield Road, Waltham Cross, Essex, wheeling her sixteen-month and four-month-old babies in a second-hand pram – she couldn't get a new one – with shopping basket on the handrail, is "our trusty and well-beloved Marguerite Diana Frances Smith" who once blazed away with a Sten gun at Germans hunting her down as a secret agent in France.'

The article continued: 'Not until last week did the neighbours learn that Mrs Smith was someone rather special. Then it was announced that France had awarded her the Croix-de-Guerre for "exceptional courage" and the King had granted . . . [her] an MBE.' Her husband, about to be demobbed, was to resume his job as a River Lea police inspector. The article described how Peggy had found the new house in Waltham Cross and had paid the £50 deposit on the spot. 'She and her husband had about £400. It was enough for the full down payment and some furniture. She bought a Utility suite for the bedroom, and wandered far afield picking up second-hand odds and ends to fill the other rooms – "I couldn't have all Utility. It would have looked like a barrack room,"' she told the reporter, Sidney Rodin.

Peggy's main concern now was to beat the shortages imposed by Austerity. 'You can get plenty of milk jugs, but you can't get cups and saucers. I have been looking everywhere for a mixing bowl for puddings. For two months I had to use a milk bottle to roll pastry, because I couldn't get a rolling pin. The extra soap ration for babies stops at one year, but that is just the age they start crawling and get twice as dirty. I would go with less food to have more soap. I am sometimes at my wits' end to do my washing.'

On 19 September 1944, Thomson wrote by hand a letter of appreciation to SOE: 'In the early days, after the invasion, before the need for a courier arose she took her place on the staff of Jean-Marie [Frager] exactly as one of the men. She marched with them and took her turn at sentry with them, always as a volunteer.' Later on, travelling great distances by bicycle as a courier, 'she was quite fearless and undertook work on roads which were known to contain enemy barrages with a nonchalance which was the admiration of us all.'

The final word can go to SOE. 'First-class, sensible and courageous girl. Showed lots of good sense and intuition in most dangerous and awkward situations. Determined, wise and eager, simple, charming and modest. One of our outstanding girls.'

Chapter 11

PAOLA DEL DIN

Like Violette Szabo and other famous SOE agents, Paola Del Din felt the burning call to serve her country after the death of a loved one in action. Following the Armistice of 1943, her brother Renato, who was just one year older than her, had made soundings among friends to form a patriotic Resistance group. It was not communist, as many were, and it had no particular political association; only a desire to hoist the red, white and green Italian flag, ridding Italy of both Germans and fascists. She explains: 'When I saw our soldiers coming back from Russia and Greece I thought why, why did they have to go? Africa we could understand, yes, as we had been there for generations. But not the others.'

Born on 22 August 1923, Paola has lived most of her life in the north Italian city of Udine, the historic centre of the prosperous Friuli region. Her father, a lieutenant colonel in the Alpini regiment, had been captured in Albania on 16 December 1940 and was commandant of his prisoner-of-war camp in India.

She relates: 'All that summer of 1943 we collected arms, hiding them at home. From the autumn people met in our house and hid there. My brother had tremendous stamina. He never said, "I'm tired or thirsty or hungry".' Renato and his colleagues named their group the Osoppo brigade after a nearby fortress that in 1848, the year of national uprisings across Europe, had held out for months against the Austrians. Eventually the Austrians had allowed the defenders to march out with their colours to Venice.

Early in March 1944, Renato left for the mountains to start active resistance against the Germans. The next month, on 25 April and aged just twenty-two, he had led a surprise attack on the ancient walled Alpine town of Tolmezzo, forty-eight kilometres north of Udine, the first of its kind. Hit twice, he was 'Primo Caduto', the first to fall for freedom, as the plaque states in the street named after him. In an impressive display of passive resistance, his funeral in Tolmezzo was attended by a large crowd, some said as many as 3,000 people, despite a German ban on the event.

On Renato's body the enemy found a handkerchief with his initials, R.D. A search began immediately. A friend of Renato's mother, Signora Dall' Armi, had been taken to the SS Command and shown photographs of Renato, whom the Germans suspected was one of her sons. As it happened, both her sons were already in prison, but the face was familiar and she soon warned Paola: 'You must tell your mother as she can't fail to recognise Renato when she sees the photograph.' Paola and her mother did not receive the dreaded confirmation of Renato's death until the beginning of June. 'I then offered my services to the cause for which he had given his life,' she says.

She took the code name Renata after her brother – it carries a subtle double entendre as *renata* in Italian means reborn. In working with the partisans, Paola faced none of the prejudice that some women agents had to endure in France. Both she and her sister had attended university, which in Britain would have been quite unusual at this time. Paola was in her fourth year, reading Literature at Padua University. Until 1943 she had studied at Bologna University but had transferred to Padua because of the dangers and difficulties of travelling so far south. 'At first everybody was amazed to have a girl but when they saw I was not a hindrance, they became very friendly,' she says.

She had already carried out a number of minor but still

highly risky missions for Fiamme Verdi, another group of partisans to the west, who took their name from their leader. On 1 May 1944, she went on their orders to Padua 'to arrange for a rendezvous between representatives of the Osoppo Command and a patriot from the Florence movement who was in contact with Padua and Milan'. Then on 22 July, Verdi, whose true name was Candido Grassi, sent for her and entrusted her with a much bigger and more dangerous mission, to go alone to Florence as a courier, carrying secret documents for the Allies who were expected shortly to take the city. This was a job for which SOE's French Section's brave women couriers received extensive training. Paola had just four days' notice.

Her mother gave consent to the mission, saying: 'You must go. Or your brother will have died for nothing.' Paola recalls: 'I was full of enthusiasm and expectations. I wanted to do something wonderful for our country.'

On 24 July she was given the documents and 12,000 lire for expenses; this was later increased by a further 5,000 lire from her mother.

One of the papers entrusted to Paola on her five-hundred-kilometre journey south was a recommendation from Major Beckett, the British liaison officer working with the Osoppo, for the award to her brother of Italy's highest honour, the Medaglia d'Oro al Valor Militare. It read: 'With only ten men, he entered Tolmezzo . . . where at that time there were some 800 German and fascist soldiers . . . [he] succeeded in entering the barracks inflicting numerous losses on the enemy before being killed himself. This exceptional act of heroism which cost him his life merits the highest decoration.'

Even then the family was being watched. 'There was a man who used to sit in a café for hours outside our apartment drinking nothing . . . wherever we went he would appear. When my mother and I went from one shop to another looking in vain for a pair of shoes for me to wear on my journey, he was there waiting outside every shop.'

'If you succeed the war may be finished by November,' she was told half jokingly by Beckett, who was known to his Italian companions as Manfredi. Beckett was one of SOE's many remarkable characters. His real name was Squadron Leader Manfred Czernin, and he was born in Austria, the son of one of the last Foreign Ministers of the Austro-Hungarian Empire. In 1938, as Hitler marched into Austria, the young Czernin fled to Britain. SOE dropped him blind by parachute into northern Italy in June 1944. A contemporary, Patrick Martin-Smith, recalled: 'Manfred was a Squadron-Leader in the RAF but wore a kind of skiing cap, with a large peak that made him look as though he had transferred from Rommel's Afrika Corps.'

The growing strength and boldness of the Osoppo brigade contradicted Kesselring's widely reported press statement on 9 April that 'Bands are melting away like the snow.' After the war Kesselring, the German commander in Italy, acknowledged that by June 1944 the partisans had become a serious menace. By May, six of the twenty-five German divisions in Italy had to be diverted to northern parts to fight Italian patriots or Yugoslav partisans on the borders of Venezia Giulia.

Following the fall of Rome in early June, partisan activity sharply increased in central and northern Italy. German intelligence estimated that in June, July and August, there had been 30,000 casualties at the hands of the partisans, either killed, wounded or missing.

In the summer of 1944 British and American liaison officers with the partisans told them confidently that the Allies would break through the Gothic Line in north Tuscany in September, rapidly spreading out into the Lombardy plain towards Milan, Turin and the Veneto. These high expectations were not realised: the Gothic Line held after the Americans removed seven divisions in Italy for the South of France landings in August 1944 – much against the wishes of Winston Churchill and Field Marshal Alexander. Indeed, Kesselring wanted to withdraw to the Alps but Hitler would not agree. Hitler's strategy paid off; when the last Allied assault on Bologna was repulsed at the end of November 1944, all plans for further Allied offensives were postponed until the spring.

SOE's strict security procedures discouraged couriers from carrying written messages, whether in code or in clear, and one of the puzzles about Paola's mission is that Czernin had a radio operator, Lieutenant De Felice, described by Paola as 'aged about 25, blond; smooth hair; tall and well-built'. Czernin sent a signal through De Felice to SOE in the south, giving Paola's details and the date of her departure from Udine. Why could not the material she was carrying – which would have brought almost certain death and probably torture if she had been discovered – have been communicated by wireless?

Paola believes her mission may have been connected with the plans, strongly supported by Churchill, for an Allied landing at the top of the Adriatic, aimed at making a thrust into Austria that would enable the Allies to reach Vienna before the Russians. Even if Allied divisions had not been taken from the front to serve in the South of France landings, an attack on Istria would have met formidable opposition from the Germans. Hitler had reacted swiftly to the Italian Armistice of September 1943 by placing the north Adriatic coast, including Friuli, under direct German command. For the German forces in Italy, this was both a vital supply line and an evacuation route.

The letters Paola carried were written on very thin paper. Her mother made for her a special waterproof envelope of guttapercha, a form of rubber used for insulating cables, in which to carry them. This was concealed beneath her dress and was completely invisible even when she moved. 'In those days we wore more clothes. And I was very thin,' she recalls.

Paola carefully rehearsed her story: that her father was a

prisoner of war in India (which was true); that her mother was in Florence and she had to join her. Her fencing training, she says, helped a lot. 'In fencing, you have to check yourself, to think and plan, not lose your head. It makes you very exact.' She was also very fit. 'My father, who was in the Alpine regiment, used to take us mountaineering, bicycling, skiing.'

Paola set off on the 8 a.m. train from Udine on 26 July. As the train crawled slowly southwards, she noticed that the long stone bridge over the River Tagliamento had been damaged by bombing. Arriving in Padua at 3 p.m., she hastened to the convent where she had stayed while at the university and was put in touch with a priest who had helped numerous Jews escape. The priest lent her both his car and his driver, a loyal fascist from Sardinia who was on his way to visit his family in Bologna and who exhausted Paola with his constant rantings during the journey. 'This priest maintained his cover by appearing on friendly terms with the Germans. At the end of the war he was imprisoned for five years for collaborating. If only we had known, we could have vouched for him,' says Paola.

They had to cross the River Po under cover of darkness. The bridges had been destroyed and, as night fell, a barge that had been hauled out of sight during the day began to ferry across the large numbers of lorries waiting to go to the front. Later Paola was able to tell the Allies of this and of another barge at Crespino, which took all the traffic going north. Once across, the Sardinian driver stopped until first light, fearing that their tiny Fiat Topolino might be hit by a passing lorry during the blackout.

Arriving in Bologna, she was concerned that the Sardinian, who now believed her to be a Jewess, might betray her where-abouts. So she asked to be dropped ahead of her destination and made her own way to the convent of the Campostrini nuns, where her sister had lived while at university. She then went into a travel agent to ask about ways of continuing to Florence. Impossible, she was told. Further enquiries among friends at the university suggested that her only hope was to go boldly to German Command and ask for a pass.

Paola continues the story:

I went there and told them a long story about how my mother was ill in Florence, having fled Rome where she had gone to try to arrange for the liberation of my father who was a prisoner of the English in India. After some hesitation, they told me they could not give me a pass as the city was about to fall. However, a German woman in the office said I was a 'dumme Gans', a stupid goose, insisting on asking for something that could not be done. As she went out of the room, a man who was in clear disagreement suggested I should go and wait at a famous landmark in the centre of the town, the Due Torri, the two towers known as 'Asinelli' and 'Garisenda', around 2.30 p.m. and ask if any of the German cars, which were always there, were going to Florence.

Here she found an ambulance driven by two old soldiers who took pity on her and agreed to take her at sunset when there was less danger from air attack. They could carry her as far as Filigare, where she would have to stop another car. They falsified an old pass, changing the name and the date for her. When they were stopped at a road block as they left Bologna, she explained, as agreed with the two old soldiers, that she worked at the Military Chemical Institute in Florence and had to go to Filigare to bring back some equipment. 'In front of the ambulance drove a big tank, as this was "bandengebiet" or bandit territory.' At Filigare the soldiers found her a lorry that was ferrying ammunition to Arezzo, putting in good words for her to the SS guards accompanying the lorry. Her fate was now in the hands of the Germans all around her.

At the turn-off for Arezzo, the SS guards entrusted her to two policemen guarding the crossroads. It was now nearly midnight and they began to question her in German. 'I was exhausted and made a slip, contradicting myself. They immediately became suspicious. I knew I had to divert their attention so I produced some beautiful fresh fruit I had in my bag. Immediately they became more friendly, stopping a car and persuading the officer to take me. The officer had been drinking and I had some difficulty making him stay on his side of the car. I was lucky. We say in Italy there is always an angel for children.' Otherwise his groping might quickly have alerted him to the papers concealed beneath her dress.

Half an hour after midnight on 30 July she was dropped in total darkness at the gates of Florence. A lorry immediately drew up, its driver demanding to be told the way to Pisa. 'They swore furiously at me when I failed to give the answer. I had never heard such language. In those days people did not speak as they do today,' she says.

She heard voices and, walking towards them, suddenly found herself at the gate of a large garden that had been taken over by the Germans as a parking area. She had intended to continue on under cover of darkness into the city itself but when the sentry challenged her, she explained that she simply wanted a place to sleep. Seeing how young and vulnerable she looked, he allowed her through. 'They made me leave my small suitcase and gave me two blankets to sleep in the garden. The guard woke me very punctually as I requested precisely at five o'clock.'

Leaving her suitcase at the parking area, she went to 64 via Gioberti in search of the one person she had a chance of contacting, a Professor Chieffo, Professor of Letters at the school of the Daughters of the Sacred Heart. Her hope was that he would recognise her because she looked so like her brother Renato, who had been a friend of the professor's son.

Paola had arrived at a critical moment in the vital battle for Florence. Rome had been treated as an open city by the Germans, and was left unoccupied and undefended, but in Florence the prospect loomed of a street-by-street battle, causing devastation to churches, palaces and houses. The River Arno, running through its heart, formed the German defence line. Only days after Paola's arrival in Florence, Kesselring blew up all the bridges across the River Arno except the famous covered Ponte Vecchio. To ensure that this was completely unusable he had blocked the ends with a mountain of rubble provided by dynamiting nearby houses along the river. Hundreds of landmines and booby traps were strewn through the debris to make it impassable even on foot.

On 5 August, a daring British officer working for SOE, Charles Macintosh, succeeded in laying a telephone cable along the 914-metre Corridoio del Vasari, an overhead gallery built in the sixteenth century to allow the Medicis to cross the river from the Palazzo Vecchio to the vast Pitti Palace, unobserved and safe from potential assassins. The Germans had systematically knocked out the floor of the gallery immediately above the bridge but Macintosh worked his way across, using the broken beam ends as footholds. Once the cable was in operation, the partisans north of the river were able to report on German movements and helped guide British artillery fire.

The professor explained that he and his wife had neither water nor electricity, so after returning with Paola to the parking area to collect her suitcase from the German guard, he took her the next day to the Sacred Heart college. She remained there for eleven days until the buildings were requisitioned by the Germans and everyone had to move to another college run by Barnabite monks. The monks, she says, 'were really tremendous. The place was full of refugees and everyone slept on top of the other, on the steps or in the open air without blankets or mattresses.'

On 3 August at 1400 hours a proclamation by the German commander of the city of Florence was issued, stating the following:

1. From this moment it is forbidden to walk the streets and squares of Florence.
2. All doors and windows including those of shops are to remain closed.
3. The population should take cover in the inside rooms of main buildings.
4. The patrols of the German armed forces have orders to fire on anyone found on the streets or looking from the windows.

Thrilled to be in the centre of the action, Paola paid scant regard. 'As I knew some German, I wandered about the Occupied Zone, asking soldiers for news. I must have been protected by some saint as many people were killed walking about the streets or looking out of their windows.' The danger was all the greater because she had to keep her documents with her at all times as there was no safe place to put them.

I could never forget that my friends in Friuli needed me to be fast. Florence had been supposed to fall rapidly. On 7 or 8 August the partisans rose and liberated part of the city. But the area towards Fiesole, where I was, remained in tenacious German hands . . .

On 15 August I heard by chance that one of the monks had got a pass from the Red Cross to take a madman to a hospital in a part of the city taken by the Allies. I asked if I could go with them and after some negotiations with the Germans, this was agreed . . .

The front line that day was between the Pino bridge and the Piazza Donatello and we had to go down the very street that the Germans were controlling from the Sacred Heart college. No shots were fired as we crossed. As soon as we were on the other side, two British officers called the madman over. He was not mad at all, I think. He spoke with a Florentine accent but I never saw him again.

From here she went to the British High Command in the Hotel Excelsior where she asked for No. 1 Special Force (SOE's operational name in Italy), producing her passport and Czernin's letter of 23 July 1944. A copy is preserved in her personal file. It runs: 'The bearer of this note has messages of importance to deliver and must be taken immediately to the nearest Field Security Section on the showing of this note, without prior questioning by any unauthorised person.'

She had been told to ask for the 'Blond Major', Charles Macintosh, and also presented a note sent to the partisans by SOE's Captain Patrick Gubbins (now a security officer in Florence), in front of whom she now stood. 'He looked at me in amazement and exclaimed, "I never thought they would send such a young girl on a mission of this kind".'

Czernin had told her in July that 'in one week Florence will be free', but the advance had proved slow. On 14 August, the day before she crossed the front line, the Americans landed in southern France.

The officer who interrogated Paola after her transfer to Rome three days later concluded:

I see no reason to doubt the good faith of this 'courier'. She gave the 'Maggiore Biondo' password, and delivered a roll of dispatches and documents which included a 1 page report from the B.L.O. [British Liaison Officer] and a somewhat longer report in Italian from Commandante Verdi. She also had sundry specimens of German passes, including a TODT membership card, and a number of blank sheets of headed paper suitable for making out permits re employment with German War Industry etc. She showed courage and resourcefulness on the journey. The inspiration and incentive must have come partly [from] the death of her brother. I do not know whether she is aware of the suggestion of the B.L.O. that her P.W. father should be released sooner. I naturally did not broach the question for fear of putting false hopes into her head. But if this had been mentioned to her it would certainly have provided an even more powerful incentive to help carry her through.

Paola explained that the whole Udine–Trieste area was a prohibited zone and that anyone moving into it needed a permit. She said that anyone issued with a *carta d'identità* for the Udine area should have 'a 1944 card, as 1943 cards are checked up on carefully, especially for men of active age'. She also provided the name of a German informer in Udine, Enrico Natlachen of Via Marinoni, who had lived in Austria till 1938. Natlachen, whom she described as 'tall; thin; pale; hair blond, sparse' with blue eyes and gold-rimmed glasses, was housebound following a parachute injury but had 'numerous visitors . . . his guilt is not yet proved, but he is very suspect'.

Paola had been very disturbed that the Lieutenant Donaldson who interrogated her did not fit the description of the blond major and at first refused to hand over the documents. 'I was afraid I was under suspicion but the lady I was billeted with suggested I had no alternative except to hand them over.' After she had done this, she was promptly sent off by air to Brindisi and then on to Monopoli, arriving on 19 August. Here she was taken to one of a series of villas behind the town that had been appropriated by No. 1 Special Force. 'The one I was taken to at the beginning, if I'm not mistaken, had the code name Museum. I was told it belonged to an ambassador to Japan and had a wonderful library,' says Paola.

Here she ran into further trouble because the documents she had brought at such risk from Udine could not be found. Donaldson, she learnt later, had put them in the safe, gone off to a party and forgotten about them.

Nonetheless, SOE was clearly impressed with Paola and rapidly provided security clearance. The file report of 22 August 1944 reads: 'This girl is extremely capable . . . She was interrogated and cleared as quickly as possible . . . wishes to return to her area . . . She is quite willing to continue her work for us and does not merely want to return for family reasons.' She was also given permission to make a three-minute call to her sister Maria in Palermo, who was promptly summoned to British High Command so that they could speak on the telephone.

At Monopoli, the colourful head of No. 1 Special Force, Commander Gerry Holdsworth RNVR, had established an arrangement of training units based on those at Massingham, the SOE base outside Algiers. There was a parachute training school near Brindisi airfield at San Vito dei Normanni; a paramilitary battle school at Castello di Santo Stefano, a few miles down the coast from Monopoli; and a wireless training school nearby at La Selva. Paola's hopes of returning home before winter, as she had promised her mother, rose when she was sent on the parachute course, making the required four jumps in four days.

Meanwhile her father had arrived back home in October. 'He had gone out in the bottom of a ship with thousands of prisoners – he came back by plane in four days,' she says. Gerald Thistlethwaite, the officer looking after Paola, later recalled: 'In October 1944 I met Colonel Del Din in full Alpini uniform and took him to his daughter. At this dramatic reunion she had to break the tragic news to him that his only son Renato had been killed.'

She was now assigned as courier to the Bigelow mission. The commander of the mission, Gianandrea Gropplero di Troppenburg – code name Freccia – recalls his astonishment when on the commando course he saw Paola, his former schoolmate, walking towards him. As his radio operator he chose Dumas Poli – code name Secondino – who had been in the navy.

Unfortunately, the heavy losses of planes sent from southern Italy to assist the Warsaw uprising in August 1944 were not made good for six months, and as a result SOE was able to make fewer air sorties to northern Italy. Even so, over the winter, Paola and her companions made no less than ten tantalising abortive sorties. 'First an engine caught fire, then another one stopped. One time the pilot could not find the landing ground, another time the wings iced up. Or we ran into bad weather – but we were never able to jump,' she says.

Meanwhile, in Friuli conditions had deteriorated with the quartering of 20,000 Cossacks to winter in the province. The Germans, angered by partisan attacks that endangered their supply route across the Alps (and their line of retreat), brought the Cossacks in to drive the partisans out. Hitler had approved the creation of a Cossack army with its own generals in March 1944, promising that if the war did not allow them to return to their own lands, he would meet their needs in Western Europe. The Cossacks arrived in July and August by train via Villach in Austria. This was not a mechanised army. Their transport was drawn by horses, mules, bullocks and even camels. As winter approached, the Cossacks relentlessly pushed the partisans back into the mountains, often sacking whole villages in the process.

Finally, on the night of 9 April 1945, Paola and her companions took off from Rossignano Solvay, south of Livorno and close to No. 1 Special Force's new base at Siena. Ronald Taylor, who put her into the Dakota that dropped her some eight kilometres north of Udine, recalls: 'She looked just like a fifteen- or sixteen-year-old, her blonde hair plaited round her head. Tiny, but fearless.' A wireless message, 'Kisses to Mafalda,' was sent to announce their arrival. The pilot identified the dropping area from signals made with bicycle lamps by the waiting partisans.

Dakotas had a very big door and were first class for jumping. Unfortunately, Paola had forgotten to remove the woollen gloves that she had been given 'because of her small size' and found it impossible to manoeuvre her parachute ropes. As a result she landed with a fearful thud and found it difficult to walk for several days. 'I was shorter by five centimetres,' she laughs.

Returning home, she found that, after she had left, her mother had been imprisoned by the Germans without any charge and then released forty-two days later, without any reason given.

Freccia promptly formed a new brigade of partisans, the Giustizia e Libertà brigade, operating as part of the Osoppo division. They went into action repeatedly in the following weeks, losing a tenth of the 450 men they recruited. On 16 April Freccia's brigade set out to attack the retreating Germans at Buia but were spotted by Cossacks who immediately opened fire. Despite fierce resistance, Freccia and his wireless operator, Secondino, were wounded and captured. Freccia was then interrogated by an SS captain and three Cossacks. He refused to provide any information and was badly beaten, reopening his wounds. 'I suppose this could have been called torture but, with fresh wounds, it did not seem to hurt and I held out,' he said. Brought before a firing squad in the courtyard, Freccia recalls: 'I spoke to the women who had gathered round to watch the execution and urged them to tell their children that the freedom of Italy was worth dying for . . . I had never felt so happy, knowing I was going to sacrifice my life for my people and my country.'

But at that moment, in Hollywood style, his comrades fired a mortar into the courtyard, scattering the enemy. The execution was postponed. Freccia and his comrades were trussed up and thrown into a cart to be taken to the fortress at Osoppo and shot. On the way the partisans attacked again. The Cossacks threw themselves into the ditch and the horse bolted; Freccia was able to get loose and grab the reins. Ingeniously he then concealed himself in a cesspit where few were likely to come looking for him, using grappa to disinfect his wounds.

Learning of their predicament Paola strove to find a place where they could recover; Freccia was wounded in the thigh and Secondino in the head. Initially Freccia was moved from one barn to another but there was a constant threat of new round-ups. One evening just before curfew Paola and two young men boldly took Freccia by car to Udine to the house of a Red Cross worker whose family had looked after many wounded partisans. She also recovered a radio, enabling

Secondino to re-establish contact with No. 1 Special Force. 'During this time Renata [Paola] maintained contact with the mission and acted as courier in Udine and other towns in the area.' Freccia adds: 'Renata did her best to establish order amongst the different units, acting with great courage.' To Paola, although only a very young courier, fell the task of keeping up the morale and cohesion of the group. 'I gained their respect by showing that neither danger nor fatigue could stop me. They had to be kept ready to ward off attacks from retiring troops, and I had to supply the messages for the two transmitters in the area,' she says.

On 28 April the partisans in Friuli launched a concerted uprising. Paola recalls:

A heavy rain poured all night. Cossack or Turkestan carriages passed through the town in a long file. I had been told to be in Buia at S. Stefano by 8 a.m. I left Udine in the morning by the early trolley-car to Tarcento, got off at Collalto and walked the last eight to ten kilometres to Buia. Soon I was so drenched that my skirt was sticking to my legs, making it impossible to walk fast. As soon as I reached Buia and passed the barrier guarded by German sentries, the church bell rang eight times. I was on time.

Shooting began from all directions. The final battle with the Germans had begun. She immediately asked for a gun, hoping to finally avenge her brother. But this time her age counted against her and her request was met with a strict 'no'.

Paola's gallantry was recognised in the award of the same medal, the Medaglia d'Oro al Valor Militare, that her brother had received posthumously. She also proudly retains her parachute wings. Paola took her degree at Padua later in 1945. She then won a Fulbright Scholarship to the University of Pennsylvania where she spent two years. Returning to Italy to become a high school teacher, she married a doctor who worked in the hospital at Udine and quickly settled down to have a family of three girls and a boy.

Today she is one of forty-five survivors who bear the high honour of the Medaglia d'Oro. Every April she attends a ceremony in Tolmezzo in honour of her brother's uprising, on the anniversary of his death.

Chapter 12

ALIX D'UNIENVILLE

Oronte has the highest opinion of this girl and is most anxious that she should be awarded a British decoration if possible. She has already been proposed on the French side but this is taking some considerable time.

SOE memo of 8 August 1945

'She is discreet and inconspicuous – the last person to be suspected,' wrote Major John Wedgwood, the chief instructor at Beaulieu when Alix d'Unienville completed her course early in 1944. Unusually, Alix had been allowed to forgo the usual paramilitary training. It was not considered necessary for the civil mission she was to undertake: organising the reception and transmission of messages for de Gaulle's Free French *résistants* in the Paris area.

Born in May 1919 in Mauritius, Alix left the island with her family when she was six or seven and went to live in Brittany, near Vannes, and in Morbihan, where at different times the family had two châteaux, Nedo and Kerozee.

When the family were seeking to leave France from Bordeaux shortly after the government fell, she heard the famous broadcast of de Gaulle on 18 June 1940, calling on the French to fight on. Finding the British consulate at Bayonne shut, they took a taxi to Saint-Jean-de-Luz where they had heard the consulate was open. It was 23 June. Every room was full, but the d'Unienvilles finally found a family *pension* willing to take them, allowing Alix, her parents and her brother to sleep on banquettes in the hall. Hearing the Spanish border was shut, they went the next day to look for a ship. The last English boats were boarding Polish troops. They waited all day, then another, until finally all the troops had boarded. Then it was the turn of British civilians. Suddenly the officers relented. The crowd rushed forward pell-mell and had to mount by the pilot's ladder. The baggage followed, some of it falling into the sea. Men slept on the deck, the women in the hold. The Polish Red Cross served a hot meal to the soldiers; what was left was given to the women and children. In the afternoon the British provided tea for all. After that there was nothing to eat or drink and only the crew were fed. But Alix's mother, who spoke good English, returned with some bacon and potatoes for her children. On the third day, the little cargo ship left the convoy and on 28 June they at last saw the English coast. They arrived in Plymouth a few hours later, to be given drinks and sandwiches by the Red Cross.

London fascinated Alix; it was her first opportunity to explore a great capital city. With her brother she spent hours exploring the underground, entranced by the lights of the stations, sparkling like Christmas trees, as the trains emerged from the tunnels. Part of the excitement was that the station names in the suburbs had been taken down, and it was too risky with their foreign accents to ask for help.

Everyone was braced for an imminent German invasion, but what struck Alix most was the extraordinary calm. The memory of the rout in France, the chaotic exodus, the defeated looks on people's faces, all left a bitter taste. By contrast the British, desperate though their situation still was, were determined to fight to the end. 'I remember a poster that showed a Tommy at prayer – "We only kneel before you, O Lord," it said.' The authorities had learnt lessons from the streams of refugees who had cluttered the roads in France. Radio, newspapers and posters all carried a single message: 'Stay put!'

At that time there was still hope that the governors of the

French colonies would rally to de Gaulle. Then, on 3 July came the news of the bombardment of the French fleet by the Royal Navy at Mers-el-Kébir, followed a week later by the bombing of the *Richelieu* in a British raid on Dakar. 'After our enemies, our allies turned to crush us,' she says.

In 1940, provisions in England were still relatively plentiful. Bread was not rationed. Ration cards were not required in restaurants. Textile coupons were only introduced in July 1941. Alix discovered the shade of Hyde Park, the placid pelicans of St James's, the guard at Buckingham Palace, the counters at Woolworth's and the pleasure of banana splits. Sunday lunch among the French included soufflés, veal roasts, ice creams and fresh fruit with cream.

Then the blitz began. 'The first days we counted the raids, proud of our scores. But soon we lost count . . . I remember my first bomb. I was alone in the house, in my room on the top floor. It was daylight. I heard an aeroplane and immediately an enormous explosion. Despite the instructions to stay clear of the windows I rushed to look. The block opposite had simply disappeared. A whole new view had opened of other houses and courtyards. I was stupefied and fell on my bed as my legs would no longer support me.'

London houses, she observed, were without shutters.

The carillons of glass falling on to the pavements as entire façades collapsed were the high notes of the symphony of the blitz. The bass notes came with the crumbling of masonry and the bursting of bombs on the streets. The English remained stoical, whole families would descend to sleep in the underground stations. Each morning they emerged to discover a new capital pierced with unexpected views, choked with debris amidst which the buses improvised new routes every day. Inside disembowelled buildings, flowered wallpapers, bathrooms, furniture were all on view while curtains flapped in the wind.

The underground trains, unlike the metro in Paris, did not stop during the raids. On one occasion, she was unaware that a raid had commenced and she emerged as incendiary bombs were crashing down in front of the station, turning night into day as the whole quarter burned.

Wartime London seemed not drab but brilliantly colourful. 'The display of uniforms was an astonishing spectacle. On the pavements of Piccadilly and Oxford Street one saw the battledress of the British, the Poles, the Belgians, the *képis* of the French, the great hats of the New Zealanders, the Scots in kilts and the skirts of all the women in uniform.'

On their arrival in London, her brother had gone straight to de Gaulle's office to join the Free French. In October he was ordered with a friend, Henri Montocchio, to undertake a secret mission that would prepare the way for Madagascar and the island of Réunion to rally to the Free French. They were to broadcast from Mauritius to Réunion, an operation that the *Daily Sketch* pronounced one of the greatest propaganda successes of the war. Alix also wrote several broadcasts, which were accepted by the French section of the BBC. She was asked to address herself to French youth her own age. This was part of a policy that persuaded people from all walks of life – students, sailors, farmers, postal workers, nurses, plumbers, apprentice pastry-cooks – to speak of freedom to their fellow French men and women.

Alix went to work as a secretary at de Gaulle's headquarters in Carlton Gardens. Her boss was a Lieutenant d'Ollonde, whose real name was d'Harcourt. He had already lost a leg in the war but this did not deter him from going on a mission to France, from which he returned alive.

She moved on quickly to work on the production of propaganda leaflets destined for the groups of Free French all over the world. Some were to be dropped over France by the RAF, others were produced at the request of different Resistance movements. One simply carried the date 1918, announcing to the Germans that their day of reckoning was once again approaching.

Alix was familiar with the offices of the Free French special services in Duke Street, but one day in 1943, an officer gave her the top-secret address of their British counterpart and told her to go there for an immediate interview with a captain who was expecting her. Out in the street she realised that in the excitement she had not taken in the address. 'There was not the shadow of a name in my head,' she recalls. She could not return to the officer of the Bureau Central de Renseignments et d'Action who had briefed her; they would lose confidence in her at once. Risking all, she decided in desperation to turn to a London taxi driver. Did he know of a top-secret British establishment where foreigners went? 'A hush-hush office round here?' he said, a little mystified. She watched him walk over to a group of colleagues. Their gestures and guffaws showed they were highly amused. She said to herself, 'They don't know, or if they do they won't drive a foreigner there.' But no, he came back, started the engine and took her straight there.

Her captain was waiting and she was not even late. Her SOE training began in midsummer 1943 with a stay 'at an agreeable villa in the country'. Although she did not know it, this was one of the large houses in the grounds at Beaulieu. 'Our class was scarcely numerous, eight pupils in all: a young female radio operator, a British officer who had lived in France, a young surgeon, a young man whose real name was Davout d'Auerstaedt, three Frenchmen and myself.' The weeks that followed were the gayest and the most amazing she ever spent in England. The only work she could not cope with was the coding, 'interminable alphabetic juggling, until the message suddenly appeared before your eyes as if by magic but where a minuscule error demolished the whole structure irredeemably'. Their instructor was a Captain Drake whom she remembers as slim, lively, full of humour and speaking excellent French. He retained their attention with amusing examples. 'Suppose you have a rendezvous at a station with an unknown agent.

Do not approach him and whisper in his ear a phrase like "Pink elephants do not fly at night". Imagine you have made a mistake and the man cries "Au fou".'

Information about conditions in France was crucial. 'I was ignorant of life under the Occupation, I had never seen Germans, as during the exodus we were always fleeing before them.' One English officer on the course worried her; he spoke perfect French but his accent, although slight, was immediately perceptible. His bearing was also redoubtably British. She did not dare mention it to Drake, but spoke to her comrades. Then they were reassured; he was a sabotage expert who would go straight to a Maquis encampment.

'Specialist instructors came to teach us how to make false keys, to break locks, break into properties, poison dogs, survive in hostile conditions, in thick forests, and to find our way without a compass. I have often thought that if afterwards I had put these skills to work, my life would have been more amusing and profitable.'

The gun training unsettled her at first.

I am methodical, even a little slow. I like to take my time. It was just this that we were forbidden to do, on the principle that the first to fire wins the day. To acquire a good technique we practised in front of a glass. In one movement one had to turn, draw and shoot. Ten, twenty times it was necessary to start again because the turn was too slow, the legs in the wrong position or the arm too high or too low . . .

We shot also with live ammunition, with Stens and pistols at moving targets. Sometimes, faced suddenly with groups of mannequins we had to open fire, making sure we aimed only at our enemies. This exercise allowed us to test the speed of our reflexes. During one of these sessions, my pistol jammed. I heard the door open behind me. Drake took me by the arm. 'Well, you're dead, that's for sure.'

They went to sleep early, exhausted by the day's work and the intense physical exertions.

Innocently we thought this was the end of our work, leaving us in peace till the next morning. That was what our instructors intended. One evening, there was a mighty din. Drake beat on the doors. Those who were already asleep had to jump out of bed. Everyone was ordered downstairs to an interrogation. The pretend Gestapo attacked us at once, bombarding us with questions. All our stories of course were false but we had to defend them to the end, never to crack or contradict our accomplices.

It was, she says, a double anguish as their interrogators were also their examiners, on whom their missions depended. But this they forgot as the scene became more intense. 'We were prisoners, victims seeking desperately to parry the blows. "What were you doing at six o'clock? Why did you go out? Were you meeting a friend? His name! What were you wearing? Your accomplices have confessed. We know everything. You lie, you lie . . ." In their rage it would have been a small step to beat the truth out of us.'

Their course concluded with a training exercise in a neighbouring town. 'Our activities were so suspicious, especially in a time of war, that they could have placed us in serious trouble. To protect us, we all carried a hidden letter in case of arrest or major incident, but we were only to produce it as a last recourse. None of us had to.'

Next came parachute training.

We were very numerous but just two of us were French. The first day my fellow countryman broke his leg, and I was alone and the only woman. But many of the Poles spoke French. There were also two Belgians to whom I was instinctively drawn. But they held me in utter contempt. One of them was vastly taller than the other and they made a terrifying pair. They were professionals, real killers who had been in commando operations. The stories of their gunfights set my heart racing. Yet men of war sometimes offered strange contrasts. In the evening after the training sessions, the leader would sit at the piano, his colleague beside him. His big hands would play delicately on the keys and he sang with the voice of a nightingale.

Alix gives a vivid account of her feelings and fears.

When there were women in the line of parachutists, they jumped first. 'To give courage to the men,' they said. The red lamp lit up. 'Action stations,' cried the dispatcher. The plane was at 400 or 500 metres. One sat on the edge of the trap, feet dangling in the void, hands flat on either side. Houses, fields, roads, pylons glided beneath. In thinking of it after all these years, I still feel the blood beating in my ears while crying no, no, no. I sense the wind of the abyss whistling between my legs. The plane wobbles. It is not stable at so low an altitude. I sit on the extreme edge of the trap because my parachute is enormous on my back and I am always afraid that it will get caught. But it is vital not to lose balance and fall too soon. The plane wobbles more and more. My fingers tighten on the metal. Sweat floods over me. The green flashes on. The dispatcher does not shout, he roars 'Go! Go! Go!' until the last has jumped. He knows that force aids us. An order roared is like a trigger. At the moment of the jump, there is a sense of absolute emptiness. Then the shock of the parachute opening brought me back to consciousness. I felt an unexpected joy, a peace, a miraculous silence.

Alix had to do her practice jumps in February in bad weather, when there was the added problem of hauling in the parachute in strong winds. Generally the parachute dragged you along head first on your stomach, she says. Easy, explained the instructor: 'You turn onto your back and twist yourself round so your feet are in front. Then hold the straps firmly and the parachute will pull you back onto your feet. All you have to do then is to run rapidly towards it and turn it round. It will then collapse by itself.'

The instructors were as fearful of broken limbs and accidents as their charges. 'Keep your feet together as you jump,' they would say repeatedly. The practice night jump was the most difficult, but it went well for all, and as Alix gathered in her parachute she heard one of the instructors call to the others, 'The girl is all right' – a solicitousness that touched her. As they set off to the railway station the next day, with no broken limbs and no parachutes that had failed to open, a sudden warmth broke out. The Belgians started to sing, all the others joining in the refrains.

Back in London, the agonising waits began as the moon started to rule her life. During each fourteen-day moon period, she would stay close to the phone every morning until twelve o'clock; if she had not heard by then, she knew the operation had been postponed – for another day at least.

Alix remembers first a surge of relief and then, little by little, a renewed anxiety. She would wander through the streets, turn to go into a cinema and walk out just as quickly. Back at home, she would sit close to her mother, who knew she was on the verge of departure but thought she was destined for North Africa, which at that time was already safely in Allied hands. BCRA, without being prodigal, gave them sufficient funds to go and enjoy themselves. She recalls: 'For the first time in my life I had some money, which I spent as if there was no tomorrow.'

'Don't believe you will be so exposed. The Allied soldiers who disembark on the coast of France will be in much more danger than you,' Drake had said one day.

'He was right. Yet many of my comrades were arrested, many are dead. Of others I know nothing, and I never will know anything because I have forgotten their names. Only here and there floats a young face, a gesture, a word, a smile, an anecdote. All the rest has plunged into the shadows.'

On 31 March 1944, the moon entered its first quarter and Alix was again on the alert. She had flu but in the morning she made a routine call to BCRA. No, she was told, it would certainly not be today. She returned to her bed. Just before midday the telephone rang again. The operation was on. She was to present herself in uniform. Could an agent invoke the *grippe* as a reason for delay, she wondered. No, she would not even dare speak of it.

She put on a shirt and a khaki blouson, together with flat-soled shoes specially chosen for the jump, from which she had carefully erased every mark. Then she called a taxi and set off without luggage – that had all been prepared long before and was held by the British dispatchers. The driver took her to the BCRA offices in Dorset Square. From here she was driven off in a car by British officers, with a French comrade who was to jump with her. The message announcing their arrival had already been broadcast by the BBC: 'Deux anges viendront faire de la dentelle ce soir' – two angels will make lace this evening. Dentelle was the name of the dropping ground to which they were being sent in the Loir-et-Cher.

The details of the drive out of London are forgotten but she remembers well the large agreeable country house where they were taken. Her destination was Paris, which she remembered crossing on her way to Brittany as a child. Not wishing to be taken for an ignorant provincial, she declared she knew the capital well and carefully memorised a list of rendezvous in places that meant nothing to her. Several agents were already waiting, killing time by playing cards and walking in the pretty English garden.

She and her male companion were immediately taken to different rooms, where they put on their civilian clothes, which had been made to measure by the British. For her, they had prepared a grey dress and grey coat. It was all simple enough but also infused with meaning, for at that moment they became Francs-Tireurs, soldiers without uniform whom no treaty protected. A young woman in uniform searched her gently and conscientiously to ensure there was no label in her clothing, no paper, no ticket, no wrapper, nothing capable of betraying her.

Rejoining her companion, she was conducted into a large and beautiful dining room. It was early and they were alone. One excellent dish followed another but it was not a gay occasion, and during the dessert an officer brought them their cyanide pills. She recalls how they were assured that the pills were very well wrapped. If necessary they could hold them in their mouths and even swallow them without ill effect. Only if they bit hard would death be upon them.

To don their parachutes they were taken to a building beside the airfield. For her practice jumps Alix had worn small leather boots, which provided good support. Now she had to jump in flat soles, but they bound her ankles to strengthen them and she slipped on cloth boots to protect her from the mud. Agents had to be able to emerge from the dropping ground with their clothing unsoiled to avoid attracting attention. Their overalls had a large pouch at the back designed to take a sizeable packet. This was filled with 2 million francs in small denominations, which Alix had to carry with her, conveniently serving as a cushion.

Each agent received a silver compass and a silver flask filled with rum. Their helmets were of thick rubber and they had to carry two pairs of gloves, silk within a thicker lined pair. All of these were too big to fit her, so she ended by taking her own leather gloves.

Next came the choice of a pistol, a dagger or a knife. Although tempted by the magnificent dagger, she chose the knife as its narrow handle better fitted her hand. The dagger was usually carried against the leg, the knife in a pocket of the overalls. These also contained a torch, medical dressings and even a shovel, should she need to bury her parachute or equipment.

Against the shovel, Alix rebelled. Several dozen containers were being dispatched with them, not to mention a suitcase containing 40 million francs, which she had to deliver to Paris. If the reception committee was not there, what was she to do, she reasonably asked. Finally she was given her pistol. If all went well she was to hand this to the reception committee. With so many controls carried out on the trains and metros, guns were considered a liability. Alix thought this was debatable. When one of her comrades was arrested by two Gestapo officers, he took out his gun, shot both of them and successfully escaped.

Night had fallen when they boarded the Halifax. Alix was so heavily laden that she had to be helped in. Then began a long uncomfortable journey shut off from the world outside, the noise so loud you had to shout to be heard. She had been told that sandwiches, even rum, were served to help pass the time but none appeared. No one spoke. As a woman, she was to jump first. As the light went green, the dispatcher said 'Go', hardly raising his voice. For a fraction of a second she hesitated. Outside the moon shone feebly – it was the first day of the first quarter.

In the dim light she appeared to be plunging towards a meadow. It was only as she touched the first branches that she realised it was a wood. Protect your face, keep your legs together and allow yourself to fall freely, she had been told, should she drop into trees. As she bounced to a halt in the tree canopy, her first feeling was of relief. She had broken nothing. Dogs barked furiously, a bad sign suggesting there were houses nearby. Without success she sought to release the buckle of her harness. Instead she seized her knife, which cut like a razor through the straps, allowing her to descend to the ground.

Making her way out of the wood into the moonlight she found her companion who, like her, had landed in the trees. On the far side of a ditch they suddenly fell on a heap of bicycles. An instant later the reception committee surged out of the darkness.

The young men who met them were simple, lively and brave. They took them to a farm where they were served a second dinner for which they had a better appetite. Alix was astonished by the big pots of rillettes on the table and the pails of milk along the length of the wall behind them. Was this how the French were dying of hunger, she wondered. The night was well advanced by the time they were taken to a long-closed hotel, which the patron had opened specially for them. The next morning she looked out through the slatted shutters on a village street where people were talking, looking up to the windows and laughing. The whole village seemed to know of their arrival.

Several hours later the 'chef du terrain' arrived. He had been in Paris when the BBC had broadcast the message announcing their imminent arrival. His *nom de guerre* was Seigneur; this was appropriate, says Alix, as he was tall and slender with the profile of an eagle. Towards the evening her luggage and her millions of francs arrived, and she set off on the train to Paris, escorted by Seigneur and his assistant. But soon they were being pestered by a man who seemed more like an agent provocateur than a simpleton; he talked loudly of the 'tourists' who took 'our butter, our wine, our girls'. Seigneur was evidently equally uncomfortable and made straight for the Feldengendarmerie post on the platform in Paris, explaining that the poor young girl with him was exhausted and frozen. The soldiers took pity and let Alix bring in her suitcases as well. There they sat, occasionally smiling and exchanging gestures.

De Gaulle's Comité de la Libération was represented in Paris by a *délégué général*, Alexandre Paroli, residing in Paris, and two *délégués adjoints* for the north and south zones. Alix was to be attached to Roland Pré, the *délégué* for the northern zone. They knew that the Allied landings were imminent, and one of the principal tasks of the Delegation was to devise administrative structures that could be put in place as soon as the government changed. The Delegation's headquarters was above the Épicerie Luce in the place de Passy. It was entered through a block in the rue Duban, although there was an escape exit through the grocery should the Gestapo suddenly arrive.

Between London and Paris, Alix says, the gulf was total. London had been alive and cosmopolitan, Paris was oppressive and silent. The streets echoed to the sound of wooden clogs and German voices, and German music played every morning in the Champs Elysées. Only the sound of the sirens and the bombing raids were familiar. In London, fashion had been extremely strict during the war, inspired by the military dress. Skirts were straight, cuts classic and hats like peaked caps. By contrast, many people in Paris wore old clothes, even made out of the living-room curtains.

She was struck most by the air of resignation. Even those who knew she had come from England showed no curiosity about life in the free world. To them the war already seemed to have lasted an eternity.

Part of Alix's job was military – the organisation of radio transmissions – and she had been given the rank of Lieutenant. SOE provided her with an identity in the name of Aline Bavelan, born on the island of Réunion in 1922, who had come to France in 1938 to continue her studies in Paris. In France she received a new identity, that of a young wife whose husband was a prisoner of war. With false papers it was vital to constantly remember dates of birth and first names; for this Alix remembers that agents often kept their actual birthdays and first names, except where they had borrowed the identity of a real person, which was sometimes the case.

The agents of BCRA, or RF Section as it was known in SOE, had Resistance names like F Section agents, in their case taken from literature, science, history and zoology. Her group drew their names from Molière; her chief was called Oronte. She was Myrtil. For their comrades in France they had yet another name: Alix was Marie-France. Prudent agents, she says, chose common names but too many had exotic or bizarre ones – like Polygone, Espace or Crocodile – which were picked up by inquisitive ears all too easily in restaurants. Although the British had furnished her with textile and clothing coupons, she had no food ration tickets and was not registered, as she needed to be, at a particular point of sale. So, all the time she was in Paris, she ate at black market restaurants; however, even here it was necessary to present bread tickets. But by 1944 there was a well-established system by which a group of *résistants* would descend on a provincial *mairie* at the beginning of each month and steal the bread tickets, which quickly arrived in Paris.

Her most dangerous moments would come at each rendez-vous. The scenario had been described to her many times: 'You are waiting at the chosen place and suddenly two men are beside you. "Your papers," they demand, but this is a pretence and a car glides up and you are hustled in and you are lost.' The principle was that both parties arrived at a rendezvous exactly on time so that neither had to wait, although usually, says Alix, there were a few pained moments before the contact rushed out of the metro, or appeared breathless at the end of the street. Between two rendezvous there could be a long wait, which Alix would occupy by walking in parks and public gardens. On one occasion she felt she was being followed. She found a bench near the fountain basin in the Tuileries gardens and, sure enough, her pursuer sat down opposite her. She stood up and walked off, not so fast that she appeared to be in full flight, but still he followed. She went to the Palais Royal and decided to try the metro ruse – jumping out of the compartment as the doors closed. But he was ready. Back on the platform, she was expecting the dreaded demand for her papers, although by now the shabby-looking man no longer looked like a Gestapo agent. 'Mademoiselle, you are in a rush, I see. But even so you have time for a drink,' he said. Such a thing had never occurred to her. She looked at the little man with sudden sympathy; he had momentarily brought her back to a world she had long forgotten.

In the evenings, after the last rendezvous of the day, life changed and suddenly became gay. She was still in contact with Seigneur, who 'lived life with insolence and a magnificent aplomb'. They went to nightclubs where champagne flowed. Yet no one danced, a simple measure, she says, which avoided fraternisation between conquerors and conquered. They would dine to music and cabarets would follow. Then there was the rush to be home before the curfew, to find a hackney carriage or bicycle taxi. Seigneur always stood aside as she gave her address, which he took care not to know. One night, when the hour of the curfew had already passed, Seigneur persuaded the hackney carriage driver to take her by giving him a huge tip. The horse walked painfully slowly. She looked out in terror, expecting to see German patrols, but the city was completely empty, silent and dark.

At the beginning of June, they heard on the radio the long-awaited phrases, announcing the invasion. On the morning of 6 June, leaving her apartment, she stopped for a moment to look at the sky. The weather looked unsettled so she went back to fetch an umbrella. As a result of this slight delay she chanced on a member of the Delegation as she left.

'It's begun,' he cried.

'Where?' she asked.

'In Normandy,' he replied.

Her instinct was to stride out and tell everyone, street by street, that the first French soil was already free. But there was work to be done. Her first rendezvous was outside the Bon Marché store with Tristan and two comrades. She walked down the rue Babylone. No one was waiting in front of the shop. She was hesitant to leave straight away and passed time looking at the hawkers' baskets outside the store, pausing to buy a ball of wool. Two men passed in front of her. A voice in her subconscious said, 'The Gestapo.' But she set such worries aside and, strolling slowly, returned to the rendezvous opposite the exit of the metro. This time she saw Tristan accompanied by a friend.

She had just said excitedly, 'The Allies have landed,' when a voice barked out, 'Your papers.' They were surrounded. A car drew up alongside the pavement. It was exactly as everyone had described it. Her thoughts turned immediately to her cyanide pill. To take it, or let it drop through a little hole in the pocket of her coat into the gutter? She did neither. This turned out to be a grave error as it was later found in her possession. Fortunately, as they were bundled into the car, a girl who had come to meet them arrived in the square. Retreating hastily, she was able to alert their colleagues and cancel the meetings for the rest of the day.

They had been arrested by Himmler's Sicherheitsdienst and were taken to the notorious SD headquarters in the Avenue Foch where so many SOE agents were held, male and female. The Germans interrogated them together. Alix was much surprised that they knew her code name, Myrtil, and that of Tristan too. The joint interrogation helped, as she heard Tristan's responses.

She was photographed. A woman went through her pockets. She was wearing the clothes in which she had left England two months before, which had been so meticulously searched before she set off. Yet two years later, unstitching a seam in the coat, she was to find a note of the London tailor with her English measurements. Her pockets now yielded both the key to her apartment and the cyanide pill. The latter was irrefutable proof that she was working for the Resistance, especially as the Germans knew these pills were issued almost exclusively to agents from London. Her bag was seized and locked up, their fictitious names and addresses taken down. Every agent, she said, had an emergency address, a real one, to give if captured, which would not compromise others. Finally they were asked if they were Jews. The Germans, she noted, were highly agitated, not just because of the invasion but also, as she was later to learn, because they had just embarked on a massive round-up of which she and Tristan were the first victims. As a result their interrogation was mercifully curtailed. Then they were bundled into a prison van with individual cells and taken to the infamous gaol at Fresnes. Here she was thrust into a dark solitary cell, thoughts of imminent torture preying on her mind. After several hours she was moved to a new cell that was already occupied by two prisoners.

The next day the van took her back to the Avenue Foch. The same Germans awaited her – giving her the impression that a single team was charged with each investigation in its entirety. Her bag was brought out and the contents emptied on the table. Inside was a vast sum of money destined for their radio operators.

Where did the money come from? Who was it intended for? She replied vaguely that it was her own. Indeed, she could hardly concentrate as all her attention was focused on a single object – a metro ticket. On the back of the ticket she had scribbled an address, not of a Resistance comrade but of a doctor she was going to contact on behalf of a friend. She had been trained never to write anything down but her memory was so full of addresses that at that moment she had felt she could remember no more. Her fear was that the doctor would promptly be arrested.

For a moment the German turned away. In an instant Alix leant forward, stretched out her hand and seized the ticket. When he turned back, she was sitting immobile just a fraction closer to the table. He noticed nothing. She demanded to go to the lavatory. He refused but she persisted with such vehemence that he finally took her. Waiting outside, he stood with his foot in the door but a blind angle allowed her some freedom. She thought first about flushing the ticket down the lavatory but, fearful that it might resurface, popped it into her mouth and chewed the hard dry paper. As she stood up, the German pushed the door violently but it was over. She had swallowed the ball of paper.

Now her worries were centred on the key and the cyanide pill. By a miracle they said nothing of the pill, but they had taken the key to the decoy address she had given, found it was necessary to force the lock and now demanded to know what door the key was supposed to open. She had no idea what to say to hide the real address from them. Then she remembered a Resistance colleague who, in a flash of inspiration when faced with this same dilemma, had explained that keys were used as recognition symbols by the Resistance, who were given matching keys to enable them to identify themselves to colleagues.

Almost immediately another catastrophe was upon her. The German began to talk of the apartment used by the Delegation in the place de Passy. How had they discovered this address? She could not understand. With horror she heard him say that they had descended on the office and arrested everyone. It was only after the Liberation that she heard what had really happened. At the emergency address she had given, a comrade had left various papers, among them a receipt for the rent at the Delegation. The moment that news came of her arrest, they had remembered the incriminating receipt. As the SD van drew up outside the block in the rue Duban, her colleagues were evacuating the office and all its contents through the grocery. But they left a scrap of paper, saying: 'Madame Clément demande à Myrtille d'aller la voir.'

Again, the Germans failed to press her about 'Madame Clément' or the Delegation and turned instead to her own details. Suddenly she had to fill in the four years she had spent in England. She should have been prepared but had trusted in luck. So she chose Normandy where hopefully the Germans would no longer be able to check anything. She placed herself in Rouen where she had never been, fabricating details of family, friends, activities. She gave them an address of 10 route de Paris, believing that there must be a route de Paris somewhere on the outskirts of Rouen. No. 10 was the number of the family home in Devonshire Terrace, London.

When the Germans demanded to know her rendezvous, she invented several, pretending to reveal them with reticence and pointing out that they would no longer be used. Her interrogation took place in an atmosphere of shouting, threats and harrying. But the idea that she might have come from London never dawned on her interrogators. They never demanded to know her codes. Instead they concentrated their brutish efforts on her comrade. Tristan was cruelly tortured. Twice, to break his resistance, they carried out mock executions. In final desperation he prised open a ring in which a dose of poison was hidden, only to find that a member of his family had removed it. Although scarred for life, Tristan was to survive, jumping from the railway wagon that was taking him to Germany.

The Germans who arrested and interrogated her all spoke very good French, even if certain intonations and turns of phrase revealed their nationality. More unpleasant still was the evident fact that Frenchmen were working with them. Even today Alix asks herself how so many of her compatriots could be among their accomplices, not only collaborators and profiteers of every type but people about whom nothing suggested they would be informers.

At Fresnes she was not isolated but kept with three or four others in a cell designed for one. The day began with a summons for all those to be interrogated by the Gestapo or the SD. No one knew what stage their inquisition had reached. There were prisoners who appeared to have been forgotten for months or years. Some of those whom Alix came to know had nothing to do with the Resistance, but had been arrested for black marketeering, or through having dealings with the Germans, or had simply been denounced.

In her first cell a strict discipline reigned, instilled by a lady who had been long in prison. 'She considered herself at home. We were her guests,' says Alix. The woman had discovered that by rubbing the wooden floor with sufficient energy it could be made to shine like wax. Every morning they were set to work armed with the handles of spoons until the whole floor sparkled like the parquet of a salon.

'We were dying of hunger. In the morning we received a black mixture called coffee and at lunchtime half a loaf of bread and a bowl of warm water with a few potato peelings floating in it. In the evening there was nothing.' They lost count of the hours and days; no one had a watch in prison. Through filthy windows the light glowed faintly as from another world. Messages were passed from one cell to another through ventilators, sometimes travelling the whole length of a block. News from the outside world, brought by new prisoners, also circulated but the progress of the Allies seemed slow, the same names of towns being repeated again and again.

One day she received a visit from the German chaplain, the Abbé Stock, 'an admirable priest who was in touch with the social service of the Resistance', which had asked him to make contact with Alix.

She was suspicious but through him felt a feeble link to her comrades. A problem now pressed upon her. She knew that the Germans had discovered one of their emergency apartments at Alfortville. It was all but empty and contained nothing compromising, but it figured on a list of places where a lorry could make deliveries of food as the Allies approached Paris. If the Germans laid a trap and caught the driver, they could wrest from him a list of other depots, prompting a cascade of arrests. The chaplain asked if she needed food or clothes and, while she talked, she thought feverishly of an apparently anodyne message she could ask him to convey. It sounded so strange that he made her promise that it had nothing to do with Resistance work. She had lied to him but it was to protect the lives of her comrades. Later she heard that her message was so obscure that her colleagues could not understand it. The Germans set the trap and the lorry duly arrived, but the concierge alerted the driver and he fled with both his lorry and his list.

All the time Alix dreamt of escape. There are two kinds of escapes, she decided. Some prisoners approach it full of guile and method, watching every movement of their captors. For others it is simply a matter of audacity and seizing the moment.

She turned these ideas over in her mind, lying on her mattress with her face to the wall, while her companions interminably played cards. Being methodical and patient, she felt her best chance lay in the first method. Her reactions might not be swift enough for the second, nor did she have the physical strength that might be required. Either way, it was evident that no escape was possible from Fresnes. To begin, therefore, she had to be transferred elsewhere. There was no hope of simulating an illness. Even when prisoners were in extreme agony the Germans would not move them. She concluded that only madness – *la folie* – offered her a chance. The mentally deranged were not kept at Fresnes but were sent to Sainte-Anne. It was a dangerous strategy. The Germans might incarcerate her in a psychiatric hospital and subject her to horrific experiments, or simply kill her.

She began by shutting herself away from the world, creating a universe of complete solitude. Her role model was a servant that the family had had in France who would chat away, leaving the iron to burn a hole in the clothes while utterly unaware of what was happening around her. 'I noticed that she never looked anyone in the eye, always beyond or through them. That was the key, never to have eye contact,' she says. To her surprise, both her companions and her wardresses became fearful of her state. Only once did a warder assert that it was a pretence. Another wardress, a large motherly lady with a round face, began to take pity on her. She squeezed Alix against her chest, muttering to her in German. One day she brought Alix an orange.

Her companions became frightened for her, and during the hours of darkness the warders looked more often through the eye in the door. She would utter cries in the night and her companions would try to summon the warders. When they came she would throw herself upon them. Such was the element of surprise that several times she succeeded in escaping onto the gallery, pursued by the Germans. They did not treat it as a real attempt at escape, merely the action of a deranged girl. Next she refused to eat. She pretended that her captors were trying to poison her. First it was the soup, then the bread. As she became feebler she lay on her bed, imagining the strident Hindu music of her youth. The feeling of hunger quickly disappeared.

The doyenne of her cell spoke a little German and the length of her stay gave her a certain status with the warders. One afternoon as Alix appeared to sleep on her mattress, she heard the doyenne confiding that Alix would soon depart for Sainte-Anne.

The next day two wardresses and several soldiers came to collect her. One after another the iron gates along the interminable corridors were opened and at last she saw Paris again in the light of summer, the leaves of the plane trees beginning to turn yellow, the wide streets and occasional passers-by in light clothing.

Alix arrived at a hospital pavilion. But once again there were dirty walls and German uniforms. She had been brought not to Sainte-Anne but to the hospital-prison of La Pitié, associated with the most brutal atrocities of the Gestapo. They took off her clothes and gave her a short shirt. She was in a cell with two beds but the other one was empty. There were no warders in the pavilion, only soldiers under the orders of an Austrian officer who did not appreciate his role. In the cells there was neither water nor a WC, as at Fresnes. Only at night was she out of the gaze of the soldiers who at any moment might look through the slit in the door. Each day a young man, accompanied by a soldier, came to empty the pots. She took him for a German, but one day when the guard had retreated they exchanged a few words. He was French, a *résistant* condemned to death and waiting to be shot.

At first, silence reigned in the pavilion. In the depths of the night she could just hear a clock strike. Then one night there was an appalling clamour. She could hear men being tortured and dying in nearby cells, and again and again the words, 'Tu parleras, tu parleras,' you will speak, you will speak.

After several days a woman was brought into Alix's cell. The soldiers undressed her and laid her down because she was incapable of any movement. Her body was covered in horrendous black and blue lacerations; there were burns on her face and breasts; her feet had been burnt. Her paralysed arms hung limply; she had been suspended too long by her wrists. Her long hair was thick with blood. She was a Pole who belonged to a circuit formed in France by her compatriots. The first day the Austrian officer fed her with a spoon like an infant. After that Alix took over. 'You are the first human being I have seen since my arrest,' the woman said. For her, Alix renounced the absolute silence she had imposed on herself and admitted that she was not mad but merely simulating madness. She learnt that the woman had revealed nothing to the police who had inflicted such suffering on her. 'I always kept sufficient sang-froid to suppress the moments when I suffered most. Instead I screamed when the pain eased to direct the Germans to the least sensitive parts of my body.' Alix promised herself to remember the advice. When the woman could bear no more, she had attempted suicide by trying to tear at the veins of her wrists with her teeth but her bonds had held her back.

One morning Alix's guards returned her clothes and she was driven in a van to Sainte-Anne. At last she was at the hospital she had intended. But all did not proceed as she had hoped. There was no consultation, no hospitalisation. At no point was she put in contact with doctors or French patients. She was in a German wing; even the lunatics were German soldiers. At midday she would lunch in their company in a vast communal hall, shepherded in by a wardress and two soldiers. Her appearance produced an astonishing effect. 'This band of madmen, thrilled to see a mad woman, made friendly signs to me and shouted compliments from afar.'

A young doctor then examined her. To the numerous questions that he posed through a nurse, she gave a mix of reasoned and bizarre answers, repeating that she was not mad at all in the belief that this was the best means of persuading them to the contrary. After listening to her chest he pronounced, to her alarm, that she had a rattle in her lungs.

That evening she was taken back to the Pitié in a canvas-covered truck, accompanied by a single soldier. At one moment the soldier put down his rifle to attach the canvas flap at the back. Both his hands were occupied. She thought of hurling herself on him and pushing him out, then slipping out herself further on, unseen by the driver in his cab. She hesitated. The moment passed.

Back in her cell she found her companion still unable to wipe away her tears because of her paralysed arms and agonised by the sounds all day long of one of her comrades being tortured to death in a neighbouring cell.

Now Alix began gradually to abandon her madness, finding it had not helped towards an escape. She started to eat again – since her arrival they had been threatening to feed her by force. Here, instead of a thin gruel, they offered a ragout and slices of bread spread with lard. When she appeared to have sufficiently recovered her reason, they took her back to Fresnes.

One by one the iron gates closed behind her. Now she was shut in a new cell where one of her companions had passed the greater part of the war, keeping fit with regular exercises every morning. This second stay at Fresnes was brief. She learnt that she was to be transferred to the camp at Romainville. It was both good and bad news, for Romainville was simply a transit camp on the way to Germany.

Life at Romainville was less painful than at Fresnes. Although they were famished, by day they could circulate freely within the encampment. By night they were eaten up by bedbugs, but it was summer and they could breathe in the fresh air. She made friends. One, Marie, was a German communist who had spent years in prison. With another, Annie Hervé, she formed a plan of escape. Their camp was within the fort of Romainville, surrounded by a deep ditch. To descend into the ditch they needed a rope, which they made from thin strips torn from the black curtains in the empty top floor of the building in which they slept, hiding them in their mattresses.

They slept in adjoining beds. In the middle of the night when they were sure their neighbours were asleep, they sat on the edges of their beds in the dark, without a word, making the rope. One held the ends of the strips, the other plaited them three by three. Then they attached them to the rest of the rope.

One day a gathering wave of whispers spread through the camp: the Americans were marching on Paris. They would arrive within hours. Prisoners fell into one another's arms, laughing and crying at the same time. Women did their hair to greet their liberators. Those who could changed their clothes. Lipstick, hidden for months, emerged. There would be so many Yankees to embrace.

Hours passed. Night came. They were shut in their dormitories. The searchlight of the watchtower flashed along the barbed wire. The Allies did not arrive.

When the rope was finished their thoughts turned to the details of their escape. They decided to make the attempt in daylight when soup was being distributed and everyone was preoccupied. They smuggled out the coil of rope to the latrines and pushed it out through a ventilator where it lay hidden in long grass. Then, the evening before the day they had fixed on, Annie was deported to Germany. Alix remained behind, she knew not why. Shortly afterwards their rooms were searched. She watched the guards turning the mattresses, thinking of the black cord, which she was to find again after the war where they had left it, coiled like a boa.

One of the prisoners, a PT instructor, organised exercise sessions every morning, which Alix joined to build up her strength. She also spent hours walking the length of the barbed-wire enclosure. Now her thinking turned to an escape during transit to Germany. She imagined herself camping in the woods, scaling mountains, swimming across rivers, eating wild berries and snaring game as her English instructors had taught them. It was a fashion in the camps for prisoners to embroider their clothes with the names of the places in which they had been incarcerated. Alix decided against it, as it was hardly a camouflage for an escape.

On 15 August the last great convoy from Romainville began. The Germans were emptying the camp as the Allies approached. When previous convoys had left the remaining prisoners would gather to sing:

> Ce n'est qu'un au revoir, mes soeurs,
> Ce n'est qu'un au revoir . . .

This time there was no one to sing for them, only a small group of women and children. The Germans brutally pushed them back, grabbing a boy and hauling him up but relenting amidst the cries of the prisoners. As the convoy started, prisoners cast out little balls of paper on which they had scribbled messages, hoping that they might somehow reach their loved ones.

They were being transported in Paris buses, the vintage kind unseen in the war known as à l'impériale, with an open balcony at the back. The convoy drove to Pantin, where they were herded into cattle wagons in an abominable state. Sitting on the floor, they were packed so close it was scarcely possible to move. No one knew how long the journey would be. Nothing was known of the conditions in the German camps. When the doors of the wagons closed they were plunged into darkness. Only a narrow slit, threaded with barbed wire, let in a little light and air. It was stiflingly hot. There was nothing to drink. The train progressed slowly, along tracks repeatedly damaged by sabotage and bombing.

By evening they had scarcely passed Meaux. Finally the train ground to a halt in a tunnel where they spent the night and most of the next morning. When at last the train began to move, Alix scarcely noticed that it was rolling backwards. Suddenly it lurched to a halt. German voices were calling for everyone to get out. They found themselves amidst fields. The soldiers prepared them to continue on foot. She held on tightly to her little bundle of clothes, which contained a small packet of provisions from the Red Cross. Might this compromise her if she escaped? She kept a tin of sardines and some sweets but threw away the rest. Their long cortège, escorted by soldiers, stretched out along a plain. At regular intervals were placed machine-gun batteries. Suddenly she understood. The railway bridge across the River Marne had been cut by Allied bombardments. They had to cross the river by a road bridge and rejoin the tracks where another train would be waiting. But why, for what possible reason, were the Germans expending so much effort in transporting exhausted, enfeebled women back to Germany?

They passed a group of houses under the horrified gaze of the residents. Children looked on stupefied and the starving deportees, anxious to kindle any spark of humanity, threw them precious sweets they had saved.

The road bridge crossed the Marne at a great height. Alix, walking beside the parapet, looked down at the water running between reed-filled banks. Could she jump? The bridge was too high, the guards too close. Soon the bridge was behind her and they were approaching a new cluster of houses, the little village of Méry-sur-Marne. This was her last chance. There was a drinking fountain on the outskirts of the village. Prisoners pressed forward to use it. The guards rushed to stop them. Alix saw her chance and this time she would not lose it. In the confusion she was able to take a few steps away from the column. A few steps more and she was beside a door. She pushed. It opened. She entered a darkened room in which a man and a woman looked on aghast without saying a word. Outside the window, a few metres away, the crowd of prisoners and guards pressed on. Finally, the man came towards her. They whispered a few words and he took her up to the first floor, telling her to stay away from the window. She waited, listening, expecting every moment to hear yells and the pounding of feet on the stairs. But the minutes passed. There was no sound except the thumping in her temples.

Soon after she decided she must leave her refuge. The Germans still felt too close. Outside, the stream of deportees continued, but her group had passed. Now neither the prisoners nor the Germans would recognise her. Following the instructions of her host, she crossed a courtyard and walked out into the country. Peaceful, empty meadows stretched before her. She found an apple tree surrounded by fallen fruit and ravenously began to eat. Several hours later she was to feel horribly ill but that lay in the future. Next she came upon a woodcutter in a little wood on the edge of the meadows. His heavy German accent terrified her. 'You are from the convoy. You have escaped,' he said. She froze.

Suddenly his face shone with warmth and compassion. Unable to deny it, she decided to confide in him. He found her a hiding place in the wood and went off to tell his family. Returning, he explained that there were some people living nearby whose trustworthiness concerned him, and that she must wait. He continued his work. Then when everyone was at lunch he took her to his home. The family received her with delight and gave her water, soap, a comb, clean clothes. Lunch was served. It seemed a feast. This was a region where food was plentiful.

Conscious of the risk they were all running, she moved the next night to another village nearby, Saacy-sur-Marne. Here she stayed with the Thouvenot family who lived in a large house with a garden behind, full of fruit and vegetables. For a time she had to remain hidden. Then Madame Thouvenot decided on a ruse. Giving Alix an empty suitcase, she let her out of the end of the garden, instructing her to walk round and enter the village along the main street. Madame Thouvenot was waiting on the doorstep and ran towards Alix with open arms, greeting her as a long-lost cousin and presenting her proudly to the neighbours.

Listening to the BBC, they followed the progress of the Allies but, even though there were Germans about, the village remained lost in the torpor of summer. Across the fields on the Route Nationale they could see the German army in retreat: armoured vehicles, lorries full of troops and even horse-drawn transport, requisitioned or stolen from the farms. One day the Germans left the village with hardly a sound. They were free. But no one knew where the Germans were or whether they would return. No vehicle of any kind appeared. One morning, when picking mushrooms, they saw the Americans. They dropped their baskets and rushed forward to wave but the Americans hurtled through, alert, hurried and ill-at-ease, shouting back no more than a few words of greeting.

The great fête of the Liberation came a few days later, when a large troop of Americans arrived in the village. Flowers cascaded down on the armoured vehicles; fresh fruit was thrust into the hands of the young soldiers who threw them chewing gum and cigarettes in return. Wine flowed. Everyone rejoiced. Then the reckoning began. A girl who had consorted with the enemy was hustled forward and her hair was cut off in great tufts. Alix, her heart hardened by war, felt no pity till she saw a young American soldier turn away with a grimace and walk off. That is a lesson for me, she thought.

Several days later she returned to Paris in an American army jeep. It was a journey of just sixty kilometres, through the same landscape she had glimpsed as the train inched forward towards Germany. The verges of the road were lined with abandoned vehicles. Soon after they entered Paris, the Americans left her at a street corner. She had no idea where she was. The map that she once used to carry was still in her bag at the Avenue Foch. It took her hours to cross the city, past the debris of barricades, burnt-out vehicles and fallen trees. At last she arrived in the Boulevard des Invalides in front of her apartment. The concierge looked at her in amazement. Suspiciously, she gave her a spare key. Have you been in the country, she asked. Yes, said Alix. I have been in the country.

After the war Alix spent several years working as an air hostess for Air France. From her experiences she wrote a book, *En vol: journal d'une hostesse de l'air*, published in 1949, which enjoyed a huge success. Five years later, another volume, *Les Mascareignes: Vieille France en Mer Indienne*, was published, followed by a novel, *Le Point Zéro*, set on the island of Rodrigues. Alix returned to see her rescuers, the Thouvenots and Monsieur and Madame Haus into whose cottage she had stumbled when she slipped away from the prison column. Today she lives in a modest apartment with a pretty pocket-handkerchief of a garden, overlooking the intense blue of the Mediterranean.

Alix was awarded the MBE Military, the Légion d'Honneur and the Croix de Guerre. Yet she never received another decoration, which she equally deserved – the much-prized Médaille des Évadés, the medal for escapers. She says wistfully: 'It was the only one I really wanted, and I never got it.'

EPILOGUE

You have come to kill me. It would make such a good end.
Countess Clémentine Mankowska to the author, March 2001

This book has told the story of ten women agents. Of course there are many others. Some are well known like Odette Sansom, some are hardly known at all, especially those who worked outside France where so many of these women served.

There is Lela Karayanni in Greece, heroic mother of seven children, five of whom worked with her, organising intelligence, sabotage and the first escape of British servicemen to Egypt. She was arrested in October 1941 but was released after six months. Immediately she resumed her clandestine work, continuing until she was betrayed in March 1944. Under torture she remained silent. She was executed by the Germans on 8 September 1944. Posthumously she was awarded the King's Commendation for Bravery and the Award of Heroism and Self-Sacrifice by the Academy of Athens. But of the 10,000 personal files of SOE staff and agents that survive, none apparently bears her name.

Or there is Sylvia Salvesen, a brave Norwegian woman who founded the Bluebells, a Resistance group gathering information and helping escapees. She was sent to Ravensbrück and describes the twenty months she spent in this 'Hell for Women' in her book, *Forgive but Do Not Forget*. In Hamburg at the trial of sixteen camp staff she served as a leading witness.

The Dutch girl, Jos Gemmeke, was dropped into Holland

on the night of 10/11 March 1945, with instructions to make her way into Germany, under cover of serving as secretary to a Dutch businessman. Her mission was to make contact with Dutch workers there in the hope of organising resistance. By 1944 there were nearly 1 million forced labourers from the Low Countries in Germany. Jos had earlier played a brave role in circulating underground newspapers in Holland before escaping to England and being sent for training at Beaulieu and Ringway. But although she rapidly made many contacts, the war came to an end before the mission was truly under way.

There is Hannah Senesh, a Hungarian Jewess. No sooner had she reached the safety of Palestine than she volunteered to be sent back with others to help exfiltrate Allied airmen and help other Jews to escape. She was trained under British Command in Palestine with 31 other Jewish volunteers and sent to the Middle East Training Centre for Parachutists. Dropped into Yugoslavia from Brindisi, she was arrested almost as soon as she entered Hungary. Her thin SOE personal file, where she is described as Anna Szenes, quotes an unidentified source – a man who had been with her in prison.

'Source says that her treatment was appalling even judged by the standard of that usually accorded to spies, but that she managed always to keep absolutely silent. Her spirit had, however, been broken and she was not interested in any possible ways of saving herself . . . and asked him to try and smuggle something to her to enable her to commit suicide. This source refused to do so, saying that while there was life there was hope.' Later the source arrived at the prison of Margit Korut; he was told on arrival that Hannah had just been shot and saw her body lying in the courtyard. He believed she had been executed because she would not talk – all the other people he knew had received long terms of imprisonment but had not been executed.

Further harrowing details were provided by Hannah's mother in an interview with *The People* on 22 August 1971. Hannah's mother had remained in Budapest, happy that her daughter had escaped to freedom. Hannah had sent Red Cross postcards saying she was well. Then one day her mother was taken in to Hungarian intelligence headquarters. 'I had no idea what they were after. They kept coming back to Hannah and what she was doing. Finally, one of them said: "If you really don't know, I'll tell you." The door opened and I went rigid. Four men led in my Hannah, her faced [was] bruised and swollen, her hair in a filthy tangle, eyes blackened. I was shattered, all my hopes for her collapsed like a house of cards ... The Nazis watched us like hawks. Hannah tore herself away from them and threw herself into my arms sobbing. She asked me to forgive her. What for? One of the Nazis ordered me to talk to her, to persuade her to tell "everything", otherwise this would be the last time I saw her.' Hannah of course did not talk and her mother was able to meet her secretly several times in prison. When she was executed in October 1944, Hannah was still only twenty-three.

SOE's women recruits came from all levels of society. Another whose amazing story I wanted to tell is that of Maddalena Dufour, who ran a shop and small laundry business in Susa near Turin. At the age of twenty-six, she risked everything she had – as well as her life – on an almost daily basis. The report of her activities for SOE shows her astonishing tenacity and resourcefulness. Yet precisely because she was affiliated to no political party, Italian partisan associations have no record of her remarkable endeavours.

Immediately after the Italians capitulated to the Allies in September 1943, Maddalena began removing military stores from barracks and taking them to the partisans in the Alps. In April 1944, SOE's Winchester mission turned up at Maddalena's home. She housed them, provided them with food and 'pledged herself to their service, promising to carry out any task she might be given'. Her shop became a meeting place for the various partisan chiefs in the valley. Inside, 'among bundles of dirty and clean linen, many precious packages of explosives, clandestine publications, money for groups, and often essential foodstores, found their way in and out again.' With her chief, Edmeo, she robbed nearby stores at night to provide the partisans with quantities of biscuits, shoes, blankets, mess tins, water bottles, arms, explosives and personal clothing. The next morning, she loaded the spoils on a handcart and pushed them up into the mountains.

When she heard that one of the best members of a nearby partisan group had been caught in an ambush and killed, she rushed to warn her comrades who were planning a raid in the same area, saving them from encirclement and certain catastrophe. Next, finding the body of the dead partisan beside the road, she 'removed from his pockets several precious detonators to the marvel of bystanders'. Four days later she led a raid on a Republican clothing store and, personally disarming the watchman, helped her companions load 300 military uniforms and other much-needed clothing onto a cart.

In August, Maddalena carried a wounded partisan to the hospital on her bicycle and, by chatting to the Nazi guards, allowed him to be smuggled into the hospital through a concealed door.

When the whole of the local Carabinieri station was deported to Germany on suspicion of cooperation with the partisans, the danger increased. On 17 August she and Edmeo were arrested by fascist cadet officers. Interrogated for four hours, she defended herself without contradiction. Spies, however, had done their work and she was sentenced to be hanged. But the fascists decided that, as Edmeo was employed by the Germans and she did a lot of washing and ironing for them, they had better have a say in the matter. Maddalena and Edmeo were sent to German headquarters for further questioning. Once again she convinced them of her innocence and was told she could go free if she returned the next day at 1400 hours. Ten minutes after she left, the fascists arrived with fresh allegations and patrols were immediately sent out to scour the town for her. Too late. She had hidden with Edmeo in a vat in a wine cellar beneath the shop. Late at night she escaped to the mountains and rejoined her group. Next day the enemy broke into her shop and took everything.

Although her description and photograph were sent to all police stations in the valley, she continued her work, disguised as an old woman. In September, during yet another mopping-up operation, she saw her home in Vicoletto burnt to the ground by the fascists. When the Winchester mission arrived in Turin she regularly undertook the dangerous task of moving the radio set around the city, at the same time finding food for them all amidst severe scarcities. During the first three months of 1945 she carried out all the duties of one of SOE's women couriers in France, collecting information on round-ups and acting as personal courier to two British liaison officers, Colonel Stevens and Major Ballard.

At the end of the war she told SOE: 'I am left with the loss of all my material possessions, my business destroyed by the Nazi-Fascists.' After protracted correspondence, she received her discharge with a £250 bonus, a letter of support from the Allied Military Governor for a licence to reopen her shop and a recommendation for the Italian Silver Star. After that she disappears from history.

Another woman whose story emerges from files in the Public Record Office is the American Elizabeth Reynolds, who lived in Paris before being recruited by SOE. She was flown out by Hudson in October 1943 to join Richard Heslop of Marksman circuit in the Haute-Savoie as his courier. Badly compromised, she was on her way to Poitiers to be picked up by plane but was arrested in Paris in March 1944, where she had gone to stay the weekend in a safe house owned by a Swiss friend, Mademoiselle d'Andiran, who worked for the ambulance service. On the Monday she was arrested by the Gestapo under her real name as an American citizen. 'I was automatically accused of espionage and British Intelligence Service work,' she wrote on her return.

Her first night in Fresnes prison was spent in a cell with her Swiss friend. Here they were able to carefully rehearse her cover story: that, as an American citizen, she had been living in Switzerland but had secretly returned to France, living as a French citizen and raising money by selling her jewellery. Surprisingly, her next interrogation did not take place for a month, at which she received a crack on the skull. Nevertheless, she stuck to her story. At a third interrogation she found that the Germans were beginning to believe her. During these interrogations the Gestapo gave her the names of all the people who had denounced her, adding that some had been actively working for them for a number of years.

When asked about this, Elizabeth said:

The only reason I can give for this is that it was on the eve of the invasion, and the Germans have always tried to play the American card. The people responsible for my arrest were Comtesse Emmeline de Castéja of Neuilly and a Mlle Maximiliene Boréa, daughter of Vera Boréa, the big dressmaking house of the Faubourg St Honoré. I had known both these women well and had worked with them as an ambulance driver. Two years ago I signalled to the British authorities that I believed Mme de Castéja was not all she should be, but I was told I must undoubtedly be mistaken as Mme de Castéja's mother, the Hon Mrs Fellowes, was British.

Madame de Castéja, however, had a German brother-in-law,

Herr Krauss, who, Elizabeth said, acted as an intermediary between her and the Gestapo. 'Mme de Castéja was not unaware that I suspected her of anti-Allied activity and, having known me for many years and hearing from an unknown source – probably through a leakage from Switzerland – that I was once more in France, thought the best thing to do was to get rid of me.' When Elizabeth was tried in camera for possessing a false identity card, the judge told her, as he shut the dossier after judgement, that Madame de Castéja was responsible for her arrest. She believed that Madame de Castéja was also responsible for the Comte de Vogüé's arrest the previous November.

Another SOE agent who was able to conceal her British identity after her arrest was Eileen 'Didi' Nearne. When asked how long she had been working as a radio operator, she replied, three months, adding that the codes were provided by her chief. Feigning no knowledge of SOE, she said she had met her chief in a coffee shop and he had engaged her there and then. When they demanded the names and addresses of people she was working with, she made them up. Next they gave her the dreaded cold bath submersion, in which suspects were repeatedly plunged underwater and only released when their lungs were bursting. Bravely she stuck to her story. She then admitted to a rendezvous with her chief at the Gare St Lazare at seven o'clock that evening. This took the pressure off, but of course, when they went to keep the rendezvous, no one came although they waited till 7.15 p.m. Fortunately an air-raid warning sounded and she was able to claim that he must have been delayed as a result. She said: 'Then they took me back to interrogate me again. The chief of the Gestapo said he would give me a last chance. I stuck to the same story. They had found out that the addresses were false. I said I would take them there, which stopped them questioning me.'

On 15 August 1944 Didi was sent to the notorious women's

concentration camp at Ravensbrück. Here she met Violette Szabo. 'I knew Violet wanted to escape,' she wrote, but it was Didi who was to have the opportunity – on 5 April 1945, just as the Americans approached. While they were being marched through a forest in the dark, she managed to jump the line and hide, by good luck meeting up with two friends. After sheltering in a bombed house for two nights, they set off, only to be stopped by the SS who demanded papers, which they naturally did not have. 'We said we had none as we were French volunteers for work in Germany. Fortunately they let us pass.' Arriving in Leipzig, they found a priest who gave them shelter for three nights. 'On 15th April we saw the white flags and the first Americans arriving so we rushed out to meet them. I told them I was English and asked them if they would show us where the Red Cross was. However, they would not do this but put us in a house for one night. Next morning they put us into a camp.'

Now Didi was to suffer the fate of several agents who came under suspicion when they were overrun. The American Intelligence Service asked for her number and she had none. They were not convinced of her story of being a wireless operator or that she had been landed by plane in France in the middle of the night. She was cautious in talking about SOE and they concluded she was a German agent. Now she found herself in a camp with 'Nazi girls' who would 'ask the Americans for cigarettes and get them to come into their rooms'. Finally an English major arrived to rescue her.

Although it is striking how many SOE agents were young and beautiful, many older women were of course equally brave. Few more so than the Resistance heroine, Mrs Berthe Fraser, a middle-aged French woman living in Arras, who was British by marriage. When northern France was occupied she made the welfare of British prisoners her special mission. She gave them food and clothing and arranged for their adoption by the local population. This she continued to do until January 1941 when the POW camp was moved far across Germany to Pomerania. Immediately she set about organising the escape and repatriation of British prisoners still hidden in the region. Arrested by the Gestapo in September 1941, she was released fifteen months later on 23 December 1942 due to lack of formal proof and her ill health. Hardly was she out of prison when she contacted several officers sent out from England. She supplied them with a complete network of faithful collaborators, arranging their liaisons, their shelter, transport and hiding places.

Her most famous exploit was to arrange the escape of the great RF Section agent 'Tommy' Yeo-Thomas, the White Rabbit, who was to be picked up by Lysander near Arras. A German division had unexpectedly set up camp nearby. To smuggle him past the Germans Berthe organised a hearse in which Yeo-Thomas was concealed beneath the flowers. The coffin itself was filled with vital reports from the Parsifal mission, which he was to take back to England.

Another, older agent who gave conspicuous service to SOE was Yvonne Rudellat, the subject of *Jacqueline: Pioneer Heroine of the Resistance* (1989) by Stella King. Yvonne was dropped on the south coast of France in July 1942 by felucca, more than a month ahead of Virginia Hall. She was forty-five at the time, considerably older than other women agents. But she had made a good impression on her instructors. The report from Beaulieu, dated 21 June 1942, runs: 'She is an intelligent and extremely sensible woman. The first impression of fluffiness is entirely misleading. Her air of innocence and anxiety to please should prove a most valuable "cover" asset. She is extremely thorough and sincere in anything she does, and together with her persevering and tenacious qualities she will see any job through to its conclusion.'

The summary of her mission reads:

This officer was landed in France by sea in July 1942 to work as a courier to an organisation in northern France. She carried out her duties . . . for nearly a year with outstanding courage and devotion to duty. [Her] work involved widespread travelling and dangerous liaison activity between the various groups of her circuit. She had to pass numerous enemy controls, some on a bicycle with explosives hidden in a basket fixed to the handlebars . . . She personally organised a number of receptions in the Cher and the Ain *départements*. She also took part in a sabotage operation against the Chaigny power station, and was personally responsible for blowing up two locomotives in the goods station of Le Mans in March 1943. While she was waiting for a delivery of stores on a parachute dropping zone in June 1943 a large force of Gestapo men came to arrest her . . . Her circuit was one of the most able and efficient in northern France.

For this she was recommended for the Military Cross, normally restricted to men, although it was never approved. Following her arrest, she was sent to Belsen where the indefatigable Vera Atkins traced the details of her death. Yvonne, she told the War Office in a letter of 23 July 1946, was tragically one of those who died from exhaustion after the liberation of the camp on 15 April 1945. Atkins added: 'It appears that deaths following liberation were so numerous, and that the state of the camp was so chaotic that all that could be done was to bury the bodies in mass graves.' Her source was a Mademoiselle Rénée Rosier who had arrived at Belsen with Yvonne on 2 March 1945. She recalled: 'At this time Mrs Rudellat was not in bad health, she suffered occasionally from loss of memory, but she remained in good morale and she looked neither particularly drawn or aged.' On arrival both were put in Block 19, later transferring to Block 48, where Yvonne contracted typhus and dysentery and became very weak. Mademoiselle Rosier added: 'Some 20,000 persons died in the month following liberation, and it was quite impossible to keep any records of the dead.'

Among the most beautiful of all the secret agents who worked for the British was Countess Clémentine Mankowska. Like Christina Granville, she worked for Witkowski's Musketeers and she too came under deep suspicion from her fellow Poles. The Musketeers were formed on 5 October 1939 as a secret network to continue the fight against the Germans and the Soviets.

I went to see her in the small château near Nevers that is now her home. Although bedridden, almost blind and very deaf, Inia, as she is known, is still remarkably pretty and full of mischief. Beckoning me first to sit on her bed, she said conspiratorially in her deep voice, 'You have come to kill me. It would make such a good end.' Like Christina, she had grown up on a country estate – Wysucka on the Polish-Russian border – where she would go out riding with her father. She tells her story in her memoirs, *Espionne malgré moi* (1994). By 1939 she was living with her husband and two children on his estate at Winnogora, 900 kilometres to the west. For a while she was able to continue an almost normal life alongside the punctiliously polite Wehrmacht officers for whom she had to provide lodging. Then the Gestapo arrived, confiscated the estate and arrested her and her children. But her sons made friends with the German guards and they were able to slip away. Making her way to Warsaw, she joined the Musketeers and was sent by Witkowski to the coastal town of Noirmoutier, near Bordeaux, with the aim of gathering intelligence. Arriving in France in May 1940, she found a job as interpreter for the German *kommandatur*. But she lived dangerously, collecting money to help Polish soldiers escape to England. In March 1941 she was arrested by the Gestapo and taken to the Avenue Foch for interrogation. Such was her sang-froid that she was allowed to return to Noirmoutier where she found her standing had improved with both her fellow Musketeers and her German masters.

Returning to Poland, she took with her a large cache of material that she had secreted from the Germans – keys, letterheads, official stamps. Just as her luggage was about to be searched at the Polish border, she struck up a conversation with the customs officer and found he was a friend of her boss in Noirmoutier. The search was quickly forgotten but in Warsaw she found she was being courted by the Abwehr, the German military secret police. On Witkowski's orders she agreed to be trained as a double agent and sent to England. After instruction in codes at Tours she arrived in Bristol in May 1942. Giving herself up, she was promptly taken for interrogation and debriefing to the Royal Patriotic Asylum in Wandsworth. Here she provided huge quantities of precise information about German defences and installations.

Haltingly, she explained: 'General Bor-Komorowski, comm-ander-in-chief of the Polish army, told me after the war, "No other agent had supplied so much important information as you. You were recommended for a George Cross." But as I was a Pole it needed the approval of the Polish government and this was not forthcoming.'

She showed me copies of the long, closely typed pages of reports that she had provided. 'I had a very good memory,' she says. When she was in the Noirmoutier area, she said, 'I would pretend to be short of fuel, stop by an airfield.' Chivalrous Ger-man officers would promptly appear and go in search of fuel while she memorised every detail on the airfield: the planes, the hangars, the fuel dumps. Here she learnt of the splits in the Polish government-in-exile and the animosity towards the Musketeers that had so plagued Christina. General Sosnowski told her, 'They would like to get rid of you.' Witkowski himself was assassinated in October 1942.

Among SOE's women agents there were no Charlotte Grays, ducking out of service to pursue the calls of the heart like the heroine of Sebastian Faulks' novel. Pearl Witherington fought alongside her fiancé, Henri Cornioley, taking overall command of nearly 3,000 men. Few professional soldiers packed so much action into two months as Christina Granville, rushing up and down the Alps, persuading garrisons to surrender their arms and facing down the Gestapo.

Although the individual agents, both men and women, were resourceful, brave and often brilliantly successful in their missions, the bigger question of the value of SOE, its achievements and its failings, continues to be debated vigorously.

William Mackenzie concluded in *The Secret History of SOE*, an in-house assessment commissioned by the Cabinet Office and completed in 1948:

In the vulgar sense SOE showed a large military profit. In manpower directly employed it cost less than the equivalent of a division; a rather curious division, in which the officers were the pick of British youth, the rank and file were largely old crocks unfit for active service and girls deemed too young for conscription. Its private air force cannot (on the average) be reckoned at more than four squadrons: its private navy was tiny . . . SOE's cash expenditure on subsidies to [the] Resistance was probably no greater than its cash gains as a dealer in the European currency black market.

The Allied Supreme Commander, General Eisenhower, was warm in his praise of SOE to Colin Gubbins:

In no previous war, and in no other theatre during this war, have resistance forces been so closely harnessed to the main military effort . . . I consider that the disruption of enemy rail communications, the harassing of German road moves and the continual and increasing strain placed on the German war economy and internal security services throughout occupied Europe by the organized forces of resistance, played a very considerable part in our complete and final victory . . . I am also aware of the care with which each individual country was studied and organized, and of the excellent work carried out in training, documenting, briefing and dispatching agents. The supply to agents and resistance groups in the field, moreover, could only have reached such proportions during the summer of 1944 through outstanding efficiency on the part of the supply and air liaison staffs. Finally, I must express my great admiration for the brave and often spectacular exploits of the agents and special groups under control of Special Forces Headquarters.

Significantly, the daily summary reports prepared for SHAEF, the Supreme Headquarters Allied Expeditionary Force, after D-Day include a section on 'Resistance and SAS activities', following Weather, Ground, Naval, and Air reports – all compressed into a single foolscap sheet. Under 'Resistance' there is repeated mention of the delays to the 2nd SS Panzer division on its way to join the Normandy front line. On 13 June there are reports of departments largely under patriotic control, including Doubs, Jura, Hautes-Pyrénées, Indre and parts of Haute-Vienne and Dordogne. On 15 June it is noted that sufficient arms have been dropped in Brittany since D-Day to arm 3,000 men; on 1 July that concerted German counter-attacks have been made on Maquis in Dordogne and Lot; on 24 July that 850,000 litres of petrol have been destroyed in Puy and Cantal, as well as another 600,000 litres on a train, set on fire in a tunnel on the Namur–Dinant line. On 22 August came the surrender of the German garrison at Puget in the Basses-Alpes to FFI troops without a shot being fired.

Hugh Dalton himself, in his memoirs, *The Fateful Years* (1957), provides an impressive list of successful operations:

The destruction, mainly in France, but also in Belgium, Holland,

Norway, Denmark and Greece, of a large number of power-stations, transformers and power-supply arrangements; of factories important for the German war effort, such as the Ratier Air Screw factory at Toulouse, the Skefco ball-bearings works at Oslo and the Orkla pyrite mines and plant in Norway; demolition of locks on the main waterways between France and Belgium; the sinking of ships in many harbours; attacks on railways, both against the permanent way and against trains, especially in France against supply trains carrying oil to submarine bases; misdirection of railway goods wagons by re-adjusting destination labels; destruction of railway bridges; the kidnapping of the German General commanding Crete; the bringing out from Gothenburg of aircraft loaded with ball-bearings, and of five ships, which successfully ran the German blockade . . . carrying 25,000 tons of special steels.

Not all have concurred. Following the initial flurry of tales about heroic exploits by individual agents, more critical accounts began to appear – highlighting the disastrous capture of successive SOE agents in Holland, the damage done by double agents such as Henri Déricourt and the high rate of losses among agents working behind the lines, particularly the unfortunate radio operators.

John Keegan, the defence correspondent of the *Daily Telegraph*, was especially damning of SOE in a review approving Nigel West's book, *The Secret War* (1992). Keegan wrote: 'SOE was inefficient as an organisation, unnecessarily dangerous to work for, ineffective in its pursuit of its aims, and counter-productive in the results achieved.' He argued that SOE could never find enough of the right people to act either as controllers at home or agents in the field. 'Special operations cannot be improvised. It takes years to build up a control organisation and the networks it oversees in enemy territory. In 1940 such subversive expertise as Britain had was locked up in the Secret Intelligence Service (MI6). Although it had lost many of its networks, MI6 might nevertheless have been given an active operations branch as the CIA was when it was established in 1947.'

Yet Keegan has been generous in his recognition of the role of SOE's women agents, recommending that the survivors should be promoted from their modest MBEs and OBEs to become DBEs, Dames of the British Empire.

One yardstick of SOE's success is its effectiveness – or otherwise – in meeting the aims laid down at the outset. In *The Fateful Years*, Dalton said that SOE's purpose 'was to co-ordinate all action by way of subversion and sabotage against the enemy overseas. A new organisation was now to be created, which would absorb some elements of existing organisations, but would be on a much greater scale, with much wider scope and largely manned by new personnel.'

Another initial aim was to establish secret underground armies. The largest unquestionably was the Home Army in Poland, organised by the Poles themselves and then butchered in the Warsaw uprising. Long distances and bad weather made air drops to Poland especially difficult. A top-secret Air Ministry report of 3 April 1944 states: 'The Poles have been most unfortunate in their special operations since they moved to Italy. During the last two months, 17 sorties have been flown to Poland with only one success. The restrictions and failures have been almost entirely due to unfavourable weather.'

In France, early attempts at establishing secret armies proved wildly over-optimistic, and larger Resistance groups were highly vulnerable to penetration by the Germans. Yet despite repeated cases of penetration and betrayal, SOE was able to start new circuits, replacing them. As Churchill often said: 'The blood of the martyrs is the seed of the Church.'

Following Dalton's promotion to the Board of Trade in 1942, SOE set aside thoughts of a 'democratic international', making use of labour agitation, strikes and boycotts. In France,

SOE agents remained resolutely non-political, seeking alliance only with local Resistance groups that shared their aim of doing maximum damage to the Germans.

Much has been written on German penetration of SOE. The most serious instance, never likely to be fully resolved, was that F Section's air movements officer, Henri Déricourt, had worked as a double agent for the Nazi Sicherheitsdienst (SD), providing information about the arrival of agents. This allowed some to be arrested the moment they arrived and others to be tailed, with varying degrees of success, as they made their way to their contacts, with the intention of rounding up whole circuits. The evidence suggests that Déricourt was ultimately working for himself, holding some information back, and that the Germans hesitated to press him for fear of blowing his cover.

In addition there was the assiduous Sergeant Hugo Bleicher, who arrested Odette Sansom and Peter Churchill. Formerly a shipping clerk in Hamburg, he was recruited into the German Abwehr as a counter-intelligence agent thanks to his languages. He in turn recruited Mathilde Carré, the betrayer of the Franco-Polish Interallié intelligence network, as a double agent. She confessed to a member of SOE's French Section and was then taken to the UK – a move approved by the Germans who thought by this means to penetrate SOE. However, after her interrogation, she spent the rest of the war in confinement.

Equally disastrous to SOE was the *Englandspiel* in Holland, where the Germans played back captured radios, convincing Baker Street that resistance was growing while arresting new agents the moment they arrived. Over forty agents died as a result. Noor's radio set was also played back, resulting in the arrest of seven agents as soon as they landed in France. Maurice Southgate, Pearl Witherington's chief, who was imprisoned in the Avenue Foch before being sent on to Buchenwald, wrote:

You may now realise what happened to our agents who did *not* give the true check [on outgoing telegrams from the field to England] to the Germans, thus making them send out a message that was obviously phoney, and after being put through the worst degrees of torture these Germans managed, sometimes a week later, to get hold of the true check, and then sent a further message to London with the proper check in the telegram, and London saying: 'Now you are a good boy, now you have remembered to give both of them.' This happened not once, but several times. I consider that the officer responsible for such neglect of his duties should be severely court martialled, because he is responsible for the death and capture of many of our best agents, including Major Antelme for one, who was arrested the minute he put his foot on French soil.

Southgate said that most of these dropping grounds were in Normandy, where he claimed that in the month of June 1944 'up to ten organisations were all in German hands and had been receiving British material for months and months. I was amazed at HQ Gestapo to see the quantities of British food, guns, ammunition, explosives, that they had at their disposal.' Even allowing for an element of exaggeration – the Germans regularly sought to demoralise captured agents by suggesting they knew all about SOE – it is a devastating indictment.

Horrific as the losses were, they were offset by the astonishing rate at which circuits multiplied in the run-up to D-Day. Following the Allied landings, the Germans were harried from behind the lines in virtually every part of France. The seventeen-day delay inflicted on the Das Reich Panzer division by the circuits in which Pearl Witherington and Violette Szabo were involved was one formidable achievement. The safeguarding of the Allied landings in the South of France, through the prevention of flanking attacks across the mountains from Italy – in which Christina Granville was closely involved – was another. Sustained guerrilla tactics by the Resistance kept the Germans largely confined to a few strong points with the result that the landings themselves were virtually unopposed.

There is the larger question of whether the use of irregulars undermined the basic rules of warfare, established under the Geneva Convention. The Germans called resisters of any kind terrorists and treated them with extreme brutality. In the early days of the war when SOE was planning a commando-style operation to take out enemy pilots by killing them as they were driven out by bus to the airfield, the RAF had serious misgivings about ferrying men not in uniform to assassinate uniformed personnel of the Luftwaffe.

There is a distinction to be drawn between terrorists and guerrillas. Guerrillas use warfare for liberation or independence and their efforts are concentrated against the armed forces of an occupying power. Terrorists use their arms indiscriminately, killing and maiming civilians in the process. This SOE agents never did. Baker Street was extremely conscious of likely German reprisals against innocent citizens, either taken as hostages or killed randomly in massacres. The atrocity committed at Oradour is often talked of as if it were a unique crime of unprecedented horror but there are abundant examples of the Germans killing innocent civilians on an appalling scale. Christina Granville reported to SOE in 1940 that the Germans were killing a hundred people a night.

The Germans were, of course, brutal and merciless in their treatment of any Maquis they captured, often killing them in the most bestial fashion. Yet although the Maquis may have adopted the hit-and-run tactics of the Francs-Tireurs, in most cases they would willingly have put on uniforms if only they could have obtained them.

The distinctions between freedom fighters, guerrillas and terrorists are now more blurred than ever. But SOE did not invent clandestine warfare. The Boers in South Africa adopted such tactics more than half a century earlier. It was the Nazis who introduced unrestrained terror on civilians, first at Guernica, then through the Blitzkrieg tactics used in Poland and France, shelling and strafing refugees as they fled, and killing civilians indiscriminately.

In his article 'Was SOE any good?' M.R.D. Foot argues:

It was thanks to SOE's past support . . . that Tito was able to stand up to Stalin and assert the real strength of his local communist party, which had been forged in real battles with SOE's real guns . . . In France, the communists might have dared to try to seize power in the confusion of late summer 1944, had they had any orders from Moscow (they were dreadfully Moscow-bound, even then), and had there not been small arms for half a million men distributed around the rest of France by SOE – with half an eye on counter-balancing just such a coup.

Such political dangers were certainly carefully considered in London. Selborne wrote to Churchill on 19 November 1943: 'I think there is less danger in France of resistance movements becoming centres of post-war Communism than in most other occupied countries, because the French are quite capable of determining their own national policy without the promptings of an organised minority.' There is a note of 13 December in the margin: 'I agree WC'.

The bigger question of sabotage versus bombing will always be a matter for debate. Bomber Command consistently argued that bombing raids had the most direct and powerful effect on the enemy and they were very reluctant to release more aircraft for air drops to the Resistance. A note of 24 July 1943 by Air Marshal Portal, Chief of Air Staff, on the availability of aircraft for SOE, accepts the case that they are necessary to back SOE activities in the Balkans but says it would be 'a serious mistake to divert any more aircraft to supply resistance groups in Western Europe which [can] only be of *potential* value next year when these aircraft would be of *immediate and actual* value in accelerating the defeat of Germany by direct attack'. Portal said to Harry Sporborg, a senior figure in SOE, 'Your work is a gamble which may give us a valuable dividend or may produce nothing. It is anybody's guess. My bombing offensive is not a gamble. Its dividend is certain; it is a gilt-edged investment. I cannot divert aircraft from a certainty, to a gamble which may be a gold-mine or may be completely worthless.'

Early in 1944 Churchill intervened decisively in favour of SOE, writing to Selborne on 2 February: 'If through bad weather or any other reason the number of sorties in February looks like dropping below your estimate I want extra effort made to improve sorties to the Maquis when conditions are favourable.' Churchill added that even if the February sorties were fully successful they were not enough. 'Pray start at once on a programme for the March moon. I want March deliveries to double those planned for February. I am told that the stocks of ammunition in the Maquis are far below what is reasonable.'

The question – the value of sabotage versus bombing – is all the more sensitive, even today, in view of the extraordinary bravery of Bomber Command crews, faced with appalling loss of life. Almost 56,000 members of Bomber Command's aircrew were killed. With the sabotage of the Peugeot factory near Montbéliard, SOE showed that a few determined men, with inside help, could permanently disable a tank turret production line, without casualties in adjoining residential areas.

SOE's women agents reported on opportunities for widespread sabotage, many of which were never fully explored. Christina Granville heard in October 1940 from a new organisation in Poland that provided invaluable information: '. . . details of the work of German and Polish armament factories, plans of the factories . . . and very detailed information on new U-boats which were being constructed at Danzig.' During the summer of 1940 the Germans had taken a large number of workers from Poland, forcing them to work in munitions factories. Among them, the Resistance organisation had been able to place sixteen technical engineers, who were now at both factories and railway stations in Germany and were able to report almost exactly how many railway wagons left Germany, providing details of their contents and destinations.

Virginia Hall also told SOE of the possibilities of sending agents to Germany as French workmen. Given the huge number of French who were sent to Germany under the STO, the Service du Travail Obligatoire, this idea might have been explored further. Rather than develop SOE's capacity for sabotage, the War Office preferred to rely on bombing raids. Although Bomber Command's total dead numbered some four times SOE's total strength, there was no change of policy.

Selborne put his case in the quarterly summaries he sent to Churchill. The summary for October–December 1943 quotes figures supplied by a French railway engineer, showing that sabotage was eight times as effective as bombing in putting locomotives out of action. According to the engineer, locomotives immobilised by fighter attack were repaired on average in sixteen days whereas those damaged by sabotage took six months to repair.

Another report adds:

In preparation for D-Day Allied aircraft were carrying out low flying attacks with cannon and machine guns on locomotives in France. These attacks resulted in serious loss of life among French engine drivers and stokers and the damage done was often only temporary. As the entire staff of the SNCF was working for the Resistance and was already engaged in widespread sabotage, this caused a good deal of annoyance and anger. As a result of approaches made, the task of dealing with locomotives in certain areas was given to the Resistance. Figures published by the SNCF who kept complete records of every act of sabotage on French Railways show that between August 1943 and June 1944, 1,734 locomotives were attacked by the Resistance and more than 1,400 were immobilised which in most cases meant complete rebuilding.

Even if France had only been smouldering until D-Day, the stories of the women in this book demonstrate that as soon as the *messages personnels* went out to SOE circuits all over the country on 5 June 1944, France was at last truly ablaze, with a genuine popular uprising that liberated large parts of the country in advance of Allied troops, sabotaged power and telephone lines, brought the railways to a halt, blocked roads, confined the Germans largely to towns and exposed them to constant ambush and guerrilla attack, not only killing and wounding significant numbers but prompting still larger numbers to surrender.

A thick, battered volume of progress reports on special operations states for June 1944: 'Fears that repressive German measures would at best hamper and at worst cripple, Resistance and sabotage throughout France on and after D-Day were happily not realised. The action messages, including those for guerrilla activities, evoked a volume of activity which it was beyond the power of the enemy's counter-Resistance organisations to control.' A total of 609 out of 873 air sorties had been successful, dropping 125 personnel and 1,100 tons of stores for a loss of six aircraft. Simultaneously came reports that the 'Resistance movement in Italy has increased considerably and the numbers for the patriot bands seem to be limited only by the quantity of arms available.'

Both in France and Italy women played a major role in both the Resistance and the partisans, risking their lives from hour to hour by providing safe houses or acting as couriers. All too many of the men and women who acted so heroically in this way were betrayed or caught by the Germans and sent to concentration camps where they were abominably treated and often died. According to Maria Wilhelm's *The Other Italy: Italian Resistance in World War II* (1988), many women 'fought alongside the partisans: of these 35,000 women, some 5,000 were imprisoned, 650 were executed or died in combat, about 3,000 were deported to Germany, and 17 awarded gold medals for valor'.

There is an old Italian proverb: 'When women take up a cause you can assume it has been won.' When SOE began to send women agents to France the war was very far from won; indeed, when Christina Granville first went to Hungary and Virginia Hall to Lyons, the tide of the war was very much against Britain. Their achievement, and that of all the other women agents who followed them, was both simple and spectacular.

In an organisation that recruited numerous outstandingly brave and resourceful men, who repeatedly carried out the most hazardous missions in enemy-occupied Europe, constantly facing the threat of betrayal, arrest and torture by the Gestapo, these women were to show corresponding valour, determination and powers of endurance, serving alone or in very small groups. Without hesitation, they risked their lives on an often daily basis. For this they had no previous military or professional training, as many of the men had. They had to be alert, quick-witted, calm and unruffled while constantly acting a part. Women had never had such a role to play before, yet again and again they surprised their comrades with their astonishing mastery of clandestine life.

NOTE ON SOURCES

For all the losses that have taken place, the SOE archive remains a remarkable and often thrilling body of documentation, maddeningly incomplete in many respects but full of vivid detail in others. There is first of all the material in the Public Record Office (PRO). For this book I have made extensive use of the material on France and Italy (HS6), notably the circuit and mission reports and interrogations of the French Section (HS6/566–84). These consist of reports by the agents themselves on their missions, often including lists of sabotage targets. Sometimes the reports are written by the officers who interviewed the agents. In most cases the reports are to a standard format, giving details on conditions in France. Increasingly this material is being transferred onto microfilm.

The PRO guide, *SOE Operations in Western Europe*, states: 'As with most of the SOE records, these are only a fraction of what originally existed. There is evidence of fire and water damage in many of the papers. As there was no central registry and no indication of the file series it is difficult to estimate overall losses, which have been put as high as 85 per cent.'

W.J.M. Mackenzie, in *The Secret History of SOE* (an official history, completed for the Cabinet Office in 1948), explains:

Partly through inexperience, partly for reasons of security, SOE began life without a central registry or departmental filing system. Each branch kept its own papers on its own system, from the Minister down to the sub-sections of the Country Sections . . .

The original confusion was made worse because in 1945, when the end was in sight, SOE made a resolute attempt to impose on the existing chaos a proper system of departmental filing by subject. This was an immense task which was scarcely begun when the department officially came to an end: the registry staff was kept in being for some time, but the work was eventually stopped on grounds of economy when it was about a quarter done.

M.R.D. Foot, in his seminal *SOE in France* (1966), the first serious volume based on the archives, added:

As the organisation was wound up, some of the files were roughly weeded by staff officers who had helped to complete them, and took care to throw away only the least useful papers. At this stage, or even earlier, the entire archive of Massingham's AMF section [a mini country section for France at SOE's Algiers base] was burnt. The quantity [of paper] that remained has three times been heavily reduced, once wholly by accident. A fire broke out in Baker Street early in 1946, and a great many important files are said to have been burnt before it was got under control; though here again there is a conflict of evidence, and there is good reason to believe that most of the papers destroyed were – even if numerous – of trivial importance only.

Further weedings were made with the result that for France, says Foot, 'many of the files on particular circuits and operations, almost all messages exchanged with the field, all the training files, and some important papers on the early development of SOE have thus disappeared.'

The most up-to-date assessment of the archives has been made by the last SOE adviser, Duncan Stuart, in an unpublished paper '"Of Historical Interest Only": The Origins and Vicissitudes of the SOE Archive', given to a conference at the

Imperial War Museum in 1998. He related that a further re-organisation of the archive had been conducted by a professional archivist from the PRO, Mr C.B. Townshend, in the early 1970s. 'Townsend wrote in 1974 that [the fire] "destroyed an unknown quantity of records the subject of which it has been impossible to trace ... some maintain that only finance files were destroyed (and certainly these are conspicuous by their absence) ...", but he added that Colonel H.B. Perkins (ex-head of the Polish Section) complained after the War that "a great number of my records have been destroyed by fire".'

Stuart cites Norman Mott, head of the SOE Liquidation Section in Baker Street, who recalled: 'a large proportion of the FANY records were destroyed together with the entire contents of my own office where I was holding a considerable number of operational files. Some of the latter related to the activities in the Field of SOE FANY agents. In addition, all the handing-over briefs from the SOE Country Sections were destroyed as well as a good deal of material relating to investigations into blown *réseaux* [circuits].'

The other major body of the material used for this book are the PFs (personal files) of individual agents. There remain over 10,000 PFs of SOE staff and agents, which will begin to arrive at the PRO in 2003. For material on agents in this book I am much indebted to material from the PFs supplied by the SOE adviser at the Foreign and Commonwealth Office. These include training reports (with assessments of agents' characters and abilities), internal memos, correspondence and occasional telegrams, and sometimes financial details of operations.

Further material has come from the extensive records of the US National Archives and Records Administration (NARA) in Maryland and from the Archives Nationales in Paris. A film, *Now it Can Be Told*, featuring authentic SOE personnel, was made by the RAF Film Unit for the Central Office of

Information and was subsequently released under the title, *School for Danger*.

In addition I have talked to four of the agents who are still living: Lise de Baissac, Paola del Din, Alix d'Unienville and Pearl Witherington.

There is a large volume of literature on SOE, including quite a number of books by SOE staff and agents, as well as books on women agents, some tackled individually, some as groups. The early ones were naturally often direct recollections of individuals involved with SOE, but writers such as Jean Overton Fuller, and more recently Stella King, did a remarkable job in tracking down people who knew and worked with agents. Newspaper clippings are an additional source, shedding light on the way agents' stories were first told.

Max Nicholson's comments on recruitment outside the Civil Service were made during an interview with him.

A Note on SOE, pp. xiii–xv

For Julian Amery on George Taylor of SOE, see *Approach March* (1973), p. 211.

Hugh Dalton's letter to Lord Halifax is quoted in *The Fateful Years*, p. 368.

1: Recruitment and Training, pp. 1–21

'A new form of warfare was developed and has come to stay and may prove in a future War even more important than in the last one . . .' (p. 1) is from *A Brief History of SOE*, undated but written in the late 1940s – see [PRO] HS7/1.

Noor's instructor on her motivation (p. 3) is from her PF.

For Mauritian agents, see J. Maurice Patureau, *Agents secrets mauriciens en France 1940–45*.

Mary Herbert's interrogation on her return (p. 4) – by this time she was Madame de Baissac – is dated 30 January 1945 and is in [PRO] HS6/567.

Margaret Pawley's comments on Christina (p. 5) are in her book, *In Obedience to Instructions* (1999), p. 71.

Author's interview with Leslie Fernandez (pp. 6–7).

The definition of the FANYs as the 'First Anywheres' (p. 8) is quoted in Joyce Marlow (ed.), *Women and the Great War* (1998), p. 4. For details on FANYs, see M.R.D. Foot, *SOE in France* (1966), p. 48.

For Hitler's Commando Order (p. 9), see Foot, *SOE in France*, pp. 186–7. The order is quoted in Jimmy Quintin Hughes, *Who Dares Who Wins* (1998), p. 104.

An account of SOE's four-stage training (p. 14) is provided in Denis Rigden (introduction), *SOE Syllabus: Lessons in Ungentlemanly Warfare* (2001), pp. 2–8. Descriptions of SOE's Scottish Training Schools are to be found, *inter alia*, in Nancy Wake, *The White Mouse* (1985), pp. 104–5 and Stella King, *Jacqueline: Pioneer Heroine of the Resistance* (1989), pp. 87ff.

Wing Commander B. Bonsey's description of parachute training (p. 15) is in Wing Commander B. Bonsey, 'Top Secret Interlude', in the Imperial War Museum, Department of Documents, 79/22/1.

Sir Robin Hooper writes on training to find landing grounds (p. 16) in an introduction to Mrs B. Bertram's 'The French Resistance in Sussex', in the Imperial War Museum, Department of Documents, 95/34/1.

Details of the Beaulieu training (p. 16) to be found in Cyril Cunningham, *Beaulieu: the Finishing School for Secret Agents* (1998).

The details of Noor Inayat Khan's ninety-six-hour training exercise (p. 17) are also in her PF.

Mrs C. Wrench's descriptions of preparing agents for France and of the SOE shooting school (pp. 19–20) are in the Imperial War Museum, Department of Documents, 95/34/1.

2: An Agent's Life, pp. 22–48

Hitler's New Year's Proclamation on 1 January 1944 (p. 22) is cited in [PRO] HS6/379.

For descriptions of flying to France (pp. 22–3) see Hugh Verity, *We Landed by Moonlight* (for the incident with Lise de Baissac, see p. 212) and also the Hugh Verity tapes in the Imperial War Museum Sound Archive 9939. Further information has come from Sir Lewis Hodges.

The examples of BBC *messages personnels* (p. 24) are quoted from Noor Inayat Khan's PF. Information on containers and packages (pp. 25–6) is taken from Wing Commander B. Bonsey, 'Top Secret Interlude', in the Imperial War Museum, Department of Documents, 79/22/1.

Reports of drops to Pearl Witherington (p. 27) are in [PRO] HS6/587.

E.R. Mayer's description of his dropping grounds (pp. 27–8) is in his interrogation of 20 December 1944 in [PRO] HS6/576. That of Commandant Paul Schmidt's dropping grounds (p. 28) is in [PRO] HS6/579. Benjamin Cowburn's description of his reception by Octraine (p. 28) is in his *No Cloak, No Dagger* (1960), p. 13. Lise de Baissac's description of receiving agents (p. 29) is from her PF.

The mission instructions given to Noor Inayat Khan (pp. 29–30) are in her PF.

Eugenie Roccaserra's comments on the natural talkativeness of French city people (p. 30) are in her interrogation of 11 March 1945 in [PRO] HS6/578.

Lieutenant Colonel Starr's security rules for Wheelwright circuit (p. 31) are in his interrogation of 20–1 November

1944, [PRO] HS6/579. Commandant Maurice Dupont's rules for the Diplomatic circuit (pp. 31–2) are in his interrogation of 16 February 1945 in [PRO] HS6/569. For Cammaerts's description of recruitment on his circuit (p. 32), see his interrogation of 16–18 January 1945 in [PRO] HS6/568. For the interrogation of Michael Dequaire (p. 33), see [PRO] HS6/569.

Claude de Baissac's comments on the pros and cons of different types of false papers (p. 33) are in his interrogation of 13 November 1944 in [PRO] HS6/657.

Virginia Hall's description of problems with trains (p. 34) was sent to the *New York Post* and is on her PF.

For Cammaerts's views on *boîte aux lettres* and messages (p. 35), see [PRO] HS6/568, cited above.

For Eileen 'Didi' Nearne on her capture while using a radio set (pp. 35–6), see her report of 15 June 1945 in [PRO] HS6/576.

For Lieutenant Martin on direction-finding (p. 36), see his report of 19 September 1944 in [PRO] HS6/575.

For Captain Rousset's experience of being subjected to direction-finding by plane (p. 36), see his interrogation of 13 December 1944 in [PRO] HS6/578.

For Cammaerts on the work of radio operators (p. 37), see [PRO] HS6/568, cited above. For Maurice Southgate on London's failures to watch radio checks (pp. 37–8), see his undated report in [PRO] HS6/579.

For Pearl Witherington's comments on electric power for radios (p. 38), see her report of 23 November 1944 in [PRO] HS6/587.

For Madame Gruner on the Milice (pp. 40–1), see [PRO] HS6/571. For Cammaerts on police, control points and informers (p. 41), see [PRO] HS6/568, cited above.

For André Flattot, an American who got to Switzerland, on Swiss police (p. 41), see [PRO] HS6/570.

Agents' comments on lack of training in guerrilla warfare

(pp. 42–3): for Lieutenant D. Cameron, see report of Fireman mission of 4 November 1944 in [PRO] HS6/575, and for comment on railway sabotage see interrogation of E.R. Mayer of 20 December 1944 in [PRO] HS6/576.

E.R. Mayer's comments on concealing Maquis camps and sabotage (pp. 42–3) are in his interrogation of 16 December 1944 in [PRO] WO95/2208.

The comments of Major Hillier of the Footman circuit on ambushes (pp. 44–5) are in his report dated 24 October 1944 in [PRO] HS6/585.

On weapons instruction (p. 45), see the interrogation of Commandant Maurice Dupont of Diplomat circuit on 16 February 1945 in [PRO] HS1/237.

For Jedburgh teams (pp. 45–6), see E.R. Mayer, [PRO] WO 95/2208, cited above. For Major Hillier's comments on the politics of resistance (p. 46), see his report in [PRO] HS6/585, cited above.

For Miss B. Bertram on resistance to torture (pp. 47–8), see Imperial War Museum, Department of Documents, 95/34/1.

3: Christina Granville, pp. 49–110

Christina was born Krystyna Skarbek but was known throughout British forces by the name of Christine Granville, which she took when she was given a British passport in 1941. To her family she was known as Christina and I have used this name throughout the text.

Madeleine Masson's *Christine* (1975) remains a full and vivid account of Christina and contains a great deal of detail provided by her friends, in particular Andrew Kennedy.

Substantial documentation for this chapter has been supplied by the SOE adviser – including Cammaerts's report of 23 October 1944, describing her role in his rescue. In the PRO, Cammaerts's twenty-page report on the Jockey circuit contains a great deal of information on the work of the mission, as well as a description of his arrest and rescue by Christina (HS6/568).

There is also a brief mention of his rescue in [PRO] HS6/570 in the interrogation of Albert (Floiras) Cammaerts's radio operator. The payment of the ransom as part of the rescue operation is described in a taped interview with Cammaerts (Imperial War Museum, Sound Archives, 11238, reel 4).

Also in the Public Record Office, HS4/86 covers Christina's proposed mission to Hungary in March 1944; see also HS7/162 and HS7/183 for resistance in Poland. The correspondence between Sikorski and Gubbins is in HS4/279.

Descriptions of the fighting on the Vercors plateau are found in the files on the Eucalyptus military mission, HS6/361, HS6/424 and HS6/425.

The US National Archives (NARA) has material on 'Subversion of Enemy Troops' and a resumé of Christina's work for the Jockey circuit – RG 226, E 190, Box 140, Folder 844. The Archives Nationales in Paris has a Dossier Jockey, 72 AJ/39.

Lady Ranfurly's comments on SOE 'good-time Charlies' are quoted in Artemis Cooper's *Cairo in the War*, p. 45.

Annette Street's description of life in Cairo is in 'Long Ago and Far Away', among the manuscripts in the Imperial War Museum. Gwendoline Lees' comments on Cairo are in Imperial War Museum, Sound Archives, 11087.

Arthur Layton Funk, *Hidden Ally* (1992), is a detailed and richly documented account of resistance in southern France, with extensive coverage of the context of Christina's work. A new edition in French was published in 2001.

Secondary sources are mostly cited with titles and authors in the text (see also Bibliography). In addition, for A. de Chastelain's comments on Christina's husband Gyzicki, see Masson, *Christine*, p. 104, n.1; for Patrick Howarth's description of Christina, see Masson, p. 251.

French publications with relevant background material on

Christina's activities and the Jockey circuit are *Journal de Marche de la Résistance en Ubaye*, (Barcelonette [n.d.]); Jean Garcin, *De l'armistice à la libération dans les Alpes de Haute-Provence* (1983), pp. 410, 413, 419 (n.121), also pp. 400–2.]; Sapin (Jacques Lécuyer) et quelques autres, *Méfiez-vous du toréador* (1987); Guy S. Reymond, *Histoire de la Libération de Digne* (1993).

For the background to Christina's proposed mission to Poland in late 1944, and the fate of the mission itself, see Jozef Garlinski, *Poland, SOE and the Allies* (1969), pp. 216ff.

Christina's love life is discreetly handled in Masson and also more sensationally in Maria Nurowska, *Mitošnica* (1999), available only in Polish.

Articles on Christina can be found in *Time*, 30 June 1952, and *Picture Post*, 13 September and 4 October 1952.

4: Virginia Hall, pp. 111–38

The story of her wide-ranging activities has to be pieced together from many sources. I have used material from her PF for her missions to France and Spain, and her activity report of 30 September 1944 at NARA, covering her mission to France for OSS in 1944 (NARA RG 226, Entry 92, Box 296). A further account, with additional material, particularly on her early life and her work after 1945, is in Elizabeth P. McIntosh, *Sisterhood of Spies* (1998). There are numerous references to her work in France in M.R.D. Foot, *SOE in France* (1966) and Colonel E.G. Boxshall's 'Chronology of SOE Operations with the Resistance in France' (1960).

Other sources include Philippe de Vomécourt, *Who Lived to See the Day* (London, 1961), p. 212.

Ben Cowburn's comment on Virginia (from his PF) is quoted in Foot, *SOE in France*, p. 211, n.2.

For details of Gerry Morel, the insurance broker trilingual

in English, French and Portuguese, saved by Virginia, see Foot, *SOE in France*, pp. 171–2.

For more on Marcel Clech, see Foot, *SOE in France*, p. 196, and Boxshall, 'Chronology of SOE Operations'. For more on Charles Hayes, see Foot, *SOE in France*, pp. 200–1. For Virginia's help to Cowburn on his second mission, see Foot, *SOE in France*, pp. 196–7, and Boxshall, 'Chronology of SOE Operations'.

5: Lise de Baissac, pp. 139–55

This chapter is based on an interview with Lise de Baissac and on information from her PF supplied by the SOE adviser. Further information of the work of Lise and her brother Claude is provided in Boxshall, 'Chronology of SOE Operations'. See also J. Maurice Paturau, *Agents secrets mauriciens en France 1940–45*, pp. 65–8, and Freddie Clark, *Agents by Moonlight*, pp. 95–6.

Lise's report of her mission in April–May 1944, dated 13 November 1944, is in [PRO] HS6/587. Lise (Marguerite) is mentioned in an addendum to the Scientist circuit's report of 10 July 1944 in [PRO] HS6/578. Mary Herbert's interrogation of 30 January 1945 is in [PRO] HS6/567.

6: Noor Inayat Khan, pp. 156–83

Jean Overton Fuller's *Madeleine*, first published in 1952, remains an absorbing and impressive account of Noor; a new edition (1988) contains additional photographs and information on Noor's ancestry and her father. Fuller was a friend of Noor and although she was writing before SOE archives became available, she spoke to many people who knew Noor, including some of her captors. The quotations from Selwyn Jepson are taken from *Madeleine*, pp. 7–8, 60–1.

My account is written using information from Noor's PF supplied by the SOE adviser.

There is a chapter on Noor – 'Bang Away Lulu' – in Beryl E. Escott's *Mission Improbable* (1991).

Details on Noor's WAAF postings have been supplied by the Ministry of Defence, Air Historical Branch (RAF).

The quotation from Ernst Vogt on pp. 166–7 is taken from Boxshall, 'Chronology of SOE Operations', section 2, p. 2.

For the probable date of Noor's arrest, see Fuller's *Noor-un-nisa Inayat Khan* (1988) p. 207

7: Pearl Witherington, pp. 183–201

Pauline: la vie d'un agent du SOE (1996), compiled by Hervé Larroque, is based on conversations with Pearl Cornioley (née Witherington) and covers both her life and war work in considerable detail. My account is based principally on an interview with Pearl and material from her PF supplied by the SOE adviser. Further information has also been supplied by Colonel J.D. Sainsbury, including details about weapons.

The originals of Pearl's signals are now in the Imperial War Museum.

There is a chapter on her in Eric Taylor's *Heroines of World War II* (1991).

Pearl's report on her mission, dated 23 November 1944, is in [PRO] HS6/587. Maurice Southgate's description of his circuit (and his arrest and interrogation) is in [PRO] HS6/579.

8: Paddy O'Sullivan, pp. 202–17

Paddy was one of the first SOE girls in the news, rather to

the annoyance of her masters. It began when Sir Archibald Sinclair MP spoke out in praise of brave WAAF officers who parachuted into France before D-Day. The next week the *Sunday Express* carried an article, naming Paddy as one of the girls.

Mrs Wrench's recollections of Paddy and the Mayer brothers are in the Imperial War Museum Library.

I have also used material from her PF supplied by the SOE adviser. Paddy's interrogation, carried out on 29 December 1944, is in [PRO] HS6/579. Major Percy Mayer's report on the Fireman mission is dated 11 November 1944 and is in [PRO] HS6/585.

Captain E.R. Mayer's interrogation of 16 December 1994 is in [PRO] WO95/2208. A further interrogation of 20 December 1944 is in [PRO] HS6/576.

9: Violette Szabo, pp. 218–44

The story of Violette Szabo has been more romanticised than that of any other agent. R.J. Minney's book *Carve her Name with Pride* (1956) is based on interviews and correspondence with Violette's family and fellow members of SOE, but parts of the book, for example the passages describing Violette's brutal interrogation, including conversation, are without historical source.

There is a chapter on Violette in Maurice Buckmaster's *Specially Employed* (1952). Leo Marks, in *Between Silk and Cyanide*, describes his coding sessions with Violette and the poem he gave her for her code.

Mrs Wrench's description of Violette is in the Imperial War Museum Library, Department of Documents, 95/34/1.

John Tonkin's account of Violette at Hasell's Hall is quoted in Max Hastings' *Das Reich: the March of the 2nd SS Panzer Division through France, June 1944* (1981).

Major Staunton's account of his mission, with references to Violette, is in [PRO] HS6/579. With this is a citation for highest possible decoration to Violette, dated 10 October 1944. His account of the blowing up of the minesweeper in Rouen (from his PF) is quoted in M.R.D. Foot, *SOE in France*, pp. 263–4.

There is also material on Staunton's Normandy circuits in Boxshall, 'Chronology of SOE Operations'. Foot, *SOE in France*, p. 107, also quotes the cable that delayed Staunton and Violette's departure for France in March 1944 (I have rectified the spellings).

See also Freddie Clark, *Agents by Moonlight* (1999), pp. 232–3 and 255.

Philip Vickers in *Das Reich* (2000) has a chapter on Violette's arrival in France and her capture, with photographs and maps.

The statement on Violette's execution, obtained by Vera Atkins from Johann Schwarzhuber, is cited in Hugh Popham's *F.A.N.Y.* (Leo Cooper), pp. 105–6. Mary Lindell's views on Violette's death are in *No Drums . . . No Trumpets: the Story of Mary Lindell* by Barry Wynne (1961), p. 253.

On the encounter with Yeo-Thomas in the train, see Mark Seaman, *Bravest of the Brave* (1998).

10: Marguerite 'Peggy' Knight, pp. 245–65

Peggy Knight's adventures were first related in an article in the *Sunday Express* on 19 January 1947.

The account here is based on material from her PF supplied by the SOE adviser and also on information in Boxshall's 'Chronology of SOE Operations in France'.

There are further details in the report of the Bruce Jedburgh team, one of whose members was Major Colby, in [PRO] HS6/489.

11: Paola Del Din, pp. 266–82

This chapter is based on an interview with Paola Del Din, on information from Ronald Taylor and on material from the PFs of Paola, Manfred Czernin, Gianandrea Gropplero di Troppenburg and Dumas Poli.

In the PRO is a translation of a written statement by Paola on her mission, provided in April 1945, and an interrogation report of 17 August 1944, in [PRO] HS6/808 (under 'D').

See also *No. 1 Special Force and the Italian Resistance* (proceedings of the Bologna Conference). This contains, *inter alia*, 'A Young Partisan Returns to Friuli by Parachute' by Paola Del Din; 'The British in Friuli' by Patrick Martin-Smith; 'Britain and the Italian Partisans' by Massimo de Leonardis; 'The Bigelow Mission' by Gianandrea Gropplero di Troppenburg; and 'The British Sermon Two Mission to Friuli' by Ronald Taylor.

For resistance in Italy, see Richard Lamb, *War in Italy 1943–1945* (1993); for details of the fighting in Florence, see Charles Macintosh, *From Cloak to Dagger: an SOE Agent in Italy 1943–1945* (1982). For the problems of air sorties to Poland from Bari, see J.G. Beevor, *SOE: Recollections and Reflections* (1981), pp. 197–8.

See also Patrick Martin-Smith, *Fruili '44: un ufficiale britannico tra i partigiani* (1991).

12: Alix D'Unienville, pp. 283–313

This chapter is based substantially on Alix's own account of her war service, written for her family, with additional information from her PF supplied by the SOE adviser.

See also J. Maurice Paturau, *Agents secrets mauriciens en France 1940–45* (1995).

Epilogue: pp. 314–37

Interview by the author with Countess Clémentine Mankowska, March 2001.

Countess Clémentine Mankowska tells her story in her memoirs, *Espionne malgré moi* (1994).

Information on Lela Karayanni in Greece is from Special Forces Club.

Sylvia Salvesen describes her imprisonment at Ravensbrück in her book, *Forgive but Do Not Forget* (1958).

For more on Hannah Senesh, see Anthony Masters, *The Summer That Bled: the Biography of Hannah Senesh* (1972).

For more on Jos Gemekke, see M.R.D. Foot, *SOE in the Low Countries* (2001), p. 421.

For more on Maddalena Dufour, see [PRO] HS6/808.

For information on Elizabeth Reynolds, who served as courier to Richard Heslop of Marksman circuit in 1943, see [PRO] HS6/578.

Eileen 'Didi' Nearne's mention of Violette in captivity is in a typed statement in [PRO] HS6/576.

For more on Mrs Berthe Fraser, see Imperial War Museum Department of Documents, Misc 2437; M.R.D. Foot, *SOE in France*, p. 247; and Bruce Marshall, *The White Rabbit* (1952), pp. 77–9.

Yvonne Rudellat is the subject of a very full biography, *'Jacqueline': Pioneer Heroine of the Resistance* (1989) by Stella King. Information included here about her training, her death and the citation for a proposed Military Cross is from her PF.

The daily summary reports prepared for SHAEF following D-Day are in [PRO] WO106/5183.

Assessments of the value of SOE are from William Mackenzie, *The Secret History of SOE*, completed in 1948 and published in 2000, p. 745

Eisenhower's assessment is quoted in Foot, *SOE in France*, pp. 441–2.

For Hugh Dalton, see *The Fateful Years 1931–45* (1957), p. 374–5.

For John Keegan's review of Nigel West's book *The Secret War*, see the *Sunday Telegraph*, 9 February 1992.

The Air Ministry report of 3 April 1944 on problems with flights to Poland from Italy is in [PRO] AIR 19/816.

For more on Henri Déricourt, see Foot, *SOE in France*, pp. 299–306; Fuller, *The German Penetration of SOE* (1975); and Nigel West, *The Secret War*, pp. 2, 112–15, 121–5.

For more on Sergeant Hugo Bleicher, see Ian Colvin (ed.), *Colonel Henri's Story* (1954); it is readable but to be treated with caution; see also references in Foot, *SOE in France*.

For the *Englandspiel* in Holland, see references in Foot, *SOE in the Low Countries*, and also Pieter Dourlein, *Inside North Pole: a Secret Agent's Story* (1953).

Maurice Southgate's report, expressing his concerns about SOE failures to spot mistakes in agents' checks, is in [PRO] HS6/579.

For M.R.D. Foot's views on SOE as a counterbalance to the communists, see his article 'Was SOE any good?' in *Journal of Contemporary History* (January, 1981), 167.

The text of Lord Selborne's letter to Churchill on 19 November 1943 is in [PRO] PREM 3 409/7.

For the pros and cons of sabotage versus bombing, see Foot, *SOE in France*, pp. 435–9, also p. 13; the note of 24 July 1943 by the Chief of Air Staff on aircraft is in [PRO] PREM 3 408/3.

Churchill's instructions to Selborne on sorties to France are in [PRO] PREM 3/185/1. For RAF Bomber Command losses, see Ian Dear, *Oxford Companion to World War II*, pp. 898–9.

For more on the sabotaging of the Peugeot factory, see Foot, *SOE in France*, p. 287–8.

Christina Granville's reports on sabotage in Poland are in her PF.

Virginia Hall's report on the possibility of sending agents to Germany as French workmen is in her PF.

Selborne's quarterly summary on SOE activities during October–December 1943, citing figures supplied by a French railway engineer, are in [PRO] PREM 3 408/1.

The comment that the entire staff of the SNCF was working for the Resistance is in [PRO] HS 7/1.

The progress reports on special operations covering June 1944 is in [PRO] CAB 121/307.

Maria de Blasio Wilhelm's *The Other Italy: Italian Resistance in World War II* (1988) cites figures for numbers of women fighting alongside the partisans.

GLOSSARY

Abwehr	German military secret police
Baker Street	SOE headquarters from October 1940
BCRA	Bureau Central de Renseignments et d'Action
blind drop	Agents parachuting into France without a reception committee to meet them
cachette	An agent's hiding place
circuit	SOE's F Section was organised in circuits named after trades and occupations – Footman, Fireman, Salesman, Scientist, Stationer. Sometimes the head of the circuit is referred to by the name of the circuit, e.g. Cammaerts is referred to as Jockey
Combat	French Resistance group in unoccupied zone (zone libre) working with RF Section, not F Section
coup dur	Heavy round-up of suspects including house searches intended to flush out resisters and partisans. In Italy called *rastrallimenti*
D/F	Direction finding, a technique used by the Germans for tracking radios when messages are being broadcast
D/F Section	A unit in SOE operating escape lines
Deuxième Bureau	The Polish government-in-exile had an espionage and counter-intelligence

356

	service named after its French equivalent
Englandspiel	'The English Game' – playing back by the Germans of captured SOE radios, using an agent's codes, to deceive SOE that the agent was sending them
Eureka	A transponder on the ground, used by the Resistance, sending out a beam guiding a plane to the dropping ground for agents or material
FANY	First Aid Nursing Yeomanry
Feldengendarmerie	German Military Police
felucca	Small sailing ships, merchant vessels, used in the Mediterranean
'the firm'	Colloquial term for SOE
FFI	French Forces of the Interior
Francs-Tireurs (FTP)	In full, Francs-Tireurs et Partisans Français: the military wing of the communist National Liberation Front
Free French	Those working for the movement, Free France, founded in London by Charles de Gaulle, and fighting against the Axis in defiance of the armistice signed by the French government on 22 June 1940 after the fall of France
F Section	The French section of SOE
Geheime Feldpolizei	The German army's own secret police
George	Initially all SOE radio operators were referred to as George and given numbers to distinguish them
informant	The agent
Jedburgh	Army officers in uniform, parachuted into France to organise and arm the Resistance

Maquis	French guerrilla bands operating 1940–5
messages personnels	Phrases broadcast by the BBC to alert reception committees that an agent would be dropped in their area
Milice	Vichy French paramilitary police force, formed in 1943, which collaborated in rounding up Jews for deportation and hunting down Resistance groups
moon period	One week either side of the full moon when there was sufficient light for night flying
Musketeers	A Polish secret network, formed in October 1939 by an engineer and inventor called Witkowski, to continue the fight against the Germans and the Soviets
No. 1 Special Force	The name by which SOE was known in Italy
one-time pad	Rows of random numbers printed on silk (chosen for its light weight); each line of numbers was used for coding one message only, then was cut off and destroyed
OSS	Office of Strategic Services; the US equivalent of SOE (from 1947 the CIA)
PF	An agent's personal SOE file
poem code	Following Intelligence practice that agents' codes were better kept in their heads than on paper, SOE initially used codes based on famous poems and quotations, but these proved highly vulnerable to expert German code breakers

Polish Home Army	Poland's secret army
Rebecca	The instrument on board a plane that was able to receive signals from a Eureka
reception committee	A group of Resistance members who would set lights to guide planes carrying agents to the landing or dropping ground, help them on their arrival and carry away any containers or packages dropped with them
réseau	Resistance circuit or network
RF Section	De Gaulle's parallel French department to F Section
SD	Sicherheitsdienst, Himmler's security service
Section D	A special unit within SIS for carrying out dirty tricks against the enemy
SHAEF	Supreme Headquarters Allied Expeditionary Force
SIS	Secret Intelligence Service
SNCF	Société Nationale des Chemins de Fer Français – the French state railway authority
SOE	Special Operations Executive, formed in 1940
S-phone	A device that allowed pilots to talk directly to the agent on the ground
STO	Service du Travail Obligatoire (forced labour for French men in Germany)
time pencil	A form of explosive that could be carefully pre-set, allowing agents time to get away; it was activated when an agent pressed a ridge on the pencil, allowing the release of acid that ate at a predetermined rate through a wire

	attached to a detonator
Todt Organisation	The Organization Todt (OT) was named after Fritz Todt, Hitler's young engineer and chief architect, and mustered huge numbers of men for the Nazi building and production programme, using both forced labour and prisoners of war as well as some volunteers lured in by propaganda
23-land	SOE code for Spain
27-land	SOE code for France
Volksdeutsche	Communities of German minorities in occupied countries who were often suspected of acting for the Nazis
WAAF	Women's Auxiliary Air Force
Wehrmacht	A blanket term – literally 'defence force' – embracing all Germany's armed forces
Welbike	A portable and collapsible mini-bike
W/T	Wireless telegraphy

BIBLIOGRAPHY

Amery, Julian, *Approach March* (London, Hutchinson, 1973)

Astley, Joan Bright, *The Inner Circle* (London, Hutchinson, 1971)

Beevor, J.G., *SOE: Recollections and Reflections* (London, Bodley Head, 1981)

Bennett, Rab, *Under the Shadow of the Swastika: the Moral Dilemmas of Resistance and Collaboration in Hitler's Europe* (London, Macmillan Press, 1999)

Bertram, B., 'The French Resistance in Sussex' (Imperial War Museum Library, Documents Department, 95/34/1)

Boatner, Mark M. III, *The Biographical Dictionary of World War II* (Novato, CA, Presidio Press, 1999)

Bonsey, Commander B., 'Top Secret Interlude' (Imperial War Museum Library, Documents Department, 79/22/1)

Boxshall, Colonel E.G., 'Chronology of SOE Operations with the Resistance in France' (typescript history, London, 1960 – copy in Imperial War Museum Library)

Braddon, Russell, *Nancy Wake* (London, Cassell, 1956)

Buckmaster, Maurice, *Specially Employed: the Story of British Aid to French Patriots of the Resistance* (London, Batchworth Press, 1952)

Buckmaster, Maurice, *They Fought Alone* (London, Odhams Press, 1958)

Carré, Mathilde, *I Was the Cat* (London, Souvenir Press, 1960)

Clark, Freddie, *Agents by Moonlight: the Secret History of RAF Tempsford during World War II* (Stroud, Tempus Publishing, 1999)

Colvin, Ian (ed.), *Colonel Henri's Story* [Memoirs of Hugo Bleicher] (London, William Kimber, 1954)

Cookridge, E.H., *They Came from the Sky* (London, Heinemann, 1965)

Cookridge, E.H., *Inside SOE* (London, Heinemann, 1966)

Cooper, Artemis, *Cairo in the War, 1939–45* (London, Hamish Hamilton, 1989)

Cornioley, Pearl, *Pauline: la vie d'un agent du SOE*, compiled by Hervé Larroque (Paris, Editions par Exemple, 1996)

Cowburn, Benjamin, *No Cloak, No Dagger* (London, Jarrolds, 1960)

Cunningham, Cyril, *Beaulieu: the Finishing School for Secret Agents* (London, Leo Cooper, 1998)

Dalton, Hugh, *The Fateful Years 1931–45* (London, Frederick Muller, 1957)

de Vomécourt, Philippe, *Who Lived to See the Day: France in Arms* (London, Hutchinson, 1961)

Dear, Ian, *Sabotage and Subversion: the SOE and OSS at War* (London, Arms & Armour Press, 1996; paperback edn London, Cassell, 1999)

Dodds-Parker, Douglas, *Setting Europe Ablaze* (Windlesham, Springwood Books, 1983)

Dourlein, Pieter, *Inside North Pole: a Secret Agent's Story* (London, William Kimber, 1953)

Escott, Beryl E., *Mission Improbable: a Salute to the RAF Women of SOE in wartime France* (Yeovil, Patrick Stephens, 1991)

Fielding, Xan, *Hide and Seek: the Story of a War-Time Agent* (London, Secker & Warburg, 1954)

Foot, M.R.D., *SOE in France: an Account of the Work of the British Special Operations Executive in France 1940–1944* (London, HMSO, 1966)

Foot, M.R.D., *Resistance* (London, Eyre Methuen, 1976; Paladin Books, 1978)

Foot, M.R.D., *SOE: an Outline History 1940–46*, 4th edn (London, Pimlico, 1999; 1st edn London, BBC, 1984)

Foot, M.R.D., *SOE in the Low Countries* (London, St Ermin's Press, 2001)

Foot, M.R.D., 'Was SOE any good?' in *Journal of Contemporary History* (January, 1981), 167

Fuller, Jean Overton, *Madeleine: the Story of Noor Inayat Khan* (London, Victor Gollancz, 1952; new edn East-West Publications, 1988)

Fuller, Jean Overton, *The German Penetration of SOE* (London, William Kimber, 1975)

Funk, Arthur Layton, *Hidden Ally: the French Resistance, Special Operations, and the Landings in Southern France, 1944* (Westport, CT, Greenwood Press, 1992); new edn: *Les Alliés et la Résistance* (Aix-en-Provence, Edisud, 2001)

Garcin, Jean, *De l'Armistice à la libération dans les Alpes de Haute-Provence* (Digne, Vial, 1983)

Garlinski, Jozef, *Poland, SOE and the Allies* (London, George Allen & Unwin, 1969)

Gaujac, Paul, *Special Forces in the Invasion of France* (Paris, Histoire & Collections, 1999)

Hastings, Max, *Das Reich: the March of the 2nd SS Panzer Division through France, June 1944* (London, Michael Joseph, 1981; paperback edn Pan Books, 2000)

Hinsley, Harry, *British Intelligence in the Second World War* (London, HMSO, 1979)

Howarth, Patrick, *Undercover: the Men and Women of the SOE* (London, Routledge & Kegan Paul, 1980; paperback edn London, Phoenix Press, 2000)

Hughes, Jimmy Quentin, *Who Cares Who Wins* (Liverpool, Charico Press, 1998)

Johnson, Kate (ed.), *The Special Operations Executive: Sound Archive Oral History Recordings* (London, Imperial War Museum, 1998)

Jones, Liane, *A Quiet Courage* (London, Bantam Press, 1990)

Journal de marche de la Résistance en Ubaye (Barcelonette, Amicale des Marquisards et Résistants, Secteur Ubaye, n.d.)

King, Stella, '*Jacqueline': Pioneer Heroine of the Resistance* [The story of Yvonne Rudellat] (London, Arms & Armour Press, 1989)

Kramer, Rita, *Flames in the Field* (London, Michael Joseph, 1995)

Lamb, Richard, *War in Italy 1943–1945: A Brutal Story* (London, John Murray, 1993)

Macintosh, Charles, *From Cloak to Dagger: an SOE Agent in Italy 1943–1945* (London, William Kimber, 1982)

McIntosh, Elizabeth P., *Sisterhood of Spies: the Women of the OSS* (New York, Random House, 1998)

Mackenzie, W.J.M., *The Secret History of SOE: the Special Operations Executive 1940–1945* (ed. M.R.D. Foot), an official history, completed for the Cabinet Office in 1948 (London, St Ermin's Press, 2000)

Mankowska, Clémentine, *Espionne malgré moi* (Monaco, Editions du Rocher, 1994)

Marks, Leo, *Between Silk and Cyanide: a Codemaker's Story* (London, HarperCollins, 1998)

Marlow, Joyce (ed.), *Women and the Great War* (London, Virago Press, 1998)

Marshall, Bruce, *The White Rabbit* (London, Evans Brothers, 1952)

Martin Smith, Patrick, *Fruili '44: un ufficiale britannico tra i partigiani* (Udine, Del Bianco Editore, 1991)

Masson, Madeleine, *Christine* (London, Hamish Hamilton, 1975)

Masters, Anthony, *The Summer That Bled: the Biography of Hannah Senesh* (London, Michael Joseph, 1972)

Millar, George, *Maquis* (London, Heinemann, 1945)

Minney, R.J., *Carve her Name with Pride* (London, George Newnes, 1956)

Nicholas, Elizabeth, *Death be not Proud* (London, Cresset Press, 1958)

No. 1 *Special Force and the Italian Resistance*, Proceedings of Bologna Conference, 2 vols. (Bologna, University of Bologna, 1987)

O'Malley, Owen, *The Phantom Caravan* (London, John Murray, 1954)

Paturau, J. Maurice, *Agents secrets mauriciens en France 1940–45* (Société de l'histoire de l'Ile Maurice, Port Louis, 1995)

Pawley, Margaret, *In Obedience to Instructions: FANY with the SOE in the Mediterranean* (Barnsley, Leo Cooper, 1999)

Pimlott, Ben, *Dalton* (London, Cape, 1985)

Piquet-Wicks, Eric, *Four in the Shadows* (London, Jarrolds, 1957)

Popham, Hugh, *F.A.N.Y.* (London, Leo Cooper, n.d. [c. 1984])

Reymond, Guy S., *Historie de la Libération de Digne* (Digne, publisher unknown, 1993)

Richards, Brooks, *Secret Flotillas* (London, HMSO, 1996)

Rigden, Denis (introduction), *SOE Syllabus: Lessons in ungentlemanly warfare* (London, Public Record Office, 2001)

Rossiter, Margaret L., *Women in the Resistance* (New York, Praeger, 1986)

Salvesen, Sylvia, *Forgive but Do Not Forget* (London, Hutchinson, 1958)

Sapin [Jacques Lécuyer] et al., *Méfiez-vous du toréador* (Toulon, AGPM, 1987)

Seaman, Mark, *Bravest of the Brave* (London, Michael O'Mara, 1998)

SOE Operations in Western Europe (London, Public Record Office [n.d.])

Stafford, David, *Secret Agent: The True Story of the Special Operations Executive* (London, BBC Worldwide, 2000)

Stafford, David, *Churchill and Secret Service* (London, John Murray, 1997; paperback edn London, Abacus, 2000)

Street, Annette, 'Long Ago and Far Away' (MS, Imperial War Museum Library)

Sweet-Escott, Bickham, *Baker Street Irregular* (London, Methuen, 1965)

Tickell, Jerrard, *Odette* (London, Chapman & Hall, 1949)

Travers, Susan, *Tomorrow to be Brave* (London, Bantam Press, 2000)

Verity, Hugh, *We Landed by Moonlight* (Wilmslow, Air Data Publications, 1994)

Vickers, Philip, *Das Reich* (Barnsley, Leo Cooper, 2000)

Wake, Nancy, *The White Mouse* (Melbourne, Macmillan, 1985)

Wake, Nancy, *La Gestapo m'appelait la souris blanche: une Australienne au secours de la France* (Paris, Editions du Félin, 2001)

Webb, Anthony M. (ed.), *The Natzweiler Trial* (London, William Hodge, 1949)

Weitz, Margaret Collins, *Sisters in the Resistance: How Women Fought to Free France 1940–1945* (New York, John Wiley & Sons, 1995)

West, Nigel, *The Secret War: the Story of SOE, Britain's Wartime Sabotage Organisation* (London, Hodder & Stoughton, 1992)

Wilhelm, Maria de Blasio, *The Other Italy: Italian Resistance in World War II* (London and New York, Norton, 1988)

Wilkinson, Peter, *Foreign Fields: The Story of an SOE Operative* (London, I.B. Tauris, 1997)

Wilkinson, Peter, and Astley, Joan Bright, *Gubbins and SOE* (London, Leo Cooper, 1993)

Wynne, Barry, *No Drums . . . No Trumpets: the Story of Mary Lindell* (London, Arthur Barker, 1961)

INDEX